PRAISE FOR
EXCELLENCE
IN COACHING

'An outstanding resource! *Excellence in Coaching* has deservedly become one of the field's foremost textbooks, relevant to both practitioners and learners of coaching.'
Dr Christian J van Nieuwerburgh, Associate Professor, Henley Centre for Coaching and Behavioural Change, Henley Business School

'Top managers are increasingly turning to specialist coaches to help them think, earn and redirect ... This very helpful book is for those in the growing profession of coaching, the facilitative partners who are helping today's executives maximize their own performance.'
Greg Parston, Director, Institute for Public Services Value, Accenture

'The variety of chapter contributions is commendable and the cumulative effect is both affirming and edifying.'
Dr Elaine Cox, Director of Postgraduate Coaching and Mentoring Programmes, Westminster Institute of Education, Oxford Brookes University

'Offers a breadth of perspectives on the subject ... Written by experts in the different fields, it leaves the reader to judge which of these various methods are the most appropriate for their particular needs.'
People Management

'Anyone who invests in this book will not feel cheated.'
Training and Coaching Today

'If you only have one coaching book on your shelf, this is the one to have.'
Resource Magazine

THIRD EDITION

Excellence in Coaching
The industry guide

Edited by
Jonathan Passmore

ASSOCIATION
FORCOACHING

KoganPage

LONDON   PHILADELPHIA   NEW DELHI

First published in Great Britain and the United States in 2006 by Kogan Page Limited
Second edition published in 2010
Reprinted in 2011, 2012 (three times), 2013, 2014 (twice), 2015
Third edition published in 2016

2nd Floor, 45 Gee Street
London EC1V 3RS
United Kingdom
www.koganpage.com

1518 Walnut Street, Suite 1100
Philadelphia PA 19102
USA

4737/23 Ansari Road
Daryaganj
New Delhi 110002
India

© Association for Coaching, 2006, 2010, 2016

The right of Association for Coaching to be identified as the author of this work has been asserted by them in accordance with the Copyright, Designs and Patents Act 1988.

ISBN   978 0 7494 7445 4
E-ISBN   978 0 7494 7446 1

British Library Cataloguing-in-Publication Data

A CIP record for this book is available from the British Library.

Library of Congress Cataloging-in-Publication Data

Names: Passmore, Jonathan, editor.
Title: Excellence in coaching : the industry guide / Jonathan Passmore,
    [editor].
Description: Third edition. | London ; Philadelphia : Kogan Page, 2016. |
    Includes bibliographical references and index.
Identifiers: LCCN 2015040198| ISBN 9780749474454 | ISBN 9780749474461 (ebk)
Subjects: LCSH: Employees–Coaching of.
Classification: LCC HF5549.5.C53 E93 2016 | DDC 658.3/124–dc23 LC record available at
http://lccn.loc.gov/2015040198

Typeset by Graphicraft Limited, Hong Kong
Print production managed by Jellyfish
Printed and bound by CPI Group (UK) Ltd, Croydon, CR0 4YY

CONTENTS

Introduction 1
Jonathan Passmore

PART ONE The business of coaching 9

01 What is coaching? 11
Frank Bresser and Carol Wilson

02 Coaching within organizations 33
Katherine Tulpa

ABOUT THE EDITOR

Prof Jonathan Passmore is a chartered psychologist, accredited coach and coaching supervisor. He is the managing director of Embrion, a psychology consulting company and full professor of leadership and coaching psychology at the University of Evora, Portugal. He holds five degrees and is an active contributor through articles, books and conference speeches. Jonathan has worked at board level in the private, public and not-for-profit sectors and has worked for a range of firms including PricewaterhouseCoopers, IBM and OPM. Jonathan can be contacted via his research and publications website, **www.jonathanpassmore.com**.

CONTRIBUTORS

Geoffrey Abbott, PhD is Director of Executive and Organisational Coaching at the Graduate School of Business, QUT, Australia. He coaches and facilitates across GSB's corporate and award programmes, particularly in leadership development. Geoff's expertise is in coaching in complex international environments and he is a passionate advocate for action learning methodologies. Geoff is co-editor of *The Routledge Companion to International Business Coaching* (Moral and Abbott, 2011) and has numerous published articles and chapters on international coaching. He has over 10 years' experience as an executive with the Special Broadcasting Service, Australia. Geoff is a member of the Global Advisory Board of the Association for Coaching and a regular presenter at coaching and related conferences. He also runs a consultancy company specializing in international business coaching, with strong links into Latin America.

Graham Alexander is often described as a 'super coach' and has been attributed with introducing business coaching to the UK. He is one of the few people coaching at the top level of UK/international business, specifically with CEOs, boards and senior executives, and has coached more UK CEOs than anyone. Graham developed the GROW model, which has become the world's best-known business coaching framework. He is the author of *Tales from the Top* and co-author of *SuperCoaching*, and is Senior Vice President, Europe, of the Hudson Highland Center for High Performance. Graham can be contacted at **graham@grahamalexander.com**.

Dr Jacqueline Binkert is a principal of Appreciative Coaching Collaborative, LLC and co-author of *Appreciative Coaching: A Positive Process for Change*, a researched, evidence-based approach to coaching founded on the Appreciative Inquiry. She has presented Appreciative Coaching® workshops internationally. Jackie specializes in executive coaching and has worked with clients from non-profit organizations and international corporations to educational institutions and manufacturing, including the Executive Development Center of a Fortune 50 company. She can be contacted at **jbinkert@appreciativecoaching.com**.

Diane Brennan is passionate about the power of coaching. She became involved as a leader within the International Coach Federation (ICF) to expand global conversations and professionalization across the community. Diane served as the ICF global President in 2008. She is an executive coach, consultant, author and co-editor of the book, *The Philosophy and Practice of Coaching*. She holds an MBA, ICF Master Coach and is fellow of the American College of Medical Practice Executives. She was also the first Director of Training for Fielding University coaching programme. She can be contacted at **diane@coachdiane.com**.

Frank Bresser is a leading, global business expert for the successful implementation and improvement of coaching. Supported by his worldwide team, he advises companies on the effective use of coaching. His expertise is used and put in practice successfully in organizations across the globe and has set international standards in the implementation and improvement of coaching. He holds an MBA with Distinction in International Management from the University of East London. He is based in Germany and can be contacted at **www.frank-bresser-consulting.com**.

Dr Alison Carter is an independent researcher, consultant and writer on HR, organizational change and coaching. She is a Principal Associate at the Institute for Employment Studies (IES) in the UK, a Visiting Scholar at James Cook University in Australia and was formerly a Director of the European Mentoring and Coaching Council (EMCC). Alison is a popular speaker about coaching matters, including at the US Academy of Management, the British Academy of Management and the EMCC annual conferences. She can be contacted at **alisoncarterdba@aol.com**.

Dr Ann L Clancy is a principal of Appreciative Coaching Collaborative, LLC and co-author of *Appreciative Coaching: A Positive Process for Change*, a researched, evidence-based approach to coaching founded on Appreciative Inquiry. She is an executive coach and international coach trainer, offering Appreciative Coaching® workshops and presentations. She has worked with executive clients from corporations, retail companies, governmental agencies, community groups and non-profit organizations. She can be contacted at **aclancy@appreciativecoaching.com**.

Prof Sir Cary L Cooper is the 50th Anniversary Professor of Organizational Psychology and Health at Manchester Business School, University of Manchester. He is the author of over 150 books (on occupational stress, women at work and industrial and organizational psychology), has written over 400 scholarly articles for academic journals, and is a frequent contributor to national newspapers, TV and radio. Professor Cooper is the President of the British Academy of Management and outgoing Chair of the

Academy of Social Sciences. He is a Fellow of the Academy of Management (having also won the 1998 Distinguished Service Award) and an Honorary Fellow of the Royal College of Physicians and of the British Psychological Society.

Hetty Einzig is a leadership coach and facilitator working globally with individuals, teams and organizations across corporate, private and public sectors. She is a senior consultant and associate with *Transition Expertise, Leaders' Quest, Performance Consultants International* and *PC France*; she was a founder member of *Be the Change*, the social change organization, and is a team member of *Rising Women Rising World*. Her roots are in transpersonal psychology, and as a fully trained psychotherapist this understanding and experience underpins all her work. She is Editor of the AC Global Bulletin, ICF PCC accredited and holds an MA in *Organisational Consulting* from the Tavistock Centre, University of East London. She can be contacted at **webenquiries@hettyeinzig.com**.

Anthony M Grant PhD is widely recognized as a key pioneer of coaching psychology and evidence-based approaches to coaching. He has authored over 100 coaching publications, and is the Director of the Coaching Psychology Unit at Sydney University, a Visiting Professor at the International Centre for Coaching and Leadership Development, Oxford Brookes University, a Senior Fellow at the Melbourne School of Business, Melbourne University, and a Visiting Scholar at the Said School of Business, Oxford University. In 2007, Anthony was awarded the British Psychological Society Award for outstanding professional and scientific contribution to coaching psychology and in 2009 he was awarded the Vision of Excellence Award from Harvard University. He can be contacted at **anthony.grant@sydney.edu.au**.

Professor Peter Hawkins is Professor of Leadership at Henley Business School, founder and Emeritus Chairman of Bath Consultancy Group, Chairman of Renewal Associates, and a global thought leader in leadership, team and board coaching, coaching supervision, and creating a coaching culture. He teaches internationally in these areas and leads the Bath Consultancy Group training in Coaching Supervision and the AoEC training in Systemic Team Coaching. He is author of *Leadership Team Coaching, Leadership Team Coaching in Practice, Creating a Coaching Culture, The Wise Fool's Guide to Leadership* and co-author of both the best-selling *Supervision in the Helping Professions* and *Coaching, Mentoring and Organizational Consultancy: Supervision and development*. Peter can be contacted at **peter.hawkins@renewalassociates.co.uk**.

Margot Hennessy has significant expertise in partnering with and coaching international leaders to achieve performance excellence. Her remit for her last two roles has focused on developing the top 900 leaders of a FTSE top 10 organization, internationally, including emerging markets LAC, Africa, Middle East and Asia Pacific. She has experience in linking the business brand with employee value propositions to deliver commercial people and talent outcomes, with extensive networks established in all areas of HR: Transformation, Coaching, Leadership and Talent, with the purpose of sourcing best practice and knowledge. Margot can be contacted at **margot.hennessy@gmail.com**.

Allard de Jong is an international development specialist, performing team coaching, process facilitation and leadership coaching. He is currently Director of Change and Challenge, and an associate at Penna and LHH. He lectures on coaching, leadership and change throughout Spain. He holds an MA in Communication Studies and a BA in International Business Administration. Allard can be contacted at **allard@allarddejong.com**.

Kate Lanz runs a successful leadership consulting and coaching practice, after a successful career in business as an international General Manager, notably with Diageo. Kate is coaching faculty at INSEAD, the global business school. She holds a BSc in Psychology, an MBA, two earlier degrees and is currently completing a doctorate in applied neuroscience in leadership. She is a qualified coaching supervisor and has written extensively on important aspects of coaching, leadership and coaching supervision. Kate consults and coaches internationally with global corporate clients. In her spare time she has rediscovered horse riding. Kate can be contacted at **kate@lanzexecutivecoaching.co.uk**.

Ian McDermott Named one of Britain's Top 10 Coaches and described as 'the Coaches' Coach' (*Independent on Sunday*), Ian McDermott pioneered the integration of NLP and coaching. Ian is founder and Director of Training for International Teaching Seminars (ITS). For nearly 30 years ITS has been advising senior leaders worldwide and coaching the next generation to become innovative leaders. A successful entrepreneur, Ian is an Honorary Fellow of Exeter University Business School, where his focus is on entrepreneurship and innovation. His work is featured in The Open University's MBA course 'Creativity, Innovation and Change'. Ian is also External Faculty at Henley Business School. In the US he is Dean of Innovation and Learning for the Purposeful Planning Institute. A prolific author, his books have been translated into 20 languages. His most recent is *The Collaborative Leader: The Ultimate Leadership Challenge*.

Michael Neenan is an honorary vice-president of the Association for Coaching®, co-director of the coaching training programme at the Centre for Coaching, Blackheath and an accredited cognitive-behavioural therapist. He has co-written (with Professor Windy Dryden) over 20 books on cognitive behaviour therapy including the best-selling *Life Coaching: A cognitive behavioural approach*. His coaching practice focuses on both personal and professional development. Michael can be contacted at **neenanmike1@aol.com**.

Prof Jonathan Passmore is a chartered psychologist, accredited coach and coaching supervisor. He is the managing director of Embrion, a psychology consulting company and full professor of leadership and coaching psychology at the University of Evora, Portugal. He holds five degrees and is an active contributor through articles, books and conference speeches. Jonathan has worked at board level in the private, public and not-for-profit sectors and has worked for a range of firms including PricewaterhouseCoopers, IBM and OPM. Jonathan can be contacted via his research and publications website, **www.jonathanpassmore.com**.

Dr M Alicia Peña Bizama is a Chartered Counselling Psychologist and an Occupational Psychologist. She has worked both in the NHS and in the private sector, and is now the Head of Student Wellbeing at the University of Reading. She obtained her Professional Doctorate in Occupational Psychology and her research was focused on the factors that lead to an effective return to work after being off with stress, anxiety or depression. In her current role she is working with students to facilitate the development of resilience and self-efficacy to maintain health and well-being. Alicia can be contacted at **m.a.penabizama@reading.ac.uk**.

David B Peterson has been an executive coach and innovative thought leader in leadership development for over 20 years. As Director of Executive Coaching and Leadership for Google, he coaches senior leaders and manages the network of internal and external coaches. In addition to being a world-class coach, he is a highly-regarded author and speaker, known for being on the cutting edge of the profession, challenging the conventional wisdom and exploring provocative new ideas.

Philippe Rosinski is an expert in executive coaching, team coaching, and global leadership development, sought after by leading international corporations. He is principal of Rosinski & Company (**www.philrosinski.com**). He is the author of *Coaching Across Cultures* and his pioneering work in bringing the crucial intercultural dimension into the practice of coaching has won him worldwide acclaim. Philippe is the first European to have been designated Master Certified Coach by the International Coach Federation. COF is available at **www.philrosinski.com/cof**.

Alex Szabo is a qualified and accredited personal and professional coach. She is a business professional with extensive experience in strategic management and operations. Her background of psychology, training, merchant banking, and entrepreneurial experience led her to found Tailored Coaching, which provides results-orientated personal, business, executive and group coaching. Alex was a nominee for the AC Honorary Awards Influencing Coaching category and is co-founder of the Association for Coaching®, the UK's leading professional body. She can be contacted at **www.tailoredcoaching.com**.

Katherine Tulpa is the Executive Director of Wisdom8, an international coaching firm specializing in board and top-team development, and Global CEO and co-founder of the Association for Coaching®. As a sought after GlobalCoach, coaching CEOs and leaders from over 35 different cultures, she is also an author, speaker, and visiting lecturer. Some of her awards include 'Coaching Mentoring Person of the Year' by Coaching at Work, and the 'Global Leadership Coaching Award' at the World Coaching Congress. Katherine is passionate about raising the bar of coaching and stretching global leaders so that they make a positive impact in the world. She can be contacted at **ktulpa@wisdom8.com**.

Sir John Whitmore was a successful professional racing driver before moving into business. He then moved to California to study and promote the emerging psychologies, before returning to the UK to set up a tennis and ski school based on a new learning method called The Inner Game, which redefined coaching. He then teamed up with former Olympians to found Performance Consultants, bringing coaching into business. In 2004, he was made recipient of the *AC Honorary Award for Impacting the Coaching Profession* and his book *Coaching for Performance* is a business best-seller and has been translated into 14 languages. **www.performanceconsultants.co.uk**.

Dr Alison Whybrow was at the forefront of the development of the coaching psychology profession in the UK for nearly a decade, holding an executive position within the Coaching Psychology group of the British Psychological Society from 2004. She was presented with an Achievement Award for her Distinguished Contribution to Coaching Psychology from her peers within the British Psychological Society in December 2009. Alison has continued to support the development of professionalism in coaching and coaching psychology globally. She has a strong coaching and consulting practice, based on an ecological world view, and contributes as an editor and writer to coaching and coaching psychology publications. Alison can be contacted at **alison@alisonwhybrow.com**.

Carol Wilson is an international speaker, author and broadcaster. She is a Fellow of the ILM, the Association for Coaching® and the Professional Speaking Association. She designs coaching and leadership programmes for organizations all over the world in local languages, has won numerous awards, authored *Performance Coaching: a Complete Guide to Best Practice Coaching and Training* and provides coaching programmes to the charity The Ministry of Entrepreneurship. She can be contacted at: **info@coachingcultureatwork.com**.

FOREWORD FROM THE SECOND EDITION

Books about coaching generally offer the perspective of a single coach drawing on their experiences from the field. My book *Coaching for Performance* is one of those. They serve to contribute to the body of coaching knowledge and to the income and reputation of the author.

This one is different. It brings together a range of the best writings on the subject without judgement or favour. As such, it gives the reader an opportunity to sample the field and take responsibility for their own choice of which path or paths to follow or combine, or whether to carve out a new path of their own. Any coach, or would-be coach, is bound to gain from the richness that is offered, from practical experience of, and advice on, running a coaching practice to important issues such as standards, ethics and supervision; this book embraces many different methodologies.

A recently emerging theme in the coaching industry is the recognition of the need to collaborate for the benefit and the reputation of the industry as a whole and its clients, rather than maintaining the protective self-interest that has characterized much of business in the past. This book reflects this view; for example, the editor and contributors have not received any payment for their efforts, and have thereby made a genuine contribution to the industry as a whole, one that transcends personal gain.

Coaching has been established for more than two decades, and it is now coming into maturity and revealing more of its depth. At a superficial level, coaching helps people to clarify their goals, to schedule their actions and to succeed more readily at work and in life. It helps people to learn and perform better by enhancing their awareness, responsibility, self-confidence and self-reliance. At a deeper level, when undertaken well and responsibly, it helps people along their evolutionary journey towards higher or deeper levels of themselves – to discover who they really are. It is a psycho-spiritual journey that is both universal and as pre-programmed as is the Darwinian one of biological evolution.

The principle and practice of coaching is a choice of making kit on a micro scale, and let us hope that these principles will spread to the macro in time. We are a fledgling industry but, as Margaret Mead said, 'Never believe that a small group of dedicated individuals can not change the world –

indeed it is the only thing that ever has'. Is the Association for Coaching® such a group? Let us cast aside our self-limiting beliefs and cooperate towards a higher goal, higher version. This end is something to which this book contributes and of which it is an example.

John Whitmore
Author of Coaching for Performance

PREFACE

This book came about during a conversation at an Association for Coaching® event in London in 2005. Katherine Tulpa and I reflected on the need for a single guide to coaching practice that would bring current issues together.

With the help of the back of an envelope and a delayed train from King's Cross station this book moved from a vague conversation over coffee to a book proposal. The simple idea was to bring together the top English-speaking coaching writers to contribute to a single book. This book assembles two dozen of the world's top coaches, all of whom have written and published elsewhere and are experts in their individual fields. It covers issues which have not been written about widely, such as coaching supervision and coaching ethics, but which are of importance if coaching is to develop as a profession. It also aims to offer the reader a selection of the most popular coaching models, written by the leaders in each of these areas, along with guidance on getting started in coaching.

The book has subsequently been adopted by course leaders at universities and coach trainers across the world, who like the idea of a short and simple book which covers the key areas. Its popularity has resulted in multiple reprints, new editions (of which this is the third) and international translations.

The book is divided into three sections. The first is what we have called 'The business of coaching', and covers the themes of 'What is coaching?', 'Coaching within organizations' and 'Running your coaching practice'. If you are new to coaching, studying coaching or are setting up your coaching practice, this section will be of interest to you. The second section contains a selection of the most popular coaching approaches, with chapters by the leading writers in each of these areas. Most coaches use a single model in their coaching practice; by offering an accessible description of a range of models we hope coaches will be able to develop their practice further, first by reading and then securing further training in some of the specialist areas such as cognitive, transpersonal and motivational interviewing. The third section explores current issues within coaching, from supervision to ethics and diversity. Much of the material in this section is new thinking and seeks to take forward the debate in these areas.

As always with editions like this, as editor I end up frustrating authors who wanted to bring a creative touch to their writing while I attempted to create some consistency in look and feel throughout the book. On the other side is the frustrated publisher keen to move forward while I attempt to herd authors towards the finish post of the publication deadline. The result is never the perfect book, but I hope it will be a useful addition to every coach's bookshelf.

Throughout the book we have tried to use the term coachee for the person who sits in the session with the coach, and the term client for the person who commissions the coaching and pays the bill. Sometimes these are the same person; however, often in organizational settings they are different people.

The ideas and views expressed in each chapter are those of the individual authors, and do not necessarily represent my own views as editor or those of the Association for Coaching®. As the editor, a chartered psychologist, coaching practitioner and a researcher into coaching practice, I am interested to hear your views about coaching practice and coaching research.

ACKNOWLEDGEMENTS

I would like to express my thanks to Katherine Tulpa and Alex Szabo who supported the idea of the book and for their encouragement during the process. Thanks are also due to the authors who gave of their time, without payment, to contribute to this collaborative piece and for putting up with my desire for redraft after redraft.

I would like to pay tribute to my wife, Katharine, who has allowed me to spend many hours at the keyboard typing and engaged in discussions about the book and its subsequent new editions. This book is dedicated to her and to my two daughters.

Jonathan Passmore

Introduction

JONATHAN PASSMORE

Coaching: the future

The first edition of *Excellence in Coaching* was published in 2006 and has since established itself as a popular read for practitioners and those studying coaching. The book has sold across the world and is now a course text on several coaching programmes in the UK and beyond. Its popularity has led to numerous reprints and a second edition.

Since the second edition in 2010, other collected editions have been published but the popularity of *Excellence in Coaching* has remained.

In creating this third edition we have stuck to the original model: a short and accessible book for practitioners interested in how coaching works, with references for readers who want a deeper coverage of issues to follow up. The chapters from the first and second editions have been updated and new chapters added to ensure readers have the latest thinking on coaching practice.

This third edition divides the book into three sections. The first deals with the nature of coaches. These chapters cover how coaches can establish and best manage their business and how to work in parallel with clients and coachees. The second section of the book is concerned with coaching models and techniques. Rather than concentrate on a single model we have offered a number of models: behavioural, cognitive behavioural, NLP, transpersonal, solution-focused, Appreciative Inquiry and integrative. Our aim is to help coaches to extend their professional practice. Most people are taught a single coaching model in their coach training; we have tried to encourage trainers and coaches to use a diverse range of models which meet the needs of their coachee and of the issue. I have previously advocated that coaches develop a personal integrated model of coaching which blends together different approaches, and I hope that the range of models will help coaches in this endeavour. The third section of the book focuses on issues facing coaches, from working with stress to ethics, cross-cultural working and standards.

Coaching at work

Recent meta-analysis research (Theeboom *et al*, 2014; Jones *et al*, 2015; Sonesh *et al*, 2015), and a growing body of coaching research demonstrates that coaching has become a popular intervention that now ranks alongside leadership development and management skills programmes (see Passmore *et al*, 2013 for a wider discussion). Further, there is positive evidence that coaching can have an impact on individuals from improving education outcomes to addressing health-related issues, as well as in safety, driver training and organizations.

However, the ability to harness this potential takes self-awareness, self-belief, personal motivation and tools to enable the coachee to put new ideas into new ways of behaving. The role of the coach in the relationship is to facilitate and coordinate these elements, working in harmony with his or her coachee. Some have suggested that the harmonic relationship in coaching should be like conducting a band, waving the baton of the question and focusing attention on each element in turn. I would prefer to see this more like playing jazz, with the coach and coachee working together to weave a pattern that emerges from the process.

In organizations there is the added complexity of working with a second 'client': the organization sponsors. They have their own views about what needs to be delivered from coaching. Since 2006 organization sponsors have developed in their understanding of coaching: what they expect, what coaches should deliver and how to select the right coach. As the market continues to develop and HR professionals become more confident in managing coaching contracts, it is likely that organizational coaching relationships will start with tripartite meetings to set the scene and agree the objectives, and will close with a similar review. We are likely to see a continued shift to professionalization, which means a continued growth in postgraduate qualifications in coaching degrees and further developments in accreditation from professional bodies.

Well-being coaching

Well-being coaching has developed too. The market itself is even more diverse, ranging from coaches working in health areas such as smoking cessation, stress and diet management, to more traditional lifestyle work. For these health interventions, coaches with backgrounds in health services or psychology are completing coaching qualifications, often to add to their counselling qualification. The evidence is that coaching, using cognitive behavioural and motivational interviewing approaches, is well placed to help support behavioural change and enhance well-being.

Coaching training standards

While coaching has become a recognized intervention, sadly there are still no standards or licensing arrangements which are widely recognized. Professional bodies have continued to develop their own standards, but the lack of regulation means anyone can call themselves a coach.

As a result clients need to be cautious when appointing a coach. They need to ask questions about their coach's training, qualifications and ethical practice.

Whether coaching is a profession which requires regulation, or is professional and requires standards, remains a matter of debate.

Coaching competencies

In an environment where few coaches were trained, knowing which behaviours were effective was arguably of limited importance. The development of coaching and its journey towards becoming a profession brings with it the question of standards and training.

What does a coach need to learn to be effective? A small number of writers have sought to answer this question. Alexander and Renshaw (2005) suggest that a number of key competencies are important. They felt that coaching competencies should be divided into three clusters: relationship, being and doing. In the first of these, relationship, coaches need to demonstrate that they are open and honest and that they value others. In the second cluster, being, coaches need to have self-confidence to be able to work with their coachee through difficult challenges. They also need to maintain an enabling style, to avoid slipping into a directive approach with their coachee, and to be self-aware. In the third cluster, doing, coaches need to hold a clear methodology, to be skilful in applying the method and its associated tools and techniques, and to be fully present. Few of these competencies easily lend themselves to a formal training.

Research (see Grant et al, 2010) suggests that coachees have a very clear view of what they value within a coaching relationship. They expect their coaches to have strong communication skills, to be able to listen, to recall information accurately, to challenge while maintaining support for them as an individual and to direct attention through questions. The senior executives in the study also expressed the view that relationship skills were important.

In this respect, credibility and previous experience helped to establish and maintain the relationship, alongside empathy and affirming the coachee. There was also a view that knowledge about human behaviour and knowledge of the sector were valued. The second of these, sector knowledge, is often contested but this may reflect a desire to divide coaching and mentoring into neat boxes. My experience suggests that the two areas are intertwined and mixed (see Table 0.1). The table suggests pure forms, while in reality coaching and mentoring run between the polarities illustrated.

TABLE 0.1 Contrasting coaching and mentoring

	Coaching	Mentoring
1. Level of formality	More formal: contract or ground rules set, often involving a third-party client	Less formal: agreement, most typically between two parties
2. Length of contract	Shorter term: typically between 4 and 12 meetings agreed over 2 to 12 months	Longer term: typically unspecified number of meetings with relationships often running over 3 to 5 years
3. Focus	More performance-focused: typically a greater focus on short-term skills and job performance	More career-focused: typically a concern with longer-term career issues, obtaining the right experience and longer-term thinking
4. Level of sector knowledge	More generalist: typically coaches have limited sector knowledge	More sector knowledge: typically mentors have knowledge of organization or business sector
5. Training	More relationship training: typically coaches have a background in psychology, psychotherapy or HR	More management training: typically mentors have a background in senior management
6. Focus	Dual focus: more typically a dual focus on the needs of the individual and the needs of the organization	Single focus: more typically a single focus on the needs of the individual

A research study (Passmore *et al*, 2014) has offered a coach competency framework using behavioural anchored statements, allowing coaches to reflect on their own behaviours, as well as providing a framework against which external coach assessors can measure coach performance.

Table 0.2 is drawn from the 10-point Behavioural Anchor Rating scale – and shows level 9 – Moving towards mastery. The scale does not show all behaviours used by master coaches, but rather provides indicative behaviours which might commonly be used by a master coach.

The full document contains behaviours for coaches starting their coaching development journey and for those who are moving towards competence.

TABLE 0.2 Coach competencies – Indicative behaviours – Progressing towards mastery

2·1

Factor 1: Establishing a clear contract	Coach explains coaching process, their role in it and their expectations of the coachee and organization to maximize the value of the sessions.
	Coach jointly agrees the logistical arrangements for the coaching assignment and offers a coaching contract.
	Coach explains confidentiality with both coach and organization, who will receive what information, how the coaching will be reviewed and the limits of confidentiality.
	Coach jointly agrees main themes of the coaching programme with the coachee (and their organization where appropriate), and if not appropriate for coaching will redirect the coachee (and organization) to the appropriate intervention or person.
Factor 2: Building a trusting relationship	Coach uses themselves as a tool, through personal stories and insights; such stories are always for the benefit of the coachee and are explicitly linked back to the coachee's agenda.
	Coach openly answers questions raised by the coachee, but does so at a time that facilitates the learning and development of the coachee's insight, without avoiding answering.
	Coach uses listening, questioning, affirmation, summaries and reflections throughout the coaching session.
	Coach keeps their commitments made to the coachee (and the organization).

TABLE 0.2 *Cont'd*

Factor 3: Facilitating agenda	Coach jointly agrees SMART goal(s) with the coachee that reflect the length of time available, the themes agreed at the start of the assignment and previous conversation.
	Coach periodically reviews progress through the session, as well as at the end of the session, appropriately challenging the coachee if the coachee appears not to be fully engaged.
	Coach uses a range of communication skills to maintain the focus of the coachee on the goal and the pace of the session to complete the task (or agrees otherwise with the coachee).
	Coach maintains focus of the coaching programme throughout the relationship to help the coachee (and organization) achieve the wider goals.
Factor 4: Facilitating reflection and learning	Coach uses short and simple open questions throughout the session, which regularly recreates moments of silent reflection for the coachee.
	Coach actively listens to words and body language and communicates this through their body language and when reflecting back may demonstrate their understanding of the emotions and details of the situation (when appropriate), which can result in silence and/or emotional responses from the coachee.
	Coach uses complex reflections, such as amplified reflections.
	Coach summarizes to provide breaks, check understanding and support the coachee's learning for the next part of the session and/or help the coachee remain focused/remind them of content.
	Coach uses affirmation, by reflecting back or making a personal statement which validates the coachee or their work, and which contains a statement of the coach's emotions in response to the situation.
	Coach uses silence and body language to encourage the coachee to continue thinking or speaking.
	Coach uses four or more models and blends this together within their coaching practice, adapting to meet the needs of the coachee and their presenting issue.

Factor 5: Managing emotional and organizational boundaries	Coach displays (appropriate) empathic emotional responses to the coachee, and is aware of the individual, the coaching relationship, gender and cultural issues and the social context/environment.
	Coach contains their own emotions.
	Coach identifies issues with strong emotional content that require immediate or future referral to other individuals or agencies, and actively works to ensure the coachee does not come to harm.
	Coach refers skilfully where the issue is beyond the competence of the coach, or where they can identify another coach who could more effectively help the coachee.
	Coach uses their self-awareness about their own values and beliefs appropriately.
	Coach manages the boundaries between different stakeholders involved in the process, recognizing potential conflict and systemic issues.
Factor 6: Reviewing outcomes	Coach jointly reviews with the coachee the outcome of the session against the goals and supports further work outside the session, encouraging the coachee to draw support from their manager, friends and colleagues.
	Coach jointly reviews the outcome of the coaching assignment with the coachee (and the organization where appropriate) with explicit reference to the original themes agreed.
	Coach invites feedback at the end of the session, and the end of the assignment from all stakeholders, uses follow up and probing questions to gather behavioural evidence of both 'positives' and 'what could be different next time' and notes feedback for future reflection and learning in their journal.
	Coach reflects on their and their coachees' behaviours, cognitions or emotions at the end of each session and the end of each assignment and notes these in their journal, as well as identifying learning and/or future actions (where appropriate they share this with their supervisor or in their journal).
	Coach recognizes they are on their own learning journey towards mastery and actively seeks new experiences and insights to aid this developmental journey.

SOURCE: Adapted from Passmore *et al* (2014).

Conclusions

This book, we hope, will provide readers with an enjoyable, stimulating read across the current debate within coaching.

References

Alexander, G and Renshaw, B (2005) *Super Coaching: The missing ingredient for high performance*, Random House Business Books, London

Grant, A M, Passmore, J, Cavanagh, M and Parker, H (2010) The state of play in coaching, *International Review of Industrial & Organizational Psychology*, 25, 125–68

Jones, R, Wood, S and Guillaume, Y R (2015) The effectiveness of workplace coaching: a meta-analysis of learning and performance outcomes from coaching, *Journal of Occupational & Organizational Psychology*, DOI: 10.1111/joop.12119

Passmore, J (2007) Coaching and mentoring: the role of experience and sector knowledge, *International Journal of Evidence Based Coaching and Mentoring*, Summer, 10–16

Passmore, J, May, T, Badger, L, Dodd, L and Lyness, E (2014) *Coaching for Success: The key ingredients for coaching delivery & coach recruitment*, ILM, London

Passmore, J, Peterson, D and Freire, T (eds) (2013) *The Wiley-Blackwell Handbook of the Psychology of Coaching and Mentoring*, Wiley-Blackwell, Chichester

Sonesh, S C *et al* (2015) The power of coaching: a meta-analytic investigation, *Coaching: An International Journal of theory, practice & research*, 8 (2), pp 73–95

Theeboom, T, Beersma, B and van Vianen, A E M (2014) Does coaching work? A meta-analysis on the effects of coaching on individual level outcomes in an organizational context, *The Journal of Positive Psychology*, 9, pp 1–18

PART ONE
The business of coaching

What is coaching?

01

FRANK BRESSER and CAROL WILSON

Coaching: the new profession

This chapter sets out to describe the nature of coaching: its boundaries with other helping interventions, the skills required to make an effective coach and the evidence of the impact of coaching on individuals and organizations.

Coaching is one of the fastest-growing professions. Having emerged from the area of sports in the 1960s, coaching transferred to business throughout the 1970s and 1980s, underwent a high degree of diversification and popularization in the 1990s, and was characterized by further professionalization and consolidation in the first one and a half decades of this century. It is today accepted as a respected and widely used resource for personal development. Various forms of coaching (life coaching, executive coaching, career coaching, sports coaching, etc) exist. This chapter addresses the question of what is the essence of coaching, what qualities, skills and competencies a coach actually needs, what are the relevant differences between coaching and other disciplines, and what benefits coaching offers.

Defining coaching

Leaving aside the hyperbole that currently surrounds the term 'coaching', there exists a common understanding of what it actually means. Although different definitions abound, they mostly describe the same phenomenon.

> Coaching is ...
>
> - 'unlocking a person's potential to maximize their own performance. It is helping them to learn rather than teaching them' (Whitmore, 2009);
>
> - 'a collaborative, solution-focused, results-orientated and systematic process in which the coach facilitates the enhancement of work performance, life experience, self-directed learning and personal growth of the coachee' (Grant, 1999; basic definition also referred to by the Association for Coaching, 2006, 2015; today the Association for Coaching additionally provides on its website various definitions of different, existing types of coaching, 2015);
>
> - 'partnering with clients in a thought-provoking and creative process that inspires them to maximize their personal and professional potential' (ICF, 2015);
>
> - 'the art of facilitating the unleashing of people's potential to reach meaningful, important objectives' (Rosinski, 2003).

At the heart of coaching lies the idea of empowering people by facilitating self-directed learning, personal growth and improved performance.

Beyond this shared understanding, a host of issues are still under discussion within the profession. We have summarized 12 dimensions (Bresser, 2005, 2008, 2010, 2013a) that are part of this wider debate (see Figure 1.1).

FIGURE 1.1   The 12 dimensions of coaching

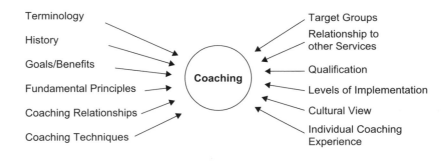

Terminology
History
Goals/Benefits
Fundamental Principles
Coaching Relationships
Coaching Techniques

Coaching

Target Groups
Relationship to other Services
Qualification
Levels of Implementation
Cultural View
Individual Coaching Experience

1. Terminology

The term 'coaching' is used to describe a wide range of interventions, which is in part a result of the absence of a legally binding definition. So, anyone is free to call anything 'coaching'. The continuing movement to professionalization of the sector will help both coaches and clients deepen their understanding of what coaching is, how it can help and when to use it.

2. History

A number of writers argue that coaching, as a one-to-one learning conversation, has existed since the dawn of civilization. A contrary approach presents this discipline as a new invention of the second half of the 20th century. Most writers recognize that although single coaching elements may always have existed, the development of models and their use in workplace environments are more recent. Questions still, however, remain about what models, methods and techniques are most effective.

3. Goals/Benefits

// Commonly mentioned benefits of coaching include enhanced personal and organizational performance, better work–life balance, higher motivation, better self-reflection, optimized decision making and improved change management. //   *1·3*

One question remains the subject of ongoing debate: whose goals – those of the coachee or the sponsor organization – should be primarily served by coaching? Some argue that above all it is in the very nature of coaching to serve the coachee's goals; others emphasize the sponsor's payment and organizational context as dominant elements and prioritize the interests of the sponsor organization. A middle view stresses the importance of professional contracting in the beginning to ensure a win–win situation all the time. In any case, an effective coach needs to be able to identify and address the issue of competing priorities.

4. Fundamental principles

Commonly agreed fundamental principles of coaching are self-responsibility, respect, acceptance, confidentiality, integrity, transparency, flexibility and neutrality. However, debate continues about the interpretation and practice of the principles. How can the coach be resilient towards external pressures? How should the coach handle possible conflicts of interest? How does the coach most effectively deal with his or her own blind spots?

5. Coaching relationships

There is a broad consensus that the coachee retains responsibility and ownership of the outcomes and is the leader of the whole coaching process, while the coach tailors the coaching around the coachee's needs and remains detached. Coaching requires a coaching contract as the fundamental basis for a good coaching relationship. This relationship is commonly described as an equal one, neither participant being superior nor subordinate to the other. But what happens in more complex relationships where coaching is used within organizations? Can a manager coach a direct report at all? What impact does delivery by human resources within the organization have on the coachee's willingness to share fully his or her story?

6. Coaching techniques

The techniques of listening, questioning, clarifying and giving feedback are essential. What other tools are admissible and how these may be applied in coaching, however, is subject to debate. Also, the pros and cons of alternatives to face-to-face communication, such as the telephone, e-mail or videoconferencing, are open to dispute. What effect do these have on the coaching process and outcomes?

7. Target groups

Coaches vary in whom they offer services to. Some coaches are willing to work across issues and sectors; others are more specialist. A debate persists over whether and to what extent coaching is equally applicable to all these target groups, what approaches work best with different issues and whether coaches are more, or less, effective when they attempt to work across all domains.

8. Relationship to other services

A clear distinction between coaching and other services (eg mentoring, therapy, counselling) is crucial and is dealt with below. Where coaching and another service are mixed, some argue that this is not coaching; others argue that the term 'coaching' encompasses every service that includes any element of coaching.

9. Qualification

Listening, questioning and clarifying skills are indispensable for any coach. Depending on each coaching approach, additional coaching skills may also be required. But how far should the coach understand the issues faced by the coachee? Should the coach have management or sector knowledge? The main source of coaching proficiency (talent/natural ability, learning/training, experience or a combination of these) is also a topic for controversy, and contributes to the debate about training and development of coaches.

10. Levels of implementation

The importance of each level is assessed differently depending on the school of thought (see Figure 1.2). However, that coaching is a professional service provided by professional coaches is commonly accepted. Whether it is preferable that such coaches are external (from outside the company) or internal (own staff) is again a matter of debate. Also, there is no doubt that companies have increasingly started to make use of coaching forms beyond the one-to-one coaching paradigm as well and to ingrain the coaching principles at the workplace.

FIGURE 1.2 Levels of implementation

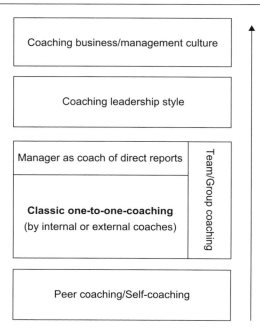

One distinction that is useful to be aware of is between managers who coach their direct reports and managers who demonstrate a coaching leadership style. While the first category are acting like professional coaches and giving formal sessions, the latter maintain their role as leaders and integrate coaching elements, such as listening, skilful questioning and empowerment, into their everyday methods of leadership. It is advisable to be very reluctant and careful about using the first category due to the inherent, likely conflicts of roles.

11. Cultural view

Coaching extends across various cultures at the global, regional, national, organizational and individual level and is a worldwide phenomenon today. There is some debate over how far coaching can be applicable to all cultures and to what extent different cultures require different coaching definitions (see Bresser, 2013a, 2013b; Frank Bresser Consulting, 2009; Passmore, 2009; Rosinski, 2003).

Coaching across the globe

Research (Bresser, 2013b; Sherpa, 2013; ICF, 2012; Frank Bresser Consulting 2009) suggests there are about 50,000 coaches operating in the world. Coaching is a global phenomenon and – irrespectively of the experienced global financial crisis of the past years – has continued to grow, especially in Asia in recent years. At the same time, first indicators are visible for a flattening growth of coaching in Western Europe and North America. Other global trends are the continued diversification of coaching (in terms of cultural diversity, coaching forms and larger technological variety in coaching delivery) and the development of best practice in coaching; unfortunately also the ambivalent situation in the actual practice of coaching in terms of quality and integrity.

12. Individual coaching experience

Each person's unique coaching experience inimitably shapes their individual understanding of coaching. People may see and define coaching in a certain way simply because of how they came across it for the first time. Reflection on and acknowledgement of one's own subjectivity regarding coaching is key to maintaining sound detachment and the right context.

Coaching is still work in progress. The 12 themes illustrate the issues that are part of the ongoing debate as the coaching profession develops. It is this diversity of approaches that provides the rich source of inspiration required for the beneficial advancement of today's coaching profession.

Coaching qualities, skills and competencies

Core elements

In his seminal book *Coaching for Performance*, which has sold over 800,000 copies in 25 languages since it was published in 1992, Sir John Whitmore defined the principles of coaching as 'Awareness and Responsibility'. The diagram below adds another seven and encapsulates the core principles as understood in coaching internationally today:

FIGURE 1.3   Core elements of good coaching

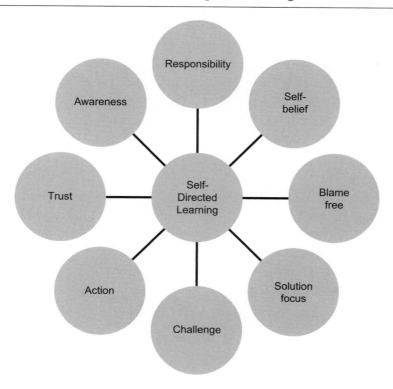

The fundamental skills the coach will use in exercising these principles are listening, questioning and clarifying within a framework of goals and actions. The most well-known framework developed for coaching is the GROW model, which was created by Sir John and his associates, and popularized through his book (**Editor's note**: Graham Alexander (see Chapter 5) was also involved in the development of the GROW model):

FIGURE 1.4   The GROW model

Focusing on solutions raises energy and makes problems seem smaller, so it makes sense to start a session by defining what it is that the coachee wants to achieve. There is a tendency to move immediately into considering what might be done to achieve the Goal; where coaching differs is in the exploration of Reality, by asking questions which hold the coachee's focus in the present, for example:

- What is happening now?
- What impact is it having on you and others?
- What have you done so far?

If enough Goal and Reality questions are asked, the coachee will usually become clear about what can be done, and Options for actions will start to present themselves without effort. The final section is W for Will rather than A for Action because it is about exploring what the coachee can actually commit to doing, rather than ending up with a list of what she or he should or would like to be able to do.

The GROW model is flexible and it is acceptable to jump backwards and forwards through its four elements within a session. It is a robust framework which can be applied to projects and plans as well as conversations. Many other coaching models have since been devised and they are broadly similar to the framework of GROW.

Role of the coach and coachee

There are two components to the coaching session: the process and the content (see Figure 1.5). The coach is in charge of the processes, such as:

- timekeeping;
- ensuring that the coachee sets clear goals, strategies and actions;
- holding the coachee accountable;
- keeping the coachee's focus on track.

FIGURE 1.5 Two components to a coaching model

The coachee is in charge of the content, such as:

- choosing the topics of the coaching;
- creating the specific goals and actions to be worked on;
- deciding upon the time frame.

If coaches allow themselves to drift over the line into 'content', for example, by giving advice or asking questions out of curiosity, they are no longer coaching. Paradoxically, there are times when the coach has some specific advice or insight to offer and, when this is the case, he or she may mark this as separate from the coaching by asking permission: 'Can I offer you some advice from my own experience?', or 'Can I share with you my insight about this?'

The coach acts as a mirror, reflecting back the coachee's thoughts, words and ideas to enable the coachee to see things more clearly and, in doing so, to work out how to move forward. Coaches believe that coachees have all the knowledge they need; the coach is there to help them tap into it.

There are countries where the locals nod when they mean no, and shake their heads when they mean yes. This is a result of their cultural background, and some big misunderstandings can result if we visit such a country without knowing about this custom. Similarly, people have different customs arising from their upbringing or experiences in life, and these are less obvious to spot. It would literally take a lifetime for a coach to map all of these differences enough to be sure of giving the right advice. However, in the space of one session, an effective coach may be able to create a thinking space that enables the coachee to uncover his or her own self-knowledge and best way forward.

Coaching skills

Listening

Clearly, the coach will expect to spend a large part of each session listening to the coachee. However, coaching is more than just listening: the coach needs to be active in the listening process through using the skills of questioning and clarifying.

I have categorized the way people listen into five levels (Wilson, 2014). Coaching happens mainly at Levels 4 and 5:

FIGURE 1.6   The Five Levels of Listening

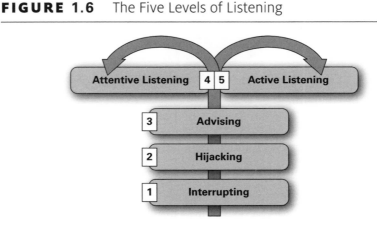

Level 1: Interrupting

> *Speaker*: 'I think we should arrange a meeting about that because ...'
> *Listener*: 'Yes, but did you see the news this morning?'

The 'listener' has prevented the speaker from finishing the sentence and has interrupted with a completely different topic.

Level 2: Hijacking

> *Speaker*: 'I don't know what to do about getting a promotion.'
> *Listener*: 'I've put in an application to move up a grade.'

This time the listener has apparently heard what the speaker said, but has hijacked the conversation by talking about him/herself.

Level 3: Advising

> *Speaker*: 'I don't know what to do about getting a promotion.'
> *Listener*: 'What you should do is ...'

Although the focus has apparently shifted towards the speaker, this is still more about the listener's agenda, and can be right off course because the listener has not explored what the speaker's real issues may be.

Level 4: Attentive Listening

> *Speaker*: 'I don't know what to do about getting a promotion.'
> *Listener*: 'Tell me more ...'

This type of listening is a great luxury which is often in short supply at work and elsewhere. The listener is encouraging the speaker to stay on the chosen topic and explore it further. Through years of research Nancy Kline (1999), a key innovator in listening techniques, identified that the single most important factor in the quality of someone's thinking is the quality of attention shown by the listener:

> 'To be interrupted is not good.
> To get lucky and not be interrupted is better.
> But to know you will not be interrupted allows you truly to think for yourself.'
> Nancy Kline (1999)

Level 5: Active Listening

> *Speaker*: 'I don't know what to do about getting a promotion.'
> *Listener*: 'Tell me more ...'

Speaker: 'I have to arrange a meeting with the boss and I never seem to find the time to do it.'

Listener: 'What's getting in the way?'

Speaker: 'Oh, I don't know. I'm busy, or she's busy. I don't seem to be able to stop long enough to work out how to do it.'

Listener: 'Is there anything else that's stopping you?'

Speaker: 'Actually, I keep putting it off because I hate asking.'

Listener: 'And what do you hate about asking?'

Speaker: 'I'm afraid she will say no.'

'Active listening' is another term for 'coaching'. The speaker's thought processes are helped by prompting and incisive questioning. In the final exchange at Level 5 the speaker has gained an important new insight – that the block is about fear of rejection rather than lack of time. At best, a coach listens at Level 5 throughout every session. This may sound like hard work, but is in fact stimulating and energizing, rather like being in a game and calculating how and when to return the ball.

Questioning

Questions are the precision tools in the coach's toolkit. The coach will skilfully intertwine open and closed questions in order to expand the coachee's learning and channel new insights into actions. Some examples of questions have already been included in the previous section, because questioning is a helpful element of active listening. Here are some further examples of how questions support the coaching process:

Coachee: 'My staff tell me I'm diversifying too much. They think we should just focus on one thing and do it well.'

Coach: 'Your staff tell you you're diversifying too much?'

Coachee: 'Most of the books I read by business gurus say you should focus on the one thing you do best and make it a success before diversifying. We're at the building stage of the business, so perhaps they are right.'

Coach: 'What is your own sense about this?'

Coachee: 'All the areas are related to our core business, so they aren't different as such.'

Coach: 'What is your overall vision for the business?'

Coachee: 'It involves several different dimensions. All my businesses have had several threads. I seem to be quite good at knitting different elements together simultaneously to make one strong business.'

Coach: 'What is your insight about that?'

Coachee: 'You know, I never saw it before, but I think my core business is diversification.'

Coach: 'Your core business is diversification?'

Coachee: 'Yes! It's not a lack of focus. I realize that now. Diversification is the right thing for me to focus on.'

Coach: 'And how can that work for you in this situation?'

Coachee: 'The way it always works. I have the ideas, test them out, follow them through, and when the framework is there I put someone in charge to look after the details.'

Coach: 'And is there any action you would like to take about that?'

Coachee: 'Yes. I'll set up a staff meeting and see if I can get them to understand it too.'

Notice how a sense of energy came into the conversation as the coachee reached the new insight that diversification was his core business. Notice also that the coach asked the coachee to move forward ('How can that work for you in this situation?') only after the coachee had gained this insight through the exploration of his current reality.

Clarifying

Clarifying encompasses the skills of:

- repeating back in different words;
- summarizing;
- reflecting back the exact words.

Repeating back in different words

Repeating back in different words enables both coach and client to understand what has been said. This is a useful tool in helping the client to gain new insights:

Coachee: *'I don't like going to the marketing meetings because everyone talks at once.'*

Coach: *'They won't let you have your say?'*

Coachee: *'It's more that I have trouble asserting myself.'*

Summarizing

Sometimes coachees get bogged down in storytelling and detail. Shortening what they have said is a polite way of interrupting and may also provide clarity in the same way as the previous example:

> *Coachee*: 'I've had the most awful day. I got stuck on the telephone, then the train was late so I missed my connection. And I'd forgotten to charge the mobile so ...'.
> *Coach*: 'Sounds like you had a calamitous start to the day. How are you feeling now?'

Reflecting

Reflecting back a coachee's exact words is one of the most powerful tools in coaching. It affirms to coachees that they have been heard, that what they have said is worth hearing, and that they can now move on:

> *Coachee*: 'I want to replace a member of my team, but I'm not sure how to go about it.'
> *Coach*: 'You want to replace a member of your team, but you're not sure how to go about it?'
> *Coachee*: 'Exactly!'

It may sound trite or awkward to a third-party listener, but the process is so homogenous in practice that the coachee does not normally notice it at all.

Another reason for reflecting back is to ensure that both coach and coachee are on the same cultural map, as we discussed earlier in this section.

Goal setting in coaching

Goals

To be effective, a coaching goal must be inspiring, challenging, measurable and have a deadline. It must also resonate and be congruent with the coachee's values and personal culture. A goal with such qualities emanates a magnetism that pulls the coachee towards it. One of the ways in which this works is through the brain's reticular activating system (RAS). This is the part of the brain that screens out 99 per cent of life's daily bombardment of the senses, allowing us to notice only what is immediately useful. A goal featuring the qualities specified above will embed itself into the subconscious and, through the RAS, we will start to notice pointers along the way that we might otherwise have missed.

Most companies rely on the SMART model for goal setting, and this works well when setting goals for other people. SMART tells the goal setter not to set the goal too high or it may demotivate the people who have to achieve it. However, a coach enables coachees to set goals for themselves, and coachees tend to set the goal too low, out of fear, lack of vision or insufficient self-belief. In addition, coachees often set goals about what they want to leave behind, rather than the destination they aspire to, for example, 'give up smoking' rather than 'get fit'.

For these reasons I created the EXACT goal setting model for coaches (Wilson, 2014), which focuses on positive goals that stretch and challenge the coachee:

FIGURE 1.7 EXACT

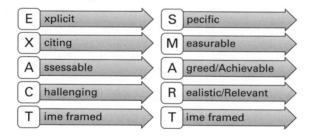

Setting actions

An important part of the coaching experience is to tie down new ideas and insights into concrete action. Setting actions in coaching is quite different from ordinary life. Actions in the real world are often regarded as chores that we want to put off. A good coach will not ask the coachee to set an action until that coachee has reached a new level of insight. Once this is reached, the insight acts as a springboard catapulting the coachee into action; indeed it would be hard to stop someone at this point. The coach's job here is simply to channel the coachee's energy into suitable, challenging and productive actions, with deadlines for carrying them out. The diagram overleaf provides a guide for coaches on setting actions (Wilson, 2014):

FIGURE 1.8   Setting actions

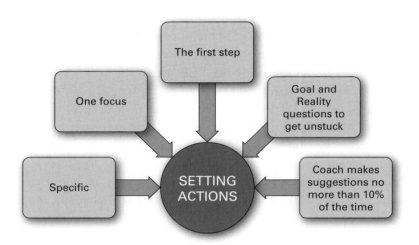

A coach who can bring both structure and the principles of self-directed learning to coaching is most likely to achieve great results. It also pays to remember that there is an underlying journey for the coachee: uncovering new awareness and new insights, and changing deep-seated habits. At the end of a series of sessions, it is often the case that whatever coachees have achieved in terms of their goals, the result that they prize most highly is the new knowledge they have gained about themselves along the way.

Coaching, counselling, psychotherapy and mentoring

Coaching draws its influences from, and stands on the shoulders of, a wide range of disciplines, including counselling, management consultancy, personal development and psychology. However, there are a number of core differences that distinguish coaching from its related fields and these are most easily highlighted through the metaphor of driving a car:

- A therapist will explore what is stopping you driving your car.
- A counsellor will listen to your anxieties about the car.
- A mentor will share tips from his or her own experience of driving cars.
- A consultant will advise you on how to drive the car.
- A coach will encourage and support you in driving the car.

1. Coaching is forward-focused

Coaching always focuses on moving the coachee forward. Counselling may be more appropriate than coaching for, say, the newly bereaved who need to explore their grief over a period of time before moving on. Psychotherapy is a broad field and is usually sought in order to fix a particular problem arising from past trauma. Although the overall effect of both of these disciplines is sometimes to move the client forward, it is not their primary focus. While therapy may be about damage and counselling about distress, coaching is about identifying and fulfilling desires.

2. Coaching is coachee-led

Psychotherapists sometimes use techniques that lead and influence the patient and which could cause damage to the psyche if applied by an insufficiently experienced practitioner. However, coaches should be trained not to lead, judge, advise or influence their coachees. Their role is to respond to the desires and expressed needs of their coachees, and to operate with the belief that the coachee has all the required knowledge to solve his or her own problem. The role of the coach is thus limited to one of a facilitator, unleashing the coachee's potential.

3. Coaching is about improving performance

The focus of coaching is about enhancing performance. In this sense, executive and personal coaching are similar to sports coaching. As a result, a key feature of coaching is behaviour, supported by cognition and motivation.

4. Coaching is not mentoring

Mentoring, while having similarities to coaching, is fundamentally different. A mentor has experience in a particular field and imparts specific knowledge, acting as adviser, counsellor, guide, tutor, or teacher. In contrast, the coach's role is not to advise but to assist coachees in uncovering their own knowledge and skills and to facilitate coachees in becoming their own advisers.

The benefits of coaching

Coaching, when properly applied, can create win–win situations to the benefit of all stakeholders. Potential outcomes of coaching – both short and long term – can be identified at an individual, team, organizational and social level. The key benefits for each level are specified below:

Individual level:

- better self-awareness and self-reflection;
- increased individual performance;
- higher motivation and commitment;
- better leadership skills;
- personal growth;
- higher quality of life/work–life balance;
- clarity in purpose and meaning;
- better management of change processes;
- improved communication and relationships;
- efficient implementation of acquired skills;
- sustainable form of personal development.

Team level:

- improved team efficiency/performance;
- clearer vision development and objectives;
- improved team spirit and conflict management;
- better communication and relationships;
- creating synergies;
- higher motivation;
- unleashing group potential.

Organizational level:

- improved organizational performance;
- higher profitability/ROI/productivity/sales;
- better staff motivation and retention;
- less absenteeism;
- buy-in to organizational values and behaviours;
- better flexibility/ability to change;
- more effective communication;

- open and productive organizational culture;
- realizing the learning organization;
- sustainable form of learning and development.

Social level:

- successful company (with the associated classic benefits for society);
- positive role model for other organizations;
- promotion of 'cleaner' high performance;
- positive, wider impact on employees' social environments;
- higher sustainability and corporate social responsibility (CSR).

The actual impact of a coaching intervention varies, of course, from case to case and is influenced by a number of factors, for example, organizational receptiveness or the coaching approach taken.

A key decision affecting the outcome of coaching is choosing the appropriate level of implementation (see dimension 10, on page 15), which can dictate the different degrees of organizational penetration by coaching (see Bresser, 2005/2006, 2010, 2013a).

Research evidence

While there was only limited research in the beginnings of coaching, the evidence that is available today is (although still not comprehensive) much more substantial and clearly confirms the benefits of well implemented coaching.

On the level of quantitative evaluation/ROI

Despite the high complexity and difficulty of calculating precise return on investments (ROI) of coaching (see eg Bresser, 2013a; Grant, 2012; American Management Association, 2008), the first noticeable attempts in this area were made a bit more than a decade ago: the return on investment of coaching was measured at 529 per cent (and at an astonishing 788 per cent when including the financial benefits from employee retention) for a coaching programme integral to a leadership programme implemented at Nortel Networks (Anderson, Dauss and Mitsch, 2002; MetrixGlobal, 2005). The Manchester study in 2001 (see Johnson, 2004) measured a return of 5.7 times the initial investment for executive coaching, and one-to-one career coaching produced an ROI of 100 per cent with enhanced staff retention (Skiffington and Zeus, 2003). According to Dembkowski (2005), US studies go so far as to indicate a possible ROI of up to 22:1. Meanwhile you find many research and case studies showing a positive ROI of coaching (see eg 2009 ICF Global Coaching Client Study; various company case studies in Bresser, 2013a).

Qualitative, perceptual evaluation of outcomes

There are plenty of research studies (eg Ridler, 2013; Sherpa, 2013; Chan, 2012; Neuroleadershipgroup, 2011; ICF, 2009) and company experiences (see eg Culture at Work, 2015; Bresser, 2013a) documenting a highly perceived value of coaching by organizations and people. Of course, this explains why coaching has become such a global phenomenon and is still growing.

Just to give an example: in 2004, 99 per cent of the organizations in the UK using coaching said that it can deliver tangible benefits to both individuals and organizations (CIPD, 2004). In Germany, 89 per cent of executives being coached and 93 per cent of HR managers saw coaching as a successful tool (Böning and Fritschle, 2005; Heidrick and Struggles, 2004). More than 70 per cent of HR professionals believed that coaching is actually more effective than training courses as a means of changing behaviour and improving the performance of senior executives and high-flyers (*Training Strategies for Tomorrow*, 2003).

Given the existing, endless number of similar sources until today and the enormous variety of coaching benefits you may be interested in, we invite you to visit the following source portals/websites for further info:

www.associationforcoaching.com/pages/publications/research

www.coachfederation.org/research

www.libraryofprofessionalcoaching.com/research

These and other findings make a strong case for coaching as a worthwhile investment leading to potentially tremendous benefits. At the same time we need to continue to develop our understanding of which coaching elements specifically support these outcomes and to use this knowledge in refining coaching practice and training. For this learning process, sound detachment and good sense are needed to allow for realistic assessments of the impact of coaching.

References

American Management Association (2008) *Coaching – A Global Study of Successful Practices*, www.amanet.org

Association for Coaching (2006) *Coaching Definitions*, http://www.associationforcoaching.com/pages/about/our-values

Association for Coaching (2015) *Coaching Defined*, www.associationforcoaching.com/pages/about/coaching-defined

Anderson, M C, Dauss, C and Mitsch, B F (2002) The return-on-investment of executive coaching, in *Coaching for Extraordinary Results*, ed J J Phillips and D Mitsch, pp 9–22, ASTD

Böning, U and Fritschle, B (2005) *Coaching fürs Business*, managerSeminare, Bonn

Bresser, F (2005) The 12 dimensions of coaching, *Coach the Coach*, **15** and **16**

Bresser, F (2005/2006) Best implementation of coaching in business, *Coach the Coach*, Dec and Jan

Bresser, F (2008) The 12 dimensions of coaching, in *Executive Coaching and Mentoring*, ed R S Wawge, The Icfai University Press, Hyderabad, India

Bresser, F (2010) *The Global Business Guide for the Successful Use of Coaching in Organisations*, www.frank-bresser-consulting.com

Bresser, F (2013a) *The Global Business Guide for the Successful Use of Coaching in Organisations*, 2nd edn, BoD, Norderstedt

Bresser, F (2013b) *Coaching across the Globe*, BoD, Norderstedt

Chan HR Consulting (2012) *Second Comprehensive Coaching Study in China*, supported by European Chamber of Commerce and APAC

Chartered Institute of Personnel and Development (CIPD) (2004) *Coaching and Buying Coaching Services*, CIPD, London, www.cipd.co.uk

Culture at Work (2015) *Case Histories*, www.coachingcultureatwork.com/case-histories/

Dembkowski, S (2005) Executive coaching – die 7 größten Vorurteile, www.coaching-magazin.de, pp 1–5

Frank Bresser Consulting (2009) *Global Coaching Survey 2008/2009 – Today's Situation of Coaching across the Globe*, www.frank-bresser-consulting.com/globalcoachingsurvey.html

Grant, A M (1999) *Enhancing Performance through Coaching: The promise of CBT*, Paper presented at the First State Conference of the Australian Association of Cognitive Behaviour Therapy (NSW), Sydney

Grant, A M (2012) ROI is a poor measure of coaching success: towards a more holistic approach using a well-being and engagement framework, *Coaching: An international journal of theory, research and practice, 2012*, 1–12

Heidrick and Struggles (2004) Führungskräfte. Manager mit Coaching, *Wirtschaftswoche*, **18**, 04/2004, p 140

ICF (2012) *2012 ICF Global Coaching Study*, www.coachfederation.org/about/landing.cfm?ItemNumber=828&navItemNumber=800

ICF (2009) *2009 ICF Global Coaching Client Study*, www.coachfederation.org/about/landing.cfm?ItemNumber=830&navItemNumber=802

ICF (2015) *Coaching* FAQs, www.coachfederation.org/need/landing.cfm?ItemNumber=978&navItemNumber=567

Johnson, H (2004) The ins and outs of executive coaching, *Training*, **41** (5), pp 36–41

Kline, N (1999) *Time to Think*, Cassell Illustrated, London

MetrixGlobal (2005) *Executive Briefing: Case study on the return on investment of executive coaching*, www.metrixglobal.net/images/pdfs/metrixglobal_coaching_roi_briefing.pdf

Passmore, J (2009) *Diversity in Coaching*, Kogan Page/Association for Coaching, London/Philadelphia

Ridler (2013) *Ridler Report*, www.ridlerandco.com/ridler-report/

Rosinski, P (2003) *Coaching across Cultures*, Nicholas Brealey Publishing, London

Skiffington, S and Zeus, P (2003) *Behavioural Coaching: How to build sustainable personal and organizational strength*, McGraw-Hill, Sydney

Sherpa (2013) Sherpa Executive Coaching Survey 2013, www.sherpacoaching.com/survey.html

Training Strategies for Tomorrow (2003) When executive coaching fails to deliver, **17** (2), pp 17–20

Whitmore, J (2009) *Coaching for Performance*, 4th edn, Nicholas Brealey Publishing, London

Wilson, C (2014) *Performance Coaching: A complete guide to best practice coaching and training*, 2nd edn, Kogan Page, London

Coaching within organizations

02

KATHERINE TULPA

The need for the human touch

This chapter sets out to provide a framework, along with success factors, for coaching within organizations. Written primarily for the executive and team coach, or companies providing coaching-related services, it is not intended to serve as an extensive 'how to' guide, but rather one that will stimulate further thinking and act as a catalyst in promoting good coaching practice.

In futurist John Naisbitt's book *Megatrends*, which inspired me while I was at university in the United States in the 1980s, there is a theme that I view as a key factor behind the remarkable growth and attraction of coaching, which is, 'The more high technology around us, the more the need for human touch' (Naisbitt, 1982).

Naisbitt declared that in order for human beings to evolve, we need to find greater ways to connect and find balance as society and technology accelerate. In other words, become more high touch in a high-tech world.

Today, we find ourselves in an even quicker, more complex society, where technology reaches most parts of the globe. Organizations need to take notice of how they lead, develop and engage their stakeholders in a climate where e-mails and remote ways of working can hamper effective communication.

We are in a society where many baby-boomers in white-collar jobs are feeling tired, unfulfilled, or are looking for deeper meaning and purpose. A society where the younger generation Y, or 'millennials' (born after 1979), are expected to have higher, more demanding expectations of their employer than their predecessors (Raines, 2002).

Added to this is an emerging need for employees to find more meaning at work. This is highlighted in a number of Gen-Y research and studies indicating that employers who create an environment that promotes a greater sense of 'self', community and challenge that is 'more than just a job' will help to increase motivation, loyalty and staff productivity. Also, there are the questions that have arisen out of the economic downturn, requesting a new form of leadership.

So what do these trends have to do with coaching? If you accept that professionals and leaders in our high-tech world will need to further connect with themselves and others in their quest for deeper meaning, balance and success, then this is both an opportunity and a role for coaches and coaching providers working within organizations.

Additionally, this creates a responsibility. As the emerging coaching profession on a global scale is still in its early growth stages, those now within it are pioneers. Our actions and ways of working will help to shape and harness the uptake of coaching services in decades to come. Our profession will hopefully be one that is not only sustainable and models excellence, but continues to provide a human touch to help our clients evolve and achieve significant, lasting change.

Organizational coaching framework

Successful coaching within organizations goes far beyond the quality of the delivery. When coaching was in the early adapter stage, there may have been more scope where the external coach and the executive could go off into a private room somewhere, enjoy six months of coaching or one-to-one professional development, then conclude the sessions with little or no reporting back to the sponsor or line manager.

Now, however, the tides are changing. Coaching, along with its perceived benefits, is much more visible across the organization; it is no longer mainly a 1:1 intervention for the most senior executives. Team coaching, along with coaching skills programmes and other forms of coaching, continues to grow in popularity. In the UK, for example, up to 90 per cent of organizations are using coaching in some capacity (CIPD, 2009), and recent market indicators have demonstrated that this trend continues. While there are variances across Europe (Tulpa and Bresser, 2009) and other countries, globally, indicators are reinforcing that coaching is on track to become mainstream. Those just entering or who are already established in this emerging profession are pleased we are in this dynamic period, for this is where alliances form to benefit all parties involved and ensure acceptable levels of standards are achieved.

As demand and usage increase, this is also resulting in organizations, in particular those driving leadership, talent or learning and development programmes, bringing in more formal coaching processes and measurements. Today, there are many examples – in particular within larger, global organizations which have established coaching as a strategic initiative – which have set up more consistent ways of working. These organizations are further up the growth curve.

Therefore, as coaching grows in demand, this also creates greater pressure, in particular for the buyers or sponsors of coaching within organizations, to investigate how they procure coaching services, how they manage them, and how they measure them. According to the CIPD (2004), the key challenges facing HR practitioners are:

- integrating coaching with the bigger picture;
- opening 'closed doors';
- meeting the needs of both the organization and the individual;
- information flow and confidentiality;
- scoping and controlling costs.

Discussions with coaching professionals and buyers of coaching suggest that challenges occur when the coaching programme or group intervention is unfocused; the right chemistry or 'fit' between the coach, coachee and company culture isn't there; or there are unclear communications as to the purpose of the programme, the way it was 'sold in', or what the outcomes are.

These are issues that will not go away immediately, but over time coaches and providers of these services can adapt their approach to be more systemic, thereby helping to close the gap and meet their client's needs. My personal view is that if we want to make a real difference and stay within the organizational coaching arena, as coaches we will need to master our game and stretch ourselves to have greater discipline. This includes aligning with the needs of not just the coachee, but also his or her manager, the sponsor and organization as a whole.

There is one more dimension, which is for the coach or provider to choose and align their services with clients that are most appropriate to their personal/business requirements. When the fit is right, this is highly energizing and one where there is the most added value. When it's not, this can deplete not only their energy and focus, but those of others, too. Having the courage to say 'no' at times is not only acceptable, but good practice.

Taking into account these points, I have illustrated an organizational coaching framework (OCF) that looks to address some of these issues, as well as other areas for successful coaching within organizations (see Figure 2.1).

FIGURE 2.1 Organization coaching framework (OCF)

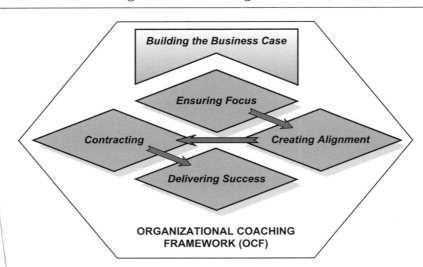

The content of the framework will be explained in further detail in the rest of the chapter; however, as an overview, the main subheadings are:

1 Building the business case

- systemic profiling;

- key challenges;

- gain commitment.

2 Ensuring focus

- maintain drive;

- identify stakeholders;

- clarify business drivers.

3 Creating alignment

- establish aims;

- matching criteria;

- best fit teams.

4 Contracting

- goals and outcomes;

- agreements;

- commitments.

5 Delivering success
- build confidence;
- solicit feedback;
- measure value.

Building the business case

In Chapter 1, the role of the coach, coaching definitions, the business return on investment and the potential outcomes at the individual, team and organizational levels were described. These are useful as a baseline of knowledge when meeting with potential clients.

To expand upon this, this section looks at helping organizations understand and buy into the real value of coaching. As there are still organizations that are not clear on what coaching is, helping the sponsor appreciate the business case will increase the likelihood of coaching being used as an effective tool for leadership and as a complement to other human resource interventions. Figure 2.2 looks at the stages involved in building the business case.

FIGURE 2.2   Building the business case

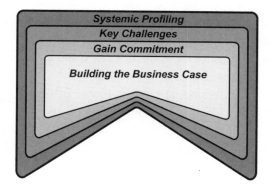

Systemic profiling

Two of the fundamental principles of attracting and working with the right kind of clients for the coach's or provider's business are: 1) knowing where to target, and 2) taking a systemic perspective. These can be referred to as 'systemic profiling'. One way of defining systemic is 'complete' or looking at a situation in its entirety. Like an investigative reporter, it involves discovering information from all angles, with a number of radars, and not accepting the first lead as truth.

On a practical level, the first step to building the business case is for the coach or provider to justify to themselves 'why' they are choosing to work with a particular organization. In other words, stepping back and identifying that the prospect or client is aligned with their vision, service offerings, capabilities and passions.

As we're currently in a market where there is more overall supply than demand, it's easy for the coaching professional to adopt the 'I'll take what I can get' approach. However, this can be very stressful, and from a marketing perspective, not very strategic.

In what areas of your business can you carry out systemic profiling?

Once the coach or provider has satisfied their criteria, this will not only give them further clarity, but help them know where to target and provide further choice. Like good coaching, it all starts with self-awareness – my suggestion here is that a coach/provider will also need self-awareness for their business.

Key challenges

When identifying 'best fit' clients, it may also be useful to investigate the client organization's vision, size, budgets, reporting lines and offerings, as well as its culture, attitudes and past experiences with coaching. A company website will give a snapshot view; the rest can come from taking a coaching approach in meetings with them.

Through the art of developing rapport, listening, asking power questions and giving feedback, a client will normally readily give this information. By taking the coaching approach, the sponsor will begin to share with you their goals and challenges, and embrace any support the coach/provider can give them in building the business case for coaching.

For others who are less receptive, it's useful to enter into discussions about their key challenges. These can be further drawn out by asking SPIN™ (situational, problem, implication, needs payoff) questions (Huthwaite, Inc). Typical challenges are listed in Figure 2.3.

Once the organizational challenges are unravelled, the client's level of awareness is raised and they form a basis for entering into discussions on how coaching may help.

FIGURE 2.3 Key challenges

1.	*Keeping employees motivated during change*
2.	*Giving our leaders and managers further skills to support the strategy*
3.	*Moving from a transactional (or task-based) culture to transformational*
4.	*Having our people stay focused during a sluggish market/low performance*
5.	*Finding ways to build leadership capabilities, innovation and strategic thinking*
6.	*Retaining our best people in a competitive market*
7.	*Discovering ways to reduce stress and increase team morale*
8.	*Identifying ways to engage our people with the company's vision and values*

Gain commitment

After coaching has been established as an appropriate tool for the client's needs, and they understand some of the benefits and what it can help them achieve, the last stage is gaining commitment. Note, the goal here is to establish an appropriate 'next step' (not necessarily to close the deal).

Again, this is where a coach's natural coaching skills are useful, as working with a sponsor to commit to a goal or course of action is not that different from working with a coachee. Commitment is defined as follows: 'the act of binding yourself (intellectually or emotionally) to a course of action' (Princeton University, 2003).

A prospective client will more than likely be making emotional decisions, rational decisions, or a combination of both. For those familiar with the Myers–Briggs Type Indicator (MBTI®), for example, or some of the techniques used in Appreciative Inquiry (ie building on strengths, 'what works'), among others, these can be useful when trying to gain greater understanding or influence a client.

What's important is to draw out options and possibilities from the client, eg 'What could building a coaching culture at XYZ lead to?', so they can witness and experience first-hand what coaching is about. From here it is useful to guide them into action, which can result in a commitment to an outcome and, if relevant, supporting them for their coaching needs.

Ensuring focus

This section explains ways to keep up the momentum gained from your initial client meetings, identify key stakeholders and, most importantly, clarify the organization's aims and objectives.

In the previous section, the focus was on getting to understand both the coach's/provider's and the client's needs (at this point, the sponsor or first point of contact within the organization). Note, there is still not an emphasis on aiming to promote or sell 'offerings', as this will evolve naturally as the coach goes through the rest of the process.

Maintain the drive

By this stage, there should have been some encouraging conversations with the sponsor and they have committed to a next step. So how does the coach maintain the drive?

One perspective is to continue with normal coaching delivery (the comfort zone), and if the sponsor likes the coach, they will call – after all, 'one wouldn't want to appear too pushy!' Another perspective is take a proactive view, staying close to the client and exploring ways to support them – an approach that models behaviours one would have with any coachee.

Many coaches love the delivery part of the business, but dread the 'selling' aspects. To overcome this block, if they can reframe their thinking and continue to focus their energy on the three key activities illustrated in the 'Building the business case' section and in Figure 2.4, this will help maintain the drive with the client.

There is an additional point too, which is important to our profession: being abundant. By taking an approach to serve, the universe has a wonderful way of giving back.

FIGURE 2.4 Key activities

1.	*Know your company's requirements, challenges and strengths*
2.	*Understand your client's requirements, challenges and strengths*
3.	*Take a coach approach, eg developing rapport, effective listening, powerful questioning, giving honest feedback*

FIGURE 2.5   Key stakeholder groups

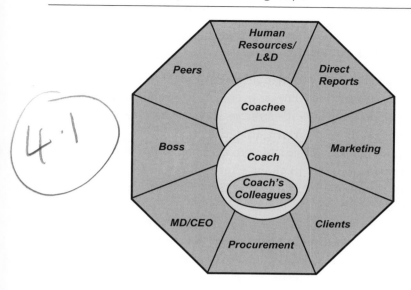

At this juncture, it's a matter of the coach taking responsibility and staying focused on helping the sponsor achieve their aims. By becoming a true partner, a coach who is abundant and shares their knowledge at the front-end can help set their service apart from others.

Identify stakeholders

To help ensure focus and support a sponsor in bringing in a successful coaching programme, it's useful to identify key stakeholders as part of an overall delivery plan. Taking a systemic view and looking at all those affected by the initiative will help the coach and the organizational sponsor adopt strategies for greater buy-in, understanding and communication throughout the process. Figure 2.5 indicates key stakeholder groups.

For smaller programmes, this is a simpler exercise, as there are fewer implications and risks. For larger initiatives, which can be time-consuming and costly, the needs of the key influencers and decision makers need to be considered. Getting the boss and/or most senior leader involved at the outset is vital, to gain top-down support.

At this time, it may be useful to discuss budgets, timelines, other talent, leadership or change initiatives planned, and any other agendas or priorities that could have an impact on the programme's success. At this stage, too, if the sponsor asks for a proposal, you may wish to defer this until there is further understanding of the drivers, purpose and aims.

Clarify business drivers

There is widespread agreement that successful coaching within organizations needs to be strongly linked to the overall strategy and business drivers. This can be a challenge where the strategy is not always clear among the leadership teams, let alone those beneath them.

With that said, in order for coaching to continue to thrive, in particular as uptake increases, it needs to show a return on investment. While we wouldn't want to lose the magic of what the human touch offers, which is invaluable, the profession is indeed getting pressure to measure how our services impact the organization's bottom-line performance. In later chapters of this book, we refer to further ways this can be done.

Some executive coaches, too, who also work in the leadership and organizational development domain, can help their clients shape and articulate their strategies. For others, whose expertise is in pure forms of coaching, it may be useful to start asking questions to clarify what the company's business drivers and, equally, the priorities are. People within the identified stakeholder groups can be a great source of answers.

This quote from *The Thin Book of Appreciative Inquiry* may inspire coaches and providers to ask the wider questions: 'The act of asking questions of an organization or group influences the group in some way' (Hammond, 1996).

Creating alignment

This section focuses on the third dimension of the OCF – creating alignment – which helps to align the coaching programme and matching process with the needs of the coachee (individual or team), the coach and the business (see Figure 2.6).

There is no doubt that coaching, when done well, can make a difference to an individual's leadership, management and communication skills (CompassPoint Non Profit Services, 2003) as well as increase confidence and job motivation (Association for Coaching, 2004). The CIPD (2004) training and development survey also states, 'when coaching is managed effectively, it can have a positive impact on the organization's bottom line'.

FIGURE 2.6   Creating alignment

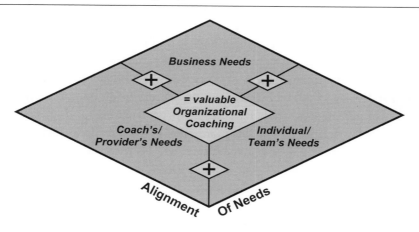

The double benefits of coaching, for the individual and the organization, are now being evidenced in numerous studies (Grant *et al*, 2010).

Establish aims

To make a difference to the organization involves creating alignment, which begins by establishing the aims and objectives, key messages, positioning, what the coaching is for, and internal selection criteria. It's also a good opportunity to reinforce the benefits, and to discuss potential pitfalls and success factors, and how a coaching approach can manifest cultural change.

To do this successfully, it's useful to facilitate a design meeting with the identified stakeholders, linking in the key challenges, business strategy, and other talent and leadership initiatives. If the group doesn't have all the answers, that's OK, as this is where a coach can bring in their knowledge, where required. The purpose is to gain clarity and buy-in from all those who can be ambassadors of the programme, to ensure it gets a first-class start. 'The most valuable coaching fosters cultural change for the benefit of the organization' (Sherman and Freas, 2004).

Matching criteria

Once the overall programme has been approved (usually a client will request a proposal to confirm the aims, content and fees) and the coach has helped the client set up a clear and upbeat communications plan (see 'build confidence'), the next stage is making sure a coach's skills and experience are aligned with the needs of the individuals or teams participating.

A number of organizations and clients that are large users of coaching recognize the value of developing a diverse and rich talent pool of coaches and providers who can accommodate the individual needs and preferences of their executive and managers. In other words, a consistent message is that one size doesn't fit all, with the matching process being one of the biggest challenges and an area where it's possible to 'get it wrong'.

As coaches or providers, the more they can do to help their clients with this concern, the better aligned they will be with their requirements. Figure 2.7 shows a model that can be used by both organizations and providers when trying to create a match.

FIGURE 2.7   Matching criteria

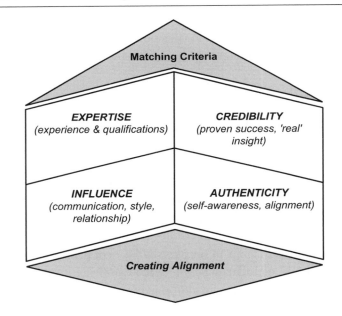

The model recognizes that a good coach, in addition to tangible expertise and credibility, also needs to possess the intangible skills of influence and authenticity.

For selecting tangible skills, some organizations have set up coach-matching systems which help managers select a company-approved coach or provider based on their expertise, preferences (eg face-to-face, location) and other search criteria (eg development need). Figure 2.8 displays components for selecting a coach based on expertise.

FIGURE 2.8 Selecting a coach

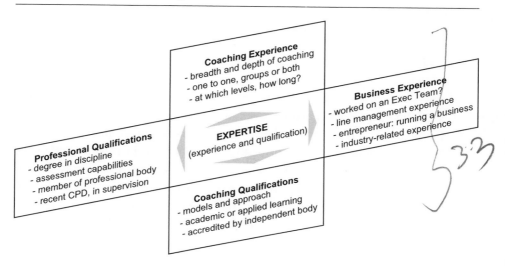

However, as with most technologies and hard data, this does not replace the need for the human perspective. Usually this means a face-to-face meeting with the manager, where the right fit is also based on instinct, the quality of the relationship and other intangibles.

Best fit teams

The concept of best fit teams is one where coaches meet with their prospective coachee for the first time to determine their needs, with the outcome being to establish whether there is a best fit. Many organizations call this a 'chemistry', or briefing meeting.

Because coaching is both a relationship and a partnership, an initial briefing is extremely valuable, for it needs to work from both ends. The main point during this process is for the coach to be honest about their experience and capabilities. It's also useful for the coach to remember that the coachee is buying into the 'whole' coach, not just their profile and knowledge base.

Taking a coaching approach during the meeting will help gain greater understanding for both the coach and the coachee. It's also useful to discuss clear ways of working, models used, and types of clients that have best suited the coach's style, and in what scenarios. This is all very useful information for both parties to determine whether there is a good fit.

There are times when coaches are not a good match for their skills and preferences; when this occurs, it's best to hold up their hand. An 'even better' way is to provide an organization with recommendations to source a more appropriate coach.

Contracting

Once there is agreement of fit, the coach/provider has been selected and the coaching needs are aligned with the business, the next stage is contracting. Sherman and Freas (2004) define contracting in the context of effective coaching as follows: 'By "contracting" we mean not just documenting the legal and financial aspects of coaching, but also defining the goals, roles, and accountability of each party. It works when each term gains the uncoerced agreement of all concerned: client, coach, and coachee.' Furthermore, successful contracting sets the psychological contract, while helping to define the outcomes, set realistic expectations and discuss 'what if' scenarios. The ultimate aim is to pave the way for a rich, highly rewarding learning experience, where all parties see the end results – one where communication and openness are a common thread throughout.

Goals and outcomes

To manage expectations, prior to the contracting session it's useful for the coach to contact their coachee to explain the purpose of the contracting session, who will be attending, and what to expect. So that they have a chance to reflect on their programme goals, it's also useful to send them a draft 'learning agreement' prior to the session, which may include:

- company aims;
- business goals (eg team, career);
- development areas;
- desired outcomes;
- any previous assessments/feedback.

At the session, these are discussed with all parties, which typically include the coach, the coachee (executive or manager) and their boss and/or sponsor (eg HR, Learning & Development).

The role of the coach is to facilitate the process and to encourage open feedback, where typically the goals, outcomes and priorities of the coachee's development programme are discussed. The group will also need to conclude that these goals are congruent and integrate with the company strategy, key drivers and aims.

Although the group shares the responsibility – often referred to as a 'triangular relationship' – the role of the facilitator is to check to make sure the goals and desired outcomes are realistic and that there is mutual clarity and understanding, and to listen intently, as terminology and the team's 'interference' (Gallwey, 2000) can sometimes get in the way.

Agreements

After the goals and outcomes are clearly defined, the next step in the contracting stage is to discuss and agree the terms. Acknowledging that the programme is an investment in the executive or manager's development, fully backed by the company, helps set the tone for the level of responsibility required by all parties. It's also useful to have a one-page overview of the draft terms at hand, to be finalized at the session.

Figure 2.9, adapted from *Coaching in Organizations* (Association for Coaching, 2004), provides some guidelines. One area worth highlighting is confidentiality. There are different views on this. Some professionals feel that any feedback being reported to the manager or sponsor needs to come directly from the coachee so that it doesn't jeopardize the amount of self-disclosure and trust required for effective coaching. Other views are that, while issues of confidentiality still need to be maintained, the client or organization is part of the coaching relationship, so a degree of reporting back is essential. This is to help support the coachee's progress and learning objectives, as well as the overall programme success. It's also a view of the Association for Coaching (2004).

FIGURE 2.9 Guidelines for agreeing contracting terms

1. **Terms of relationships** – coaching involves the coach, coachee and the sponsor paying for the coaching and/or the line manager
2. **Organization of sessions** – location, length and frequency, along with what basis contact is made between sessions
3. **Commitment to sessions** – is the assignment based on a flexible or open-ended programme, or a fixed number of sessions?
4. **Review dates** – agreed measurements and timescales, along with specifying the stakeholders involved in the review
5. **Other participants and roles** – roles to be specified and agreed
6. **Boundaries** – this links with confidentiality and should identify the purpose of the coach's role and therefore boundaries of the relationship
7. **Cancellation and payment terms** – understanding of fees, policies and agreements (NB If this is a part of an overall programme, it may be appropriate to discuss separately)
8. **Confidentiality** – basics include:
    - existing organization confidentiality agreements will be adhered to by the coach
    - the coach should be part of a professional association and abide by a code of ethics, not revealing any personal information
    - the sponsor recognizes the right to confidentiality but may ask for some success measures

So how does this work in reality? A way to handle this is to discuss in the contracting session the types of information that will be disclosed, at which levels, by whom, and how often. What's important is that all parties are transparent and very comfortable with what's agreed, paying close attention to the views of the coachee.

Commitments

After the goals and agreements are in place, the last step is to confirm the levels of commitment to the programme. This is where it is helpful to allow time for questions and discuss 'what if' scenarios, the promises of each party member, and programme success factors. Here are some typical 'what if' questions, as possible discussion points:

- What happens if there is a change of goals?
- What happens if, after all this coaching, 'x' decides to leave us?
- What happens if I require a different style of coach halfway through the programme?
- What happens if I want additional coaching for my team outside the programme parameters?
- What happens if I find it hard to make the time in my diary?
- What will a successful coaching programme look like?
- What does each of us in this room need to commit to?

There are other questions that may arise, but the important thing is that the group discusses and agrees how to respond to these, rather than the coach feeling a need to provide the solutions. Like good coaching, this helps to gain commitment.

Delivering success

By this time, the coach is finally at a stage to do some delivery of coaching – whether it's at the executive, manager or individual level, or working with teams. They have also built a strong foundation based on achieving clarity, focus and alignment. This last section looks at how to sustain and deliver success by working with all stakeholders within the programme to build confidence, solicit feedback and measure value.

Build confidence

At the very heart of coaching is a core quality that permeates the entire coaching process – building confidence. Whether this is coaching an individual at a remedial level, a leader at a transformational level or a group at an organizational level, when people or teams are looking to reach into the horizon, coaches need confidence in ample supply.

To fuel confidence, our inner power, requires a total belief, trust and respect in not only self, but the client. In 'Coaching for influence and impact' (Tulpa, 2005), a person's Centre of Power™ is one that 'inspires, engages, ignites and creates change': 'If coaches take a systemic view, in that coaching is what goes on in the space between the coach, coachee and organization, then what can happen if not only coaches are able to connect with our inner power, but also the manager/leader and the organization?'

Building confidence starts off by giving self and a client permission not to shy away from success stories. For every manager or leader that is coached, asking them to tell a story of their experience can be extremely beneficial. Communication and confidence are partners – to create larger ripples across the organization, a coaching or leadership initiative needs to be communicated widely, and often.

The real impact will come when it has top-down support. When the CEO or leader going through coaching with their team can endorse the programme, there is a greater likelihood of success. When it's seen as a reward for high performers, and helping them become even more successful, it helps to build the case for coaching and create a pull rather than a push.

Solicit feedback

Exchanging success stories isn't the only aspect of communication. To be able to deliver a successful coaching programme, adapt it appropriately and increase the coachee's learning, soliciting feedback is a key activity.

Beyond using individual assessment and 360° tools (multi-rater feedback), there are additional methods you can apply, including:

- shadow coaching;
- face-to-face feedback;
- group feedback sessions;
- organizational surveys;
- learning surveys (for the coach);

- co-coaching forums;
- informal feedback forums;
- client roundtables;
- coaching evaluation forms.

Treating the programme as one that touches and impacts various stakeholders across the organization (see Figure 2.5) can help a coach select the type required. The main points to consider are ethics: 1) adhering to confidentialities, 2) soliciting feedback on a volunteer basis only, and 3) following up with all those to whom it pertains in a specific and timely manner.

Measure value

In the introduction, I spoke about how coaching can help add a human touch to an increasingly detached world. I've also used the word 'value', one that goes beyond coaching delivery and delights all people that coaches 'touch' within the organization – the impact can be far and wide.

In Chapter 1, reference is made to ROI studies on organizational coaching. While the results for organizations are evident, and we need to continue to monitor this, it is the coachees – individuals and teams – who have gone through the coaching experience and are the ones measuring the value. They see first-hand the effects that coaching has on their skills and performance, which can leave an imprint at a deeper level.

Also, based on usage figures and commitment to spend from organizations that have seen first-hand the impression it can make on their people, coaching appears here to stay. In 2004, coaching expenditure in the United States was estimated at $1 billion per annum (Sherman and Freas, 2004), and there are now indicators that this figure has more than doubled as coaching expands globally as a key development tool for increasing performance.

That's not to say we don't have our work cut out for us – delivering value to an often complex organization is not an easy task. Green and Grant (2003) give a broader view of today's modern organization: 'An organization is a dynamic system. It is a growing, changing group of people and connections. Patterns emerge, the shape changes, only one thing is certain, it cannot remain the same.'

While we can never control a system's response to a change, we can be mindful of the currents and help to inspire and support our clients' development journeys as we 'ride the wave of change' (Tulpa, 2004).

References

Association for Coaching (2004) Summary Report: ROI from corporate coaching, http://www.associationforcoaching.com

Chartered Institute of Personnel and Development (CIPD) (2004) *Coaching and Buyers Guide*, CIPD, London

CIPD (2009) *Taking the Temperature of Coaching*, Summer, CIPD, London, www.cipd.co.uk

CompassPoint Non Profit Services (2003) *Executive Coaching Project: Evaluation of findings* (based on a study by Harder + Company Community Research), http://www.compasspoint.org

Gallwey, T W (2000) *The Inner Game of Work*, Orion Business, London

Grant, A M, Passmore, J, Cavanagh, M and Parker, H (2010) The state of play in coaching, *International Review of Industrial & Organizational Psychology*, 25, pp 125–68

Greene, J and Grant, A (2003) *Solution-focused Coaching*, Pearson, London

Hammond, S A (1996) *The Thin Book of Appreciative Inquiry*, Bend, OR

Naisbitt, J (1982) *Megatrends: Ten new directions transforming our lives*, Warner Books, New York

Princeton University (2003) WorldNet 2.0, 'commitment', http://dictionary.reference.com

Raines, C (2002) *Managing Millennials*, Generations at Work, www.generationsatwork.com

Sherman, S and Freas, A (2004) The wild west of executive coaching, *Harvard Business Review*, www.hbr.org

Tulpa, K (2004) 'Ride the wave of change', welcoming address, Association for Coaching International Conference, London

Tulpa, K (2005) Coaching for influence and impact, *Coach the Coach*, 17

Tulpa, K and Bresser, F (2009) Coaching in Europe, in *Diversity in London: Working with gender, culture, race and age*, ed J Passmore, Kogan Page, London

Leveraging the coaching investment

03

KATHERINE TULPA and MARGOT HENNESSY

Introduction

Coaching's contribution to the performance of teams, individuals and organizations has come a long way over the last decade. In many cases, coaching has become one of the most accepted forms of people development, as executive and team coaching, along with other types (eg internal coaching, coaching skills programmes, or 'leader as coach'), get rolled out as organizations look to build coaching cultures to drive business results.

Some of the questions, therefore, that are being asked from sponsors involved in leading an organization's coaching investment are: 'How do we ensure it is strategic and will maximize the business performance?', or 'How do we lead and manage the significant investment?'

In this chapter, we aim to respond to these questions, with a particular emphasis on getting the best when bringing in external coaches or coaching partners, as opposed to internally-led initiatives (although many of the same principles apply). We look to enable sponsors in achieving the best outcomes from their coaching initiatives. We also provide a strategic framework with accompanying best practice principles, which we hope will both challenge and stimulate the thinking and practice in this area.

The strategic framework is based on our shared wisdom of working with a number of global organizations involved significantly in coaching. This is based on our roles as executive coaches, coach assessors, and as an internal L&D sponsor, as well as interviewing a number of other organizations leading the way in this area.

Strategic framework for leveraging external coaching

In putting together the framework, considerations have been made for the key elements that require the sponsor's attention, if the desired outcome is to ensure that the organization is leveraging its strategic external coaching investment (see Figure 3.1).

FIGURE 3.1   Strategic framework for leveraging external coaching

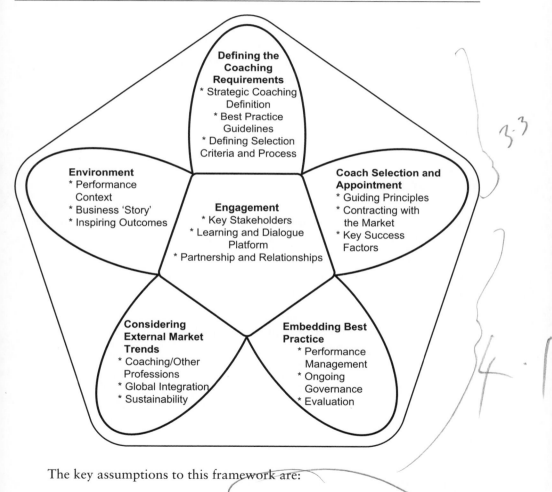

The key assumptions to this framework are:

- The organization's focus is on performance coaching vs remedial coaching. When using the term 'performance coaching', this explicitly means coaching that is focused on fast tracking the performance of an individual, group of individuals or teams, for the purpose of increasing organizational performance.

● The framework is dynamic and not intended to be a point-by-point guide. As readers engage with the different elements of the framework and review the framework holistically, the aim is that it will provoke and stimulate the development of the approach they are recommending and/or implementing.

Therefore, the proposed strategic framework, along with the recommended principles, is for a) organizations wishing to deliver greater organizational performance from the existing external coaching investment; or b) those embarking on a significant development approach, where performance coaching is a key part of the recommended learning intervention.

It is encouraged that the framework is used in a way that is integrated with the company's overall organizational development (OD) strategy. This is not only good practice, but commercially makes sense if sponsors are to drive optimum organizational performance through their external coaching investment.

Environment

As organizations continue to use external coaching to build a diverse range of capability, the more they need to focus on creating the right environment for coaching to succeed.

Creating the right environment requires setting high expectations on the financial investment, along with the anticipated results, so that there is more opportunity to leverage the external coach spend and the significant benefits that coaching can bring. It also requires the sponsor and key ambassadors (internally and externally) taking the time to proactively educate all stakeholders on 'what good looks like' throughout.

There are key areas of focus in order to cultivate this environment and achieve the greatest impact for the business. This includes the performance context, the business 'story', and inspiring outcomes, outlined in the sections below.

Performance context

Many organizations leave the briefings for the external coaching to the individuals or teams being coached. While this provides important context for the coaching, it is only part of the equation. What is often missing is the broader frame of reference, or greater understanding of the business environment, which can help coaches perform at their optimal abilities.

This knowledge, called here the 'performance context', is one of the benefits that internal coaching can bring; however, with further briefings and communication, there is no reason why this information cannot be shared with those within the coaching pool made up of external coaches/providers.

It is also recommended that sponsors take the lead on this, being proactive in defining this performance context, and communicate this to external coaches on an ongoing basis. This will enable the external coaches to focus and deliver within the broader environment, as well as the individual and team coaching context – therefore, optimizing the contribution of the organization's external coaches.

For organizations that do not provide the overall organizational performance context, a critical component, then the external coaching investment will be minimized.

Business 'story'

The term the business 'story' is used to describe what the organization has or needs to develop in respect to their growth agenda.

The 'story' is the way the organization articulates their:

- key business drivers;
- hopes, ambitions and goals;
- short- and medium-term business outcomes;
- organizational and leadership capabilities required to drive the business forward;
- other characteristics, values and attributes that will lead to success.

Essential to the story will be the relationship the organization sees between performance and talent, along with clear accountabilities that leaders and managers need to have in order to create an environment for people to perform.

For many organizations, this is the talent story; however, the business story is one that is owned by all leaders of the business, which the talent agenda is designed to deliver against. Inherent in the story is the ambition and the performance stretch that clearly define the potential which exists between current performance and the future business performance. The story needs to be succinct yet compelling.

Within the story, there is clarity about the strategic and current business outcomes and what is required to meet these objectives. There is also a level of transparency with regard to the challenges the business faces. This is balanced by a belief, or confidence, by key stakeholders that the desired outcomes are achievable.

Inspiring outcomes

While many organizations can state their strategic goals and performance plans, how they intend to achieve the outcomes is sometimes not clearly articulated to key stakeholders, including the external coaches they work with. Furthermore, when they do articulate them, they might not create the followership they require.

In creating and articulating desired outcomes, there are some key factors to draw out to include in the business 'story' to inspire and engage key stakeholders, including the external coaches. These factors also help the leaders be accountable for shaping and articulating a compelling business performance context, as defined in Table 3.1.

TABLE 3.1 Key factors for articulating desired outcomes

- Performance outcomes: how are the overarching short- and long-term performance outcomes for the business articulated?

- Environment: what is the larger 'playing ground' and greater operating environment the company is operating in? What is it looking to create and influence?

- Competitive strengths: what does the company want to strengthen and develop? What is the brand and how is it positioned in the marketplace?

- Signature strengths: what are the company's signature strengths and how will these be leveraged in order to achieve the short- and long-term outcomes?

- Measures of 'performance': what does the company expect and value in respect to delivery?

- Capabilities required to deliver the short- and long-term goals.

- Leaders' roles and responsibilities: what are the leaders' roles and responsibilities for delivering all of the above?

Engaging a diverse range of stakeholders in formulating the above to distil the most powerful messaging is recommended.

To truly leverage the external coaches' capability, the organization needs to articulate the broader business performance context in which they want their coaches to deliver. Doing this will result in key stakeholders, including external coaches, being inspired to work to the broader organizational outcomes, as well as individual or team development goals.

Defining the coaching requirements

Many organizations have yet to think through, articulate and engage their key stakeholders in defining their organization's strategic external coaching approach, resulting in a rather individualistic approach which can impact the organization's investment in this area. While this approach can deliver results to an individual/team's performance agenda, it often misses the opportunity to drive the overall organization's performance agenda. This opportunity, if taken, can drive even greater performance, leverage the commercial investment and transfer capability from external coaches into the broader organization.

Defining the external coaching requirements may well take the shape of a standalone coaching strategy, or it may form part of the organization's broader OD/HR strategy. Regardless of where it resides, in our experience, there are some key considerations that will enable sponsors to fast track their thinking in how to shape, direct and deploy the external coaching investment. These are highlighted in the sections below.

Key elements to defining the strategic external coaching requirements

There are key elements that are useful to address when defining what is required from the external coaching investment. Table 3.2 lists what are considered to be the key elements, providing a brief outline of questions needed, in order to develop a position for each. The outputs provide information and clarity that help to direct strategic decisions in all aspects of external coach selection, assessment, appointment and evaluation. It also provides the direction in order to embed best practice external coaching across the organization.

Encouraging sponsors to consult and engage key stakeholders, to create and articulate outputs around these elements is recommended. It is also

TABLE 3.2   Key elements to defining your strategic external coaching requirements

Elements	Considerations
Description – what does the organization mean by external coaching?	When leaders and people in the organization have experienced great coaching, what makes/made it great? What are the behaviours of these coaches – how do they create the performance impact? Does coaching refer just to external coaches or does it include the transfer of knowledge that consulting companies bring – eg innovation?
Outcome – what is the outcome you expect from every external coaching intervention?	What are the performance outcomes you expect from every external coaching assignment? What has been in place from external coaching assignments that have had the biggest performance impact on individual/team, eg sponsorship, line management involvement?
Organizational Aspirations – what are the stated performance aspirations of the total organization?	What are the overall performance outcomes that the business wants to drive – what capabilities are needed to drive this? What are the organizational capabilities (leadership, people, values) that are required to be embedded through development practices?
Accountabilities – clarity and articulation of organization approach – macro and micro	Is a centralized or decentralized approach to leading/managing your external coaching investment best? Is the right outcome a blend of the two? Who holds overall accountability for leading/managing? What are the roles and deliverables of key stakeholders in every coaching intervention – eg coach, coachee, and line manager?
Annual Spend – proportion of development budget to be spent on external coach	What is the right proportion of your development spend on external coaching? What percentage of this will be on team vs individual coaching? Which populations will you target with your investment?
External Coaching/ Market Trends	What is the latest thinking/practice from the marketplace? What is the latest research on coaching results?

helpful to make this information readily available to all stakeholders, including coaches, so they can perform at their best and deliver against organizational requirements. Both the conversations and the outputs from these activities will enable sponsors to lead, shape and manage the external coaching investment.

Best practice guidelines for use of external coaches

After completing the strategic coaching requirements, taking the time to create and communicate a set of guidelines on what the organization's best practice is in respect to the use of external coaches is vital. These guidelines at a minimum will establish the ground rules for engaging external coaches and outline the selection criteria and organizational expectations of each external coaching intervention.

Some suggested guidelines are to:

- Explicitly state the organization's position on the use of external coaches, including the strategic position taken on both external coaching and where the annual investment will be focused.

- Clearly define what is meant by external coaching. Not everyone has the same definition, so this alone will create change. Coaching in our experience is hard to define. Therefore providing people with a description of what the organization considers best practice coaching will fast track understanding and buy-in.

- Make transparent what external coaches' capabilities are used in selecting the external coaches. This will influence organizational users of external coaching to reflect on their coaching experiences and fast track their understanding of why the company has set the benchmark that it has.

- Identify expectations of the external coach investment. Recommend what each external coaching intervention will contain, eg length, deliverables, accountabilities of the coach, coachee and line manager.

These guidelines will provide the organization with the opportunity to reinforce the benchmark it has set in respect to the use of external coaches and promote consistency throughout the business for both team and individual coaching.

Selection criteria and process

As each organization defines and uses coaches in different ways, it's helpful to develop a set of criteria for coach selection that is aligned with the strategic coaching approach. Where this is not clear, then as a starter it needs to be aligned with the culture and overall business and people strategies, whether the need is for one-to-one coaching, team coaching, or both.

Furthermore, there are many companies that consciously select a diverse coaching pool, seeking coaches from different backgrounds and training, to accommodate the different types of leaders and the scenarios they would be working in. Others look for coaches that can demonstrate a firm grasp of their business, and/or fit in with the company's values, above and beyond the necessary coaching competencies, experience and qualifications.

Table 3.3 identifies common or basic requirements that show up across various coach selection criteria within larger organizations.

While it's easy to put out a questionnaire into the marketplace to sift through coaches' suitability to meet the basic criteria, there is a word of caution before this is done. Allowing enough time to first spend determining what to measure, along with how these areas will be evaluated is recommended.

It is also useful to determine whom to involve in the selection process. Some companies outsource this to consultancies that specialize in coach selection – and in doing so, still find it crucial to involve key stakeholders within the business, so there is ownership from within.

In terms of coach levels, typically these processes run to work with the organization's most senior leaders; however, recently we have seen organizations bringing in external coaches to work at the middle to senior management levels, at lower fees.

Coach selection and appointment

Regardless of the level of coaches sought, going through a formal selection process is a large investment of time and resources, for both the organization and the provider/coach involved. Below are defined guiding principles and other areas to take into consideration in order to maximize the return from coach selection, including success factors for what works well, in the appointment of suitable coaches.

TABLE 3.3   Coach selection – basic requirements

Ability to demonstrate a strong business acumen
Willingness to work to the organizational agenda, as well as the individual or team agenda
An accredited coach with a minimum of 3–5 years' professional coaching experience and/or a minimum of 500 coach hours*
Coaching qualifications from a credible school and/or significant related experience
In ongoing reflective practice, with high levels of self-awareness and commitment to their ongoing personal development
Certifications in various psychometrics/instruments (ie MBTI, EQ-i, etc)
Ability to hold the client 'safe' – boundary management (ie not going into therapy when not qualified, etc)
Has a 'learner' mindset – is equally comfortable as the learner as the coach
Can clearly articulate his or her underpinning beliefs, philosophy, and approach to coaching, and what informs this
Demonstrates a clear process, with proven effectiveness of his or her coaching
Has the breadth and versatility to coach in complex, dynamic environments
A member of a professional body, with a commitment to ethics and best practice

*For board-level executives, the average is typically higher – a minimum of 6+ years experience and/or a minimum of 1,000 coach hours.

Guiding principles

From our experiences, looking at a number of coach selection processes across mainly larger, global organizations, it is useful to have some guiding principles in place. These include the following, to be reinforced, in particular, by the organizational sponsor:

- to build a partnering ethos, based on trust and respect;
- to be clear and honest in communications;
- to walk the talk and deliver on promises made;
- to create a platform for learning.

When any of these are missing, there may be challenges in attracting the highest calibre of coaching in the market (if that is what the organization is seeking), or risking getting the reputation of being a company that does not take a professional or coaching approach in how they work with, or engage with, their external talent, in particular their coaches or providers.

Although there is a danger in generalizing, there have been cases where companies have mainly looked to commoditize or run the coach buying and selection through procurement, and have missed the mark in that the core coaching principles get lost. This can result in a lower overall success rate, as well as being a growing concern for the profession.

Equally, it's important to seek these same principles and related behaviours in the coaches themselves, aligned with the selection criteria and the strategic coaching approach.

Contracting with the marketplace

Before contracting with the marketplace, it's very useful to give potential coaches or providers an indication of the estimated business they would be expected to have, if they were successful in being chosen to join the organization's coaching pool, or 'academy'. This builds on the principle of establishing a partnering ethos, as many formal coach selection and appointment processes can take 2–5 days out of their diary, which is non-billable time.

As an indicator, Table 3.4 gives forms of assessment methods used, along with estimated timings they take for participants. Many experienced coaches both appreciate and use this information in their decision-making process – both the projections and whether or not the sponsor has done their 'groundwork' internally – on whether or not they put themselves forward.

TABLE 3.4   Assessment methods and timings

Phase	Method	Est. timing (with prep)
'Go to market'	Questionnaire	½ day–1 day
	Pre-interviews	2 hrs–4 hrs
Development centre	Presentations	2 hrs–4 hrs
	Live coaching demo	1.5 hrs–2 hrs
	1:1/Panel interviews	1.5 hrs–2 hrs
	Critical review/write-up	1.5 hrs–4 hrs
	Co-supervision (observed)	1.5 hrs–2 hrs
	Ethics case study	.5 hr–1.5 hrs
Follow-up/Appointment	Post-development feedback	.5 hr–1.5 hrs
	Induction/Briefing day	½ day–1 day
	Coach matching meeting	1.5 hrs–4 hrs
	Procurement conversations	1.5 hs–4 hrs

Similarly, other considerations from the coaches' and suppliers' end are whether or not the organization has given an indicator of the rate ranges or budgets, as being transparent around the budget parameters at the outset can manage expectations.

While many coaches find going through a formal selection process, when run well, to be a highly rewarding experience in terms of their ongoing professional development, it is useful to be mindful of these factors when 'going to market' to select suitable coaches. Companies who do this well have limited the ratio to no more than 1:5. In other words, if 20 coaches are required, the maximum number of entries they would be initially looking for when contracting with the market is 100, from which would be selected those invited to go through a development centre or further assessment methods.

Key success factors

In addition to what's already been mentioned – engaging key stakeholders, defining the coaching strategy and approach, establishing selection criteria that are appropriate for the business, and being clear on the estimated volume of business and rates before going to market – below lists key success factors for a winning coach selection process:

- Be mindful of not overdoing what's being called for without carefully establishing what's actually required – longer isn't always better!

- Position the coach review as a development and learning opportunity for coaches – eg having a 'Development Centre' as opposed to an 'Assessment Day'.

- Bring in expert input – eg representatives from professional coaching bodies to serve on the selection panel to provide an independent, broader perspective.

- Use both theoretical and practical forms of assessment and calibrate the two – a highly competent coach can demonstrate a combination of both.

- Write a clear brief, and communicate upfront what will be measured. This will allow some coaches/providers who do not qualify to de-select themselves.

- Set realistic timelines and meet all deadlines given – in particular, when the final decisions will be made and whether there will be follow-up feedback.

- Establish in advance a number of dates when the development days will take place, to enable busy coaches/providers to fit this into their diaries.

- Show diversity in the pool – different coaches for different needs/ leaders. Having coaches versed in different models, with different experience, can be highly useful.

- Adhere to all confidentiality and data protection policies – a coach's reputation, along with data provided, is sensitive information and not to be treated lightly.

- Create a win–win – striking the right balance between 'asking' and 'giving' at any stage throughout. This includes post-appointment, to build a longer-term relationship.

Once appointed, in order to create this win–win, some organizational sponsors have successfully recommended partners within their coaching pool to other companies looking for coaches within their wider network (typically other HR or L&D).

Although it is not recommended to take these coaches on at face value (as an appropriate coach for one organization isn't necessarily a good fit for another), it is still a good place to start, especially if the company's coach selection strategy is to initially cast a smaller net rather than a wider net that is typical when broadcasting requirements to the larger coaching community. There are strengths/weaknesses both ways.

Regardless, this is just one example of how sponsors can develop strong relationships and a partnering ethos with their appointed coaches, which will yield positive returns.

Embedding best practice

Embedding an external coaching strategic approach is important if the organization is to sustain its approach and leverage its annual investment in external coaching. Below are three areas that will provide greater traction in achieving this.

Performance management

In our experience, performance-orientated organizations who successfully invest in external coaching have a high expectation or mindset that a significant performance shift will occur as a result of every external coaching intervention. Setting this expectation is a key part of leveraging the external coaching investment that the organization can make. When this expectation is set at the outset, it helps to focus the coaching and ensures that all parties involved are committed to doing their part in making the performance shift happen.

Therefore, it is recommended that the performance outcome, specifically the behaviours the coachee is committed to making as a result of the external coaching investment, is recorded and tracked as part of the organization's performance process conversations and system. Of course, the detail of this will depend on the performance management system which exists in the organization.

In our view, one cannot go wrong by focusing on recording and tracking the following:

- The outcome the coachee or team is driving to – recording and tracking the outcome rather than the content or detail.
- Making sure the outcome is linked to the business, thereby focusing the outcome again on performance to support the end game.

- The role the line manager will play in supporting and enabling the coachee or team to make the shifts (to be tracked and recorded in their performance commitments).

- Defining key success measures on what is working in practice as a result of the coaching intervention.

- For all stakeholders to have similar expectations, with agreement to proactively use the performance management system to record the performance outcomes that the coaching is designed to deliver.

- To have key milestones along the coaching intervention. This is important, as the capability that coaching brings is to broaden the capability of the individual or team.

Experienced coaches and leaders will proactively encourage the tracking and recording of commitments through the organization's performance management system. They understand that if there is a commitment from the organization to invest in external coaching, then it needs to be matched by the individual's and team's commitment to deliver change as a result of the investment.

Each coaching assignment begins with exploration. Therefore, if performance outcomes are not written in an outcome-focused way, it can hinder the progress stakeholders make as they engage in the coaching work.

As a word of caution, it is strongly advised that the external coaches do not get involved in any form of feedback conversations that relate directly to the coachee's performance; for example, asking the coach to advise on whether or not the coachee is suitable for a potential promotion, or having the coach participate in salary or pay review discussions. Even with the best intentions, this is clearly outside most coaches' boundaries and code of ethics, as a professional coach.

Establishing ongoing governance

The role of ongoing governance is essential for embedding the strategic approach to external coaching that has been defined. Ongoing governance entails ensuring that all accountabilities associated with the external coaching investment are clearly understood and communicated. All stakeholders, including coaches, should be informed of what their accountabilities are, and where they should sit.

In addition to having the roles and responsibilities defined for each stakeholder, it is also useful to build upon the organizational best practice guidelines established for using external coaches, and create easy-to-access 'how to' guides for working with their coach or coach provider.

Here are some of the key areas to include in the guides:

- A list of the selected coaches and coaching providers, along with their contact details, geographical location and a short summary of each coach's background, strengths and style.

- Rules of engagement: eg budgeting, contracting, review process, confidentialities, cancellation clauses, etc.

- Expectations and parameters: eg if the selected coaching pool are the ones used within the company, this needs to be clearly articulated.

- Recommended length of external coaching assignments: who is to be involved in matching, and how external coaches should exit.

- When the final meeting with the coachee and line manager takes place, so that the expectations and outcomes of the coaching intervention are transparent.

These will help those responsible for choosing the right coach for the team and/or individual for whom they wish to provide a development intervention.

Some companies, too, set up a dedicated coaching portal on their internal intranet system, which makes the information widely accessible. This is especially beneficial if it is the leader or manager in the business procuring their own services for coaching, as opposed to a more centrally-led initiative.

Evaluation

The third key area which will ensure that the strategic external coaching approach developed by the organization is embedded and continually enhanced is ongoing evaluation. This evaluation needs be linked to measuring both individual and team coaching interventions, such as highlighted in Chapter 16 on evaluating coaching programmes. For the purpose of this chapter on how organizations can leverage their external coaching investment, see overleaf for a couple of recommendations in line with the systemic approach and performance orientation of the framework that is being proposed.

First and foremost, evaluating the strategic coaching approach is a prerequisite for embedding best practice. Being open to learning and incorporating the learning into a sponsor's approach will best serve the organization in its desire to maximize its investment in coaching.

The focus and design of all external coaching evaluation should be systemic, in which case it will take into consideration and evaluate the following:

- the performance impact or changes that are created as a result of the external coaching investment;
- the behavioural shifts in coachees – how they are behaving differently and contributing more to business results;
- the contribution of the external coach in enabling the coachee to make the required performance shift;
- the contribution of other key stakeholders in enabling the coachee to make the performance shift, eg line manager in contributing to the performance shift.

Ensuring that the evaluation focuses on all of the above areas will enable the organization to assess the factors that are contributing to, and limiting, the business results at both a strategic and individual/team coaching intervention level. A combination of surveys, interviews and review meetings at regular intervals will develop the organization's knowledge of coaching and the results, help to build the organization's intellectual property around coaching, and provide insights into the key levers that will inform this approach to both the coaching strategy and best practice coaching interventions.

Engagement

The levels of engagement, both internally and externally, for any significant coaching investment have a direct impact on the return of the coaching investment. In the sections below, this highlights some of the key components to encourage high levels of engagement.

Key stakeholders

The importance of involving key stakeholders both inside and outside the business as part of the evaluation process, as a source of learning, which can feed into the broader coaching agenda has already been discussed. If listened to, and dealt with effectively, this can create opportunities that can unlock further business performance.

Working with a number of organizations that do this well, they do get this balance right, establishing a partnership ethos throughout by treating the coaches as part of the company, and encouraging a number of stakeholders across the company to be accountable for the success of the coaching. If it has been positioned well as a strategic initiative, both top down and bottom up, then this makes it easier to do in practice.

This is where, too, developing the influencing skills of the sponsors initially kicking off the initiative needs to be strong. They need to have the ear of the CEO or board, and be able to translate the investment into real business terms, which adds shareholder value. This does come down to the quality of relationships established and the amount of time spent on them, as opposed to most of it being in the process or 'nuts and bolts'.

Furthermore, it's helpful to communicate to the members of the lower tiers, even those not going through coaching, why their managers are going through it, in terms of their development. This can help to create a learning environment, inspire leadership through a pull approach, and create further energy and support for the programme.

Platform of learning and dialogue

Creating and building a platform of continual learning and dialogue across key stakeholders will promote numerous benefits for both the organization and external coaches. It will also ensure that the strategic coaching approach delivers against its objectives.

Ongoing dialogue and learning requires all stakeholders to start with an intention to be open and engage in conversations where trust and transparency underpin the relationships in pursuit of organizational performance deliverables. The sponsors can take the biggest lead in this area by creating a way of working with external coaches that provides all stakeholders with a structure that will enable and inspire them to contribute fully. This structure includes many of the things being recommended as part of the strategic framework model, including providing a clear and compelling business performance context that contains a clear set of accountabilities for all key stakeholders.

Accompanying the structure must be an ethos of partnership and relationship that will establish and build a way of working that fosters learning and dialogue among all key parties. As part of the engagement strategy, building a two-way communication process between the organization and coaches that will provide the opportunity to share experience, information and learning is also encouraged.

Another key element of the engagement strategy is to ensure that all communication opportunities maximize the opportunity to deliver updates on the business performance context, along with setting up media for continuous dialogue with external coaches. These media can take the form of telecons, evaluation meetings, education forums, or even through a blog/web portal, to make the updates easily accessible.

Partnership and relationships

Having a 'partnership ethos' is another principle identified as something that needs to exist across key stakeholders in order for the results of coaching to be truly leveraged.

In companies who are leading successful coaching programmes that we studied, this mindset – followed by a set of behaviours – is prevalent. This helps in creating strong relationships, and those involved in turn become advocates for the initiative, both inside and outside the company.

In fact, even with coaches or providers who were not chosen within a selection process, if they were treated well, this created goodwill and ripples in the marketplace. This can only help a company's reputation, essential for attracting top talent, or, for example, lead to being seen as a company 'easy to do business with' as a way to secure new business or clients.

The best companies, too, involve their CEO and/or executive team as a partner in the programme – not just at the commencement of the coaching, but throughout. This commitment helps to drive coaching as an enabler to deliver business performance.

To summarize, having continuous dialogue across all stakeholder groups, with clear accountabilities, and building ongoing, trusting relationships that are aligned to the overall performance agenda are among the most essential success factors. Not taking the time to do so can be a sponsor's biggest mistake.

Considering external market trends

Owing to the dynamic, global trading economy which now touches every member of society, business leaders, more than ever, need to consider carefully the external market factors that can impact on the welfare of their business. In short, being too insular or inwardly-focused will make or break an organization, and at a rapid rate. The events of the recent banking crisis have demonstrated this.

As previously established, coaching needs to be positioned at the highest levels of the organization, as a board or strategic imperative, in order to maximize shareholder value and drive performance. This also helps in getting the right levels of engagement and support, so that over time the benefits of coaching become inherent to the company's culture.

This section identifies some of the external market factors and trends worth considering within the strategic framework, to ensure a higher return from coaching across the business.

Coaching/Other professions

As coaching evolves into a profession, demonstrating codes of ethics, best practices and standards, accreditation, evidence-based research, academic journals and shared statement of value, amongst others, those within it are continually identifying success criteria, measurements and approaches to help the profession advance.

These include a number of professional coaching bodies, such as the Association for Coaching (AC), the International Coach Federation (ICF) and the European Coaching and Mentoring Council (EMCC), which are at the forefront of these advancements.

There are also a host of academic institutions and training/service providers offering degrees and advanced certifications in coaching, along with peer-to-peer coaching forums, networks and government institutions, many of whom are pooling their shared knowledge and resources.

Furthermore, there are other industries and professions, including consulting, training, learning and development, psychology, counselling, career transition, and even executive search, which may add additional perspectives and learning into what is occurring within the wider talent, or people development, marketplace.

In short, as the coaching profession continues to grow and become more globally connected, there will continue to be a wider set of experiences and research into 'what works' – and therefore a rich source of data available for organizations investing in coaching interventions.

Global integration

According to the research (Cave and Tappin, 2008), adapting to rapid technology changes, including social networking and other virtual ways of doing business, will be one of the biggest challenges for organizations. Another is what they refer to as 'hard globalization', where competition is coming from all directions worldwide. Succeeding in this game requires leaders to have a truly global mindset.

As boundaries become blurred and trading becomes more integrated and complex, this breaks down a number of our conventional ways of working and doing business. There are not only cultural influences to consider, but language barriers and an increasingly diverse and remote talent base, which can initially hamper communications and team working.

For leaders introducing a coaching strategy that will make a real impact on the business, it is useful to consider these factors. In particular, not just the types of coaches they use, who may require more cross-cultural competencies, or working with global leaders around these areas, but also mindset. It also may require talent to be identified more locally, and/or the coach to be well versed in telephone coaching or other forms that maximize the use of technology.

Sustainability

Recent events have also influenced businesses to add 'sustainability' to the boardroom agenda. Broader than the term corporate social responsibility (which is getting a bit dated), sustainability looks at social, economic, environmental and ethical factors.

These areas are especially important as companies trade globally, so they need to be aware of international and local laws affecting these decisions. Also, there are new stakeholders to consider (eg UK banking institutions having the government as a key investor), with a shifting of power bases. Finally, there is an increasingly demanding client base starting to make purchasing and employment decisions based on the company's values and actions around sustainability. This is especially apparent in the younger generations.

With that said, offering coaching as a strategic intervention, tied into the sustainability agenda, can underpin or reinforce these considerations. Based on the Meaning and Purpose Survey (Association for Coaching/Coaching at Work), a number of coaches are seeing this show up more and more frequently in their coaching. This can only help in supporting leaders through these changes and in driving the agenda forward.

Summary

Our aim in writing this chapter was to prompt and stimulate the thinking of every sponsor who has accountability for leading and managing an organization's external coaching investment.

Much has been written about the benefits of coaching in accelerating the performance of individuals and teams and its contribution to organizational performance. However, there is also a demand to emphasize the important leadership role that organizations need to play in leveraging the external coaching investment and maximize the returns for all parties involved.

The strategic framework is systemic in its design, and takes into consideration a number of different elements that readers will benefit from as they design and embed their strategic approach to external coaching. While this chapter has focused mainly on external coaching for the purposes of this chapter, many of the principles outlined in the framework can easily be applied to internal coaching.

Finally, it is encouraged that all those who embark on this journey, design and embed an integrated approach to their strategic coaching investment, so that the results are not only sustainable, but make a lasting difference within their organizations and beyond.

References

Association for Coaching (AC), www.associationforcoaching.com

Association for Coaching/Coaching at Work (2009) *Meaning and Purpose Survey*, retrieved from http://www.wisdom8.com/resources/meaning_and_purpose.html on 4 February 2010

Cave, A and Tappin, S (2008) *The Secrets of CEOs*, Nicholas Brealey Publishing, London

Chartered Institute of Personnel and Development (CIPD) (2009) *Taking the Temperature of Coaching*, Summer, CIPD, London, www.cipd.co.uk

European Mentoring and Coaching Council (EMCC), www.emccouncil.org

International Coach Federation (ICF), www.coachfederation.org

Setting up and running your coaching practice

04

ALEX SZABO

Planning for success

The aim of this chapter is to help the self-employed and those thinking of setting up a coaching business to plan their next steps. The chapter focuses on the key elements of running a business, looking at what the individual already has in place, what areas need to be developed, and how to move forward.

According to Dun & Bradstreet and INC. magazine, 33 per cent of all new businesses fail within the first six months. Fifty per cent of new businesses fail within their first two years of operation and 75 per cent fail within the first three years. The reasons for this are usually related to at least one or more aspects of the business that are not being run effectively on a consistent basis. There may be enough clients to generate sufficient turnover, yet financial controls are lacking or the systems and administration processes are not in place. Alternatively, clients may not know who you are or what you do.

The starting point in this process is to ask yourself, what do I want? For most of us this is a difficult question to answer. What would you do if you had a coachee like you? Take time to ask yourself the same questions that you would ask them – write down your questions and reflect on what your answers would be.

In planning ahead you might also need to give some thought to a series of questions about the nature of your business:

- What do I want my business to look like?
- What stages are the different parts of my business at?

- What do I need to do to take my business to the next level?
- Why do I want my business to grow?
- Which areas of my business need to develop?
- Who needs to do that?
- When does it need to be done by?
- How is it going to happen?

Setting up a coaching practice

Company structure

When setting up your coaching practice you will need to decide on the 'trading form' it will take (see Table 4.1). The options you choose will dictate the tax you pay, the management information systems you keep and how you protect your personal assets.

TABLE 4.1 US and UK company structures

Type	Set up	Management and raising finance	Liability
Sole trader *Sole proprietor*	Register as self-employed with HM Revenue & Customs within three months of start-up. Register as soon as you can after starting your business. At the latest, you should register by 5 October in your business's second tax year. *In order to register your sole proprietorship, you'll need to file a DBA with the state or county if you're going to use a company name.*	You can make the decisions and raise funds on your own assets (*raise capital or use your own money/credit to fund your company*).	Personally responsible.

TABLE 4.1 *Cont'd*

Type	Set up	Management and raising finance	Liability
Partnership (*general partnership*) – two people +	Each partner to register as self-employed with HM Revenue & Customs. Have a written agreement. *Forming a business partnership involves filing a name statement, obtaining an employer identification number and creating a written agreement that outlines who the partners are. Contact local government agencies to obtain licenses and permits for a partnership.*	Partners to manage business and raise money from own assets. *General partners share equal rights and responsibilities in connection with management of the business, and any individual partner can bind the entire group to a legal obligation. Each individual partner assumes full responsibility for all of the business's debts and obligations.*	Each partner personally responsible (*and comes with a tax advantage: partnership profits are not taxed to the business, but pass through to the partners, who include the gains on their individual tax returns at a lower rate*).
Limited liability partnership (LLP)	Two designated members.	Members to manage business and raise money from own assets. *Because the LLP form changes some of the fundamental aspects of the traditional partnership, some state tax authorities may subject a limited liability partnership to non-partnership tax rules. The Internal Revenue Service views these businesses as partnerships, however, and allows partners to use the pass through technique.*	LLPs have two designated members who have extra legal responsibilities. *Limited liability partnerships (LLPs) retain the tax advantages of the general partnership form, but offer some personal liability protection to the participants. Individual partners in a limited liability partnership are not personally responsible for the wrongful acts of other partners, or for the debts or obligations of the business.*

Type	Set up	Management and raising finance	Liability
Limited liability company (LLC)	Incorporated at Companies House; one director and company secretary. *An LLC is not a corporation; it provides the flexibility of organization of a proprietorship or a general partnership – you don't have to have shareholders, directors, and officers.*	Directors to manage business and finance raised from shareholders, borrowing on retained profits. *Choose an available business name that complies with your state's LLC rules. File formal paperwork, usually called articles of organization, and pay the filing. Create an LLC operating agreement, which sets out the rights and responsibilities of the LLC members. Obtain licenses and permits that may be required for your business.*	Shareholders not personally responsible. *Like shareholders of a corporation, all LLC owners are protected from personal liability for business debts and claims. Because only LLC assets are used to pay off business debts, LLC owners stand to lose only the money that they've invested in the LLC.*
Limited partnership	*Not every partner can benefit from this limitation – at least one participant must accept general partnership status, exposing himself or herself to full personal liability for the business's debts and obligations. The general partner retains the right to control the business, while the limited partner(s) do(es) not participate in management decisions.*	*The general partner can be set up as an LLC to protect them. Both general and limited partners benefit from business profits.*	*A limited partnership allows each partner to restrict his or her personal liability to the amount of his or her business investment.*

NOTE:
US: text in italic relates to US practice.
UK: source info https://www.gov.uk/business-legal-structures/overview

The final structure may also depend on how much time you want to dedicate to your coaching practice and your involvement in any other activities. It is best to seek advice as to what might be right for you from your local business adviser, solicitor and accountant. Investigate resources, chambers of commerce, government websites, etc in your respective counties to get the most accurate information of a legal structure that would work for you.

Data protection

Anyone who uses a computer to keep personal information on other people will need to register the purpose for which they will use the information. This is a requirement under The Data Protection Act.

There are, however, exemptions and you would need to contact the Information Commissioner to ask for personal advice. (UK only, though there may be country equivalents.)

Insurance

Types of insurance applicable to small businesses include: professional indemnity insurance; contents insurance; and illness/loss of earnings (and where applicable, public and employer liability insurance). It must be relevant to your industry and your type of trading format in order to ensure that you have the cover that you require for your own particular needs.

Protection

Trade or service marks – the logo/design adopted by a company to identify its service or products – can be registered at the Patent Office.

Copyright – no registration is necessary; you are automatically covered if you create something original. It is advisable to use a copyright symbol © to identify it as your intellectual property. You can post it to yourself using registered post and keep it unopened in a secure place.

Assessing the business

In assessing where you are before starting out, think about your skills under four headings: Yourself; Your Operations; Your Sales and Marketing; Your Finance (see Figure 4.1).

FIGURE 4.1   Overview: Your coaching practice structure

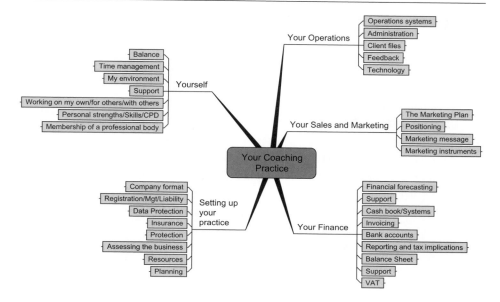

When you run your own coaching practice you need to be multi-skilled. Talk to others who have run their own businesses, and in particular talk to other coaches who run their own coaching practices:

- What is the most important thing they have learnt since starting in business?
- What would have been useful to know before starting in this field?
- If you were to start all over again, what would you do differently?

In gathering views, aim to answer five questions for yourself:

1 What should I have in each of the above categories?
2 What do I currently have?
3 What is missing in each area (skill/service/process/technology)?
4 What resources do I need to close the gap?
5 What support do I need?

All of us have gaps in our strengths when we start out: the key to success is having a plan to manage them both initially and on an ongoing basis.

CASE STUDY   Resourcing

Charlie is a successful coach. While she is intelligent and probably could have found the time to learn and develop an appropriate financial system for herself, financial management does not excite her. She recognized that this was something she needed to get on top of in order to manage her business successfully.

During her coaching supervision she explored her options. She decided that she did not want to take time to develop herself in this area but rather use the expertise of others to take on these roles. In this way she was able to use her time more effectively to coach others and spend time following her other interests. The actions for her included deciding what she was able and interested in doing, clarifying specifically what she wanted another individual to do, deciding what format she wanted the information in, researching a good bookkeeper who lived locally, getting quotes and meeting bookkeepers, deciding on who she was going to use, and making the necessary arrangements to collect her receipts and invoices in a file to be passed over to a bookkeeper to sort and log in the format she needed.

She bought in the necessary resources so that she could focus on what she needed and wanted to do:

- what: effective financial management of the business;

- why: to be aware of the financial position in order to make astute business decisions, comply legally and be free to focus on her core business responsibilities;

- who: someone who has expertise in this area;

- when: on a weekly basis;

- how: carry out the identified actions and follow a process whereby receipts and invoices would be passed over and presented back in the agreed management information format.

Planning

Follow the process for yourself, gain clarity about why you need to do this by planning effectively and setting your goals/strategies for each area, and take the relevant action. Hold yourself accountable, or ask someone you know/or a coach to do this for you, or work with someone who is going through the same process.

Success arrives much quicker if you plan things first. There may need to be several goals running concurrently, so work in a way that suits you. As a coach use your skills to outline/identify what motivates you, your values, the benefits to you and your business, and be clear about the key outcomes you would like to achieve.

Your operations

This section is about the key day-to-day functions of the business. For the purposes of this chapter it is assumed that you know how to prepare and run a coaching session.

Operations

The systems and administration processes that cover initial client contact through to the end of client contracts are known as your 'management information systems'. This consistent service should meet and suit your own and your customers' requirements. Essential elements to track include:

- Preparation:
  - details of initial contact with client including payment terms;
  - session preparation;
  - contracting: first trial session/presentation: setting expectations; coaching; confidentiality, ethics.
- Session:
  - preparation;
  - delivery;
  - coachee notes;
  - payment record;
  - setting future sessions.
- Follow-up:
  - record keeping;
  - filing;
  - logging feedback;

- post-session response to client;
- session date and utilization tracking;
- financial tracking;
- reflection, continuous evaluation and improvement actions.

Client and coachee files

Create a checklist and file for each client so the relevant information can be logged. This can include: a record of their details; contract; client notes; dates of client meetings; recording of the payments made; and an overall summary of the number of sessions. You may also want to keep brief summary details of each session.

What supporting processes do you need? As well as having checklists, know what the next steps are within the client engagement process. Consider developing a process that outlines what you need to do and by when. You may need to use a customer relation management (CRM) software package to record and achieve better customer relations.

Coachee notes need to be kept securely and recorded accurately. In particular, your notes need to be legible and laid out in an understandable format. As client notes are personal data, the coachee has a right to request to see them, so ensure that what you write is appropriate to share. A second element is the potential claim on these records by the courts. While coachees would not generally share notes with a client (such as the head of HR in an organization), if legal action is taken the courts may request access to your papers.

Remember that in your coaching work you are not giving advice, so your notes need to be simple and useful for you to help guide your journey. One mnemonic that you could use is ACT:

A: Actual or factual information that the coachee shares and is relevant to record.

C: Coaching considerations, which may be further research you need to undertake, or ideas you have during the coaching session that are inappropriate to share at that time.

T: Tasks that you agree with the coachees that they will undertake after the coaching session.

The length of time records are kept varies, and in coaching there are no definitive guidelines. The Association for Coaching (AC) recommends that records are retained for a period of at least five years.

Feedback

It is useful to obtain feedback from your clients. Such feedback can help:

- monitor the effectiveness of coaching;
- draw attention to areas of development for the coach;
- emphasize areas that still need to be addressed within the coaching engagement.

Questionnaires are a good way to collect this information.

Technology

Do you have appropriate technology? Invest in a computer with suitable hardware and software that is going to meet your needs. Keep it backed up and up to date. Organize your files methodically so that you can save time retrieving resources or the information on a project/client file that you are working on. You can improve performance by automating routine procedures and free your time to do more creative and productive work.

Your financial management

Forecasting – personal

When starting a business it is helpful to ascertain how much money you need to make from the business, to ensure that personal financial needs are covered. A realistic personal budget includes categories such as food, rent, bills, general housekeeping. Outline these in a spreadsheet and record actual expenditure against the projected expenditure, which will adjust the yearly budget.

Forecasting – business

You need to identify how much income your business will make, what the likely expenditure will be and then how much profit you hope to make.
    This can be done by:

- estimating total income from the sales of products and services;
- estimating the business-related expenditure;
- calculating salary (and dividends if applicable), including relevant tax payments.

The difference between what you are taking out of the business and your personal forecast is the sum you will potentially need to find from other sources.

Cash book/Systems

It is important to log everything that you do with regards to income and expenditure. In the early stages of your business development it is advantageous to set up a simple Excel spreadsheet to reflect everything that is coming in and going out under 'payments received in' (eg coaching sessions/ training, other) and 'payments out'. It is also important to keep all your receipts, cheque books, bank paying-in books, bank statements, copies of your own invoices and suppliers' invoices together.

Invoicing

Invoice the companies/individuals you are working with, outlining your payment terms, and ensure that your invoice arrives with them in good time, in the format they need for processing.

Set up a system whereby you check what is coming in and going out of your account. It may be helpful to have a process checklist for each client, for example:

Name

Session No

Date

Invoice sent

Payment received

Tracking date

Bank accounts

After you have decided what sort of company to set up, it would be advisable to set up a separate bank account under your company name. This will avoid confusion when reconciling your accounts. All banks provide start-up business account packs and many have a small business adviser who will be able to advise you on your particular needs. It is also advisable to get online internet banking in order to manage transactions and monitor your account.

CASE STUDY

M was an entrepreneur on his third business. When asked what he had learnt and what he would have done differently from past business ventures, he was able to identify two aspects that he could now apply to his third business: 1) check out his subcontractors' financial status (one had gone bankrupt); 2) have accurate record keeping (his second business had fines imposed on it due to late submissions and poor financial record keeping). Although the offerings of both businesses were excellent, they had suffered due to the poor financial and administration processes.

Reporting and tax implications

Depending on the structure you have chosen, there will be different administrative processes, tax and liability implications.

A balance sheet

- fixed assets – eg what the business owns;
- tangible (computers, buildings);
- intangible (goodwill, intellectual property rights (IPR), trademarks, domain names);
- current assets – eg what the business is owed (work in progress, owed by clients);
- current liabilities – what the business owes short term (overdrafts, loans, taxes);
- long-term liabilities – eg owner's capital, creditors after one year, 1 year + loans.

All financial records kept by business owners must be retained for six years.

VAT – UK

When your business turnover reaches £81,000 a year (or is expected to reach that figure), you must register for Value Added Tax (VAT) at HM Revenue & Customs.

Value added tax is a tax on the sale of goods and services which needs to be charged on sales for most businesses at the standard rate (currently 20 per cent).

You need to keep copies of all invoices and receipts and a record of all VAT you have charged and paid, and complete a VAT return on a quarterly basis.

TIP: 6 S's

System – set up financial systems which you understand and can complete on a regular basis.

Submissions – be systematic in submitting your returns on a consistent basis.

Support – get regular support from your accountant or financial adviser.

Separate – keep personal and business(es) financial files separate.

Sorted – file all aspects in an organized way, receipts in monthly files, statements in order, invoices in monthly files/client.

Security – keep all your records safe in a fireproof box and back up your electronic records weekly with a paper copy elsewhere.

SOURCE: Adapted from Business Link (2005)

Sales and marketing

According to one marketing author, the strategic objective of marketing is 'to have your clients, customers, prospects, referral sources and other stakeholders think of you first, often and well'. What would that look like in your coaching practice? If your clients think of you first, often and well, they will happily frequent your business, buy more of your services, do this regularly over a period of time – aka loyalty – and be your best advocate to new business. Prospects will give you a first crack at their business and referral sources, will talk about you often and with conviction. All of this adds up to a profitable practice with the best return on your marketing investment.

Most businesses fail because they are not properly marketed. Superior products and services poorly marketed are no match for an average product marketed with superiority. Virgin Records started with a handful of unknown brands by an unknown entrepreneur. What makes Richard Branson an exceptional entrepreneur is not the products in themselves but his brilliant and innovative marketing skills.

The marketing plan

All plans must start with an objective. Without clear objectives there is no direction; without a clear direction there is little focus and you will end up wasting time, energy and money going in directions that are unrewarding and unprofitable. Clear goals and objectives for your coaching practice are the foundation for marketing yourself. They define success so you recognize it when you arrive! Your marketing plan is really a series of questions to ask yourself.

Ten questions to build your marketing plan

1 Your goals and objectives: where are you going?

2 Your target audience: who are you going after?

3 Your offering: what are the benefits of your offering that meet the needs of your target audience?

4 Your positioning: what makes your offering different from the competition?

5 Your competition: who are you up against and what are they saying in the marketplace?

6 Marketing message: what is the core message of everything you do and say?

7 Branding: what is your identity/personality?

8 Marketing instruments: what marketing instruments are you going to use to reach your target audience?

9 Marketing calendar: when are you going to launch the prioritized marketing instruments?

10 Marketing budget: how much are you going to invest to attract and retain your clients?

Positioning

Coaches are competing with other coaches and as the market grows there is competition for the attention of clients and prospects. The noise in the marketplace is overwhelming. Ten years ago the average person was subject to over 2,000 marketing messages per day; this number has swelled to over 30,000! Consequently, not only must your message cut through the clutter, it has to be relevant, compelling and memorable, so that they think of you first, often and well.

Too many coaches try to be all things to all people, which is impossible to market with credibility and ends up being irrelevant to most. Experience suggests that coaches who are tightly focused enjoy greater success and profitability by targeting a niche and becoming the expert in that arena. In other words, make yourself 100 per cent relevant to your ideal client and you will attract more clients that resemble your principal current clients, and those who are unprofitable will disqualify themselves. Finally, your positioning must be:

- unique – different from everyone else;
- credible – easy to prove;
- defendable – no one else can easily lay claim to your positioning;
- sustainable – it will work today, next month and next year.

Your marketing message

Imagine walking into an arena where every seat is filled with your ideal prospects. Could you walk out on that stage and present to them effectively? Now let's raise the stakes. The audience is told: 'You had to come, but you don't have to stay. If this person (you) fails to keep your interest, you can simply get up and leave.' What do you think would happen? Are you really ready?

Here's what's probably going on with your audience. At any given time, 3 per cent of your prospects are currently in the market to buy your product or service and looking right now to get it. Another 6 to 7 per cent are open to it, but not currently looking. The other 90 per cent are divided into three nearly equal categories:

1 Not really thinking about it right now.
2 Think they're not interested (but might be, if you did a good job at presenting to them).
3 They know they're not interested.

So here's the real challenge. Let's imagine you have an extraordinary value proposition for your coaching, but at this time, 90 per cent of the audience isn't in the market for your coaching. At least, they think they're not interested. That means if you walk out into the arena and begin telling them how great your coaching is, 90 per cent of your audience is going to get up and leave.

What are you going to do?

So you need to 'wow' them by beginning your presentation with information that makes your prospects say: 'I didn't know that.' The focus must be on them and the things of interest to them, not you. So rule number one of your 'killer presentation' is that it must be focused on the prospect and not on you or your coaching (at least not initially).

We have seen presentations that increase closing ratios from one out of ten to eight out of ten. Also, a compelling presentation can significantly increase your ability just to get in front of your prospects in the first place. How?

Offer prospects something of value outside your product or service, something important to them. For example, a well-known marketing coach never talks about his coaching or his marketing experience and skills before telling his clients about 'The four marketing traps and how to avoid them'. Remember, 97 per cent of his prospects think they are happy with their current marketing, but he finds they can almost all relate to the pitfalls and find themselves in one or more of the 'traps', so they begin to listen and relate. Why? Because the information is of value to the prospects even if they have never heard about your offering or do not perceive a current need.

What information can you give away to your prospective clients that is above and beyond your product–service offering and would be considered extremely valuable to them?

Marketing instruments

There is no shortage of things you can do to market your practice. In fact there are over 125 ways to market your business. The point is to be selective. Pick the right 15 to 20 instruments that will best market your practice and provide the best return on your marketing investment. In fact, you need to assess marketing on a continuous basis, much like managing a financial portfolio. Inevitably you will find marketing instruments that perform well; continue to invest in these, perhaps even invest more. Then there will be those that need some tweaking. Finally, there's the bottom 20 per cent of your marketing activities that perform poorly ... throw them out and replace them with other marketing activities that could provide better yields on your investment.

Many marketing books have lists of marketing instruments, or a quick web search on 'marketing instruments' will help you.

CASE STUDY   Marketing

Luke is an accredited coach with extensive business experience. He knew he had to take the next steps to market himself and his coaching practice. He had little practical marketing experience and decided to employ a marketing coach/ consultant. His coach enabled him to achieve his goal of 'To be generating 20 prospects per week and acquiring 12 coachees in the first three months of 2005 through the development of a successful marketing plan supported by a website and a targeted marketing campaign'.

The coach identified with him the elements that would take him to the next level, from the name of his business, the method he would use to deliver his service, the branding, the website content, the stationery, the marketing message, instruments and calendar, public relations, the sales training and sales presentation, through to the growth plan. Today he is a very successful coach with a thriving coaching practice.

Luke became successful because he developed a plan and then took focused and consistent action by implementing the plan according to the agreed timescales. Luke was able to monitor his progress as he could see that everything he was doing was achieving a result. He distinguished himself from the competition and communicated a compelling and relevant message to his target audience using appropriate marketing instruments. His client base exceeded the targets that he had originally set himself.

Execution starts with a plan and is maintained by regular action and reviewing.

Sales

Why all the emphasis on marketing? Sales without marketing means you must constantly beat a path to your prospects' door. But a tenacious marketing strategy properly executed will result in prospects beating a path to your door. As long as you can develop positive relationships and you are priced fairly, you will win over many profitable clients.

Remember to nurture your clients and develop the relationships on an ongoing basis. They will buy more and more from you and also become your referral source through selling on your behalf. Don't be afraid to leverage existing clients or past contacts from another business for more business. This is your most efficient and effective marketing instrument – an active and intentional referral plan.

Yourself

To run and manage your coaching practice effectively on a regular basis you also need to identify what other areas you need to balance this with. Decide what is important to you, have a look at what is essential to keep, and identify areas you might need to let go of.

Be professional, authentic and true to yourself and your values. This includes your mindset and the brand identity you are presenting, both in appearance and your written and verbal communications. It pays to know your limitations and to take a stand for what you believe in, even if it doesn't suit others.

Balance

You can raise your commitment to a project by identifying the personal and professional benefits that will come out of achieving it.

Ten key questions

1 What are my other roles and commitments (parent, partner, work commitments, hobbies and interests, projects, spiritual needs, health, social, etc)?

2 What are the benefits of being involved in these areas?

3 How does being involved contribute towards my vision?

4 What gives me the highest return?

5 Why do I need all of these areas in my life?

6 Which areas aren't aligned to my personal and professional values and are ones that I can let go of?

7 Who needs to do that?/Who do I need to tell?

8 When will I do that?

9 How do I balance the running of my practice with everything else?

10 What process do I need to set up to ensure that I am doing everything that I want and need to be doing?

Time management

Coachees often tell us they want more balance in their lives. What questions would you ask your coachees? It is very easy to let things slip, or feel under pressure to be organized in a certain way. How do you prefer to work? What works best for you: scheduling or having flexibility? Having set days or putting things in your diary as and when? Do you need to build in 'me' time? What is the first thing that slips when you are busy? Develop an intentional plan that takes these factors into account.

Seek help either through reading, further training, or getting coaching in the areas you need to develop, such as procrastination, meeting deadlines, planning, meeting targets and working under pressure. These can be overcome and enable you to move forward and realize your and your company's potential.

Get the balance right between what you need to do for yourself personally and what you need to do for your business to grow.

Working environment

Managing the environment you work in helps you achieve your best. If your office is in part of your home you will need to ensure you have the following:

- separate defined working space;
- suitable technology (computer/fax/scanner/telephone/headset);
- desk/chair;
- filing and storage facilities;
- adequate lighting/heating/ventilation;
- bookshelf;
- set working hours.

If you are seeing coachees from home, you will also need an extra chair, to have the office clean and tidy, and ensure your insurance covers you seeing clients from your home office. Adapt your environment to maximize your potential.

Support

Tele-coaching from your home office can be quite isolating. Assess what sort of support you need (see Table 4.2).

TABLE 4.2 Support

Type of support	Support available
Meeting other coaches face to face for networking	Coach networking groups
E-mail contact with other coaches	E-mail coach forums
Learning from other coaches. Continuous professional development (CPD)	Seminars, professional forums, co-coaching events, conferences, symposiums, webinars
Working with other coaches	Professional bodies
Working for other coaches	Coaching associate companies Training companies/schools Internal coaching programmes
Business networking	Business networking forums Professional bodies

There is a vibrant coaching community, including co-coaching support groups, continuous professional development (CPD) events and coaching networking events, so there is no need to work in isolation if you don't want to. Most professional bodies should be able to put you in contact with the type of support that you need, want and will benefit from. Identify what you want as an outcome so that you can join the right group for you.

Working with others

If you find that working for yourself is too isolating or you find it difficult to motivate yourself, you may decide that you would like to work with others for a coaching associate company. If so, it's worth considering the following:

- the reputation of the company and the areas in which they work;
- the structure /team;
- the type of coaching work they would be offering, the format and to what client base;
- style of coaching;
- frequency of work;
- sales commitment;
- payment split and transparency of this (percentage to the coach and percentage to the company);
- payment terms;
- travel/other expenses;
- time commitment;
- contractual terms;
- the solvency of the company;
- client confidentiality;
- supervision/group meetings;
- trust;
- copyright ownership;
- administration processes;
- format of contact.

Personal strengths

Use your personal strengths, skills and experience to adopt a professional attitude and maintain a proactive approach in developing yourself and your coaching practice.

There is no right or wrong way to organize yourself; however, there may be more effective ways of working. Most coaches I know work differently and utilize their own strengths. Not all of us get it right all of the time, but the good thing about coaches is that we like to learn and develop ourselves. We can use techniques and interventions that will help both our clients and ourselves.

Appropriate training and skills are a requirement to be an excellent coach. I would encourage everyone to undertake continuous professional development (CPD), which is particularly important if you want to become accredited. Attendance at seminars, events, conferences and reading books all count as hours towards CPD.

Professional body

As a co-founder and COO of the Association for Coaching, I believe membership of a coaching professional body such as the AC can help and support coaches. It can guide your professional practice through its code of ethics and good practice and help you to develop yourself and your business through training and personal development opportunities. Professional bodies also provide coaches with access to a wider network of like-minded individuals and organizations who are working to achieve excellence and best practice.

Conclusions

The aim of this chapter was to see how aligned you and your coaching practice are and to ensure that the key elements of running a business were covered. The focus was on growth coming from what the individual already has in place, what areas he or she needs to develop, and how to move forward, emphasizing understanding the reasons for, and the benefits of taking relevant action, through a series of questions.

As you have progressed through the chapter, a number of essential elements of running your business have been highlighted and brought to your attention. Reflecting on the information that you have gathered can form a base upon which your coaching practice will develop to its next level.

Only you have the answers to your questions and it will be your responsibility to decide on the appropriate next step. When you are in the early stages of running a business it can useful to focus on the day-to-day aspects. However, once you are operational it can pay dividends to think about the long term and to identify objectives and implement some strategic planning around essential best practice so that you can effectively focus on your core business responsibilities.

PART TWO
Coaching models and approaches

Behavioural coaching – the GROW model

05

GRAHAM ALEXANDER

The GROW coaching model explained

The GROW model developed in the 1980s (Alexander and Renshaw, 2005) from my work with senior executives. Over the past 30 years the model has become the industry standard. A Google search conducted in March 2015 identified over one hundred and ten million internet mentions.

In the early days of coaching, although my coachees gave me positive feedback, I wasn't clear why. I questioned whether there was an implicit structure in my interactions, or whether I just made it up as I went along. When I started training coaches, including HR practitioners and middle-level managers, I was forced to clarify my methodology.

I reflected on my countless coaching sessions to understand what was going on. Gradually I saw that there was an inherent structure to what I was doing. It was not always possible to predict how it happened, but it was clear that certain milestones were reached in each effective session. My challenge was to capture them in a simple and memorable format that could be used by other coaches. GROW, a simple and effective model that can be applied to all coaching interactions, stands for Goal, Reality, Options and Wrap-up (see Figure 5.1 overleaf). (**Editor's note:** Sometimes 'Wrap-up' is replaced by the word 'Will' as in 'What will you do?' – see Figure 1.4 on p18.)

FIGURE 5.1 The GROW model

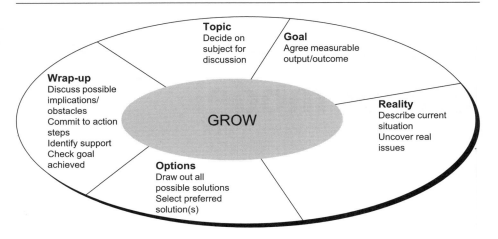

The GROW model

Effective coaches have GROW or similar models internalized so that it becomes an unconscious competence act (Howell and Fleishman, 1982). Within this framework the coaching is fluid, natural and artistic. The coachee is not subjected to a mechanistic and linear approach. While our language requires us to describe the GROW model as linear, in fact most coaching sessions are cyclical in nature. A coach recaps earlier phases of the GROW model throughout a coaching interaction, helping the coachee to see clearly and move forward.

Step 1. Coaching topic

After establishing rapport and connection, the coach asks their coachee or proposes what they would like to look at during the coaching session.

It is often the case that a coachee does not have full clarity about what they want to talk about, hence topics are presented vaguely. It's important to unravel a generalized topic and gain clarity about what a coachee really wants to focus on. In some cases gaining this insight plays a large part in resolving the topic.

Step 2. Coaching goal

Perhaps one of the most significant steps in my own coaching work was the recognition of the critical need to differentiate between the topic of a coaching session and a specific outcome. Unless the agreed topic can be distilled into a bite-sized chunk that is achievable during the agreed time frame, it can lead to a frustrating, purposeless and sometimes meandering conversation. Therefore the intention in the goal stage of the GROW model is to set a goal for the session so that the coachee can walk away with a result.

The coach should attempt to establish a goal after agreeing the topic, but the coachee may not be able initially to express it clearly and specifically. The use of further questioning and probing enables the coach to drill down into the topic until a realistic goal becomes clear.

All coaching has a defined outcome and in most cases this takes the form of an action step or steps. Coaching has a defined point to it and it is the coach's responsibility to ensure that the outcome is made crystal clear for their coachee.

Step 3. Reality

In my experience the bulk of time in coaching is spent in the reality phase. This is the time when a coach can help shine the light of awareness onto the reality of a coachee. As it is brought into sharp focus the coachee may gain new insights, raise his or her awareness and see an issue or need with more clarity. The use of open-ended questions is the primary tool that enables reality to be understood.

In the majority of cases the options for finding a solution become clearer as a direct consequence of having invested in the reality phase. The intention is to help a coachee probe into things, peel away the layers of the onion, see things specifically, clarify meaning, strip away assumptions and judgements, use precise language and provide real-world examples of assertions.

Step 4. Options

Once the coachee has described their reality in rich detail, the coach's role is to help the coachee generate some options to explore how to move forward.

In the vast majority of my sessions I have been astonished at the inherent capability of our coachees to see their way through issues, problems and development needs. In most cases it is not necessary for me to intrude too overtly into this natural process of self-discovery.

In the option phase the most effective strategy is to start by asking open-ended questions. Coaching sessions don't always have to draw out new or particularly novel ideas. Often they bring previous thoughts into sharper focus and confront the coachee with whether certain choices are desirable.

After these baseline questions, coaches can become more creative with their questioning style. The coach's aim is to flush out a variety of options to be pinned down or discarded in the wrap-up phase.

At this stage it may be that a coachee would like the coach's perspective. This can happen if the coachee feels blocked, if the solutions they have generated are inadequate, or if they are covering old ground.

The coachee now has a comprehensive list of options available, which have predominantly come from their own wisdom, experience or creativity, with some possible additions from the coach.

Step 4. Wrap-up/way forward

The coaching session now arrives at the action phase. If the coach was rigorous with the previous stages, appropriate actions may have become obvious.

Having established the coachee's immediate preferences it is important to have them describe the reason for their choices. This tests the coachee's thinking and provides greater clarity about the level of certainty and confidence they have in taking particular options forward.

The coachee may still have several options on the table, therefore the crucial thing is to narrow them down. Through this process the coachee arrives at one final option that they are ready to break down into specific action steps. This is the moment when the coach needs the coachee to be rigorous about evaluating the implications of the action, its practicality, any obstacles that could arise and any support that may be needed.

The coachee is now ready to drill down to their final action plan, including the specific action steps they will take, when they will take them, who is involved and when they will be reviewed.

This is one of the key times that taking a challenging approach can be supportive. Using a variety of closed questions or feedback can ensure that a coachee has fully checked their position.

Taking this approach will increase commitment and ensure that a coachee feels accountable for any outcome. It is the job of a coach to ensure that their coachees have made a full and complete assessment of their potential action steps and what benefit they might derive as a result.

Thus, a coachee can finally get up from a coaching session with one or more tangible steps that they have contracted to take and that will be reviewed in the next meeting.

When does the GROW model work best?

A comprehensive report in the UK (CIPD, 2004) highlights the widespread use of coaching in organizations. Almost four-fifths of respondents now use coaching in their organization (79 per cent). Use of coaching as a development tool has seen rapid growth in recent years, with 77 per cent of respondents reporting that their organization's use of coaching had increased in the last few years.

Coaching underpins the responsibilities of a manager. It is the glue that binds leadership activities with the achievement of objectives. Thus coaching has to be a large part of what the effective manager does each day (Goleman, 2002). This role of leading using coaching as a key management style has changed over the past 20 years (see Figure 5.2).

FIGURE 5.2   The changing mix in leadership

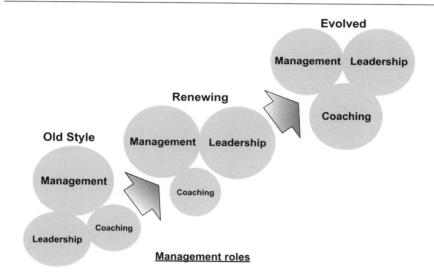

For most managers, GROW offers an excellent, accessible and comprehensible approach that allows them to respond to this new agenda. It builds on managers' existing knowledge and offers a perfect tool for a management coaching style in the workplace, alongside other management styles (Goleman, 2002). Unlike many of the other approaches, it does not require a psychologist's training or a background in psychotherapy. It assumes that the coachee is functional rather than dysfunctional and that personal development is about working with others as equals.

A second reason to select GROW above the range of alternatives – cognitive behavioural, psychodynamic or solution-focused – is that this approach plays to the organizational view of the world. GROW, as a model, is strongly suited to the world of work. One example is the growing use of leadership competencies. GROW's focus allows the coach to work explicitly with competencies and recognizes their validity as a component to develop improved performance.

Clearly, there is value in working with cognition and with the unconscious. But for many managers who are highly functional and often self-aware individuals, the desire is to reflect on all aspects of their leadership, management, effectiveness and so on through goal setting and challenge thus enabling them to be even more successful.

Tools and techniques

Within the overall framework of the GROW model and continuing to employ the core skills of questioning, listening, summarizing, offering feedback and suggestions, the following tools (Alexander and Renshaw, 2005) are very valuable.

The precision model, shown in Figure 5.3, is a useful tool that enables coaches to become highly attentive when helping their coachees decode what they are saying. I have found that coachees often use imprecise and generalized language and that each coachee has their own meaning, so coaches need to avoid making assumptions based on their own frame of reference.

FIGURE 5.3   The precision model

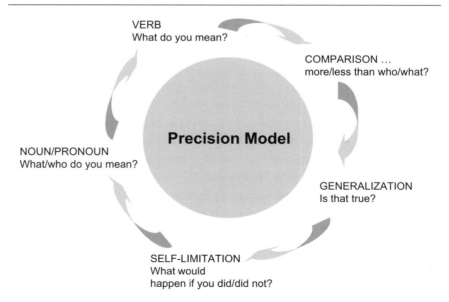

VERB
What do you mean?

COMPARISON ...
more/less than who/what?

NOUN/PRONOUN
What/who do you mean?

Precision Model

GENERALIZATION
Is that true?

SELF-LIMITATION
What would
happen if you did/did not?

If coachees use a noun such as 'the team', a coach can help them clarify who and what is meant. By asking 'Who specifically do you mean?', 'Is that all the team or some of the team?', or 'What do you mean by the team?', a coach ensures that coachees see clearly what lies behind the statement.

When coachees use a verb, 'to communicate', asking what is meant forces the coachee to give detailed thought to a broad statement, for example: 'Be briefer and clearer in what I say', 'To build understanding' or 'To say what I think'.

If coachees use terms such as 'more than', 'better than', or 'less than', the coach can clarify what they mean by asking, 'More than whom?', 'More than what?', 'Less than whom?', 'Better than what?'

When coachees generalize, saying 'I never have enough time', 'Nobody ever listens to me' or 'Everybody thinks the CEO is too remote', the precision model challenges them to think specifically about what they mean. 'Do you really mean that you never have time?' 'Do you really mean nobody ever listens to you?' 'Do you really mean everybody thinks the CEO is too remote?'

In the area of self-limiting statements it can be revealing to challenge the coachee. If the coachee makes comments such as, 'I must finish this report by 6 o'clock', 'I should have one-to-ones with my direct reports every week' or 'I have to be present at every meeting I'm asked to attend', asking, 'According to whom?' 'How do you know this?' 'What measure are you using?' 'What would happen if you didn't?' encourages him or her to test the constraint.

In summary, the precision model enables a coachee to move from making general statements to articulating exactly what is meant. This can help to re-evaluate the coachee's thinking, shed new light on an issue and ensure that before taking any action they have rigorously tested their hypothesis, saving both time and effort.

The 'structure of a problem'

A problem is a state in which coachees are 'stuck' in a situation and unclear about how to proceed. It usually involves a topic that plays on their mind, causing distraction and internal conflict. Using 'structure of a problem' helps to address a coachee's mindset and enables them to move from a 'problem state of mind' to a 'project state of mind' (see Figure 5.4). The goal is not necessarily to generate a complete solution but to tap into the coachee's internal motivation and help them feel empowered, become unstuck and see a way forward.

FIGURE 5.4   The 'structure of a problem'

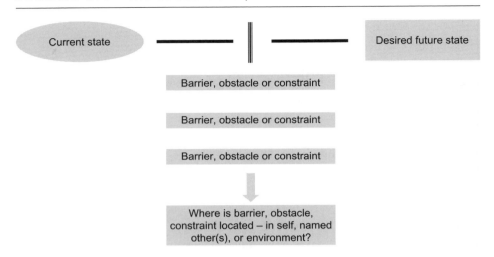

The process involves using index cards or similar to jot down various aspects, giving coachees a visual illustration of their situation. First the coach gets the coachee to identify the topic and captures the essence of the problem in a word or short phrase on a card. Next they ask the coachee to describe the current reality and summarize it in a few words. It's useful to put pace into this exercise so that the coachee doesn't get bogged down with too much detail. Then move on to the desired future state. The coach asks the coachee to describe it using sense-based language (what they want to see, feel and hear). Again, the coach captures it on a card.

Next the coach asks the coachee to identify any barriers, obstacles or constraints they perceive exists between the current state and the desired future state and jots them down, one per card. Simple questions, such as 'What barriers exist between where you are now and where you want to be?', 'What obstacles do you face?' and 'What constraints do you experience?', flush out the main interferences.

Having identified the obstacles, the coach asks where the coachee locates them in one of three places: in themselves, in another named person or persons, or in their environment. It enables the coachee to see clearly where barriers exist and thus helps them to take action where possible, and to recognize whether there are other possible barriers outside their sphere of control. Generally speaking, the coachee finds that the majority of the barriers exist within themselves and so is able to act. Once the coachee has clarified which of the obstacles to tackle it is possible to generate options and wrap up as per a normal GROW model coaching session. The coachee has moved from stuck to unstuck.

Issue resolution

Index cards can also be used to clarify large or complex coaching topics, such as organizational structural issues, managing teams or evaluating job options (see Figure 5.5). Helping coachees disaggregate the different facets of a topic onto a set of cards enables them to see the various aspects of the issue in new ways.

FIGURE 5.5   Issue resolution

The coach should encourage their coachee to jot down in short bullet points the various aspects of the issue or problem. The key is to get the coachee's inner world onto cards and laid out in front of them as quickly as possible. This act taps into the power of insight and new possibilities come into play once the coachee gains a new perspective.

'Areas of life' cards

A further use of cards is to create a pack at the outset of a coaching programme to help formulate a coaching agenda based on each aspect of the coachee's work and life. This presents an opportunity to externalize their internal reality and begin to prioritize what's most important. A coachee could have the cards shown in Figure 5.6.

FIGURE 5.6   'Areas of life' cards

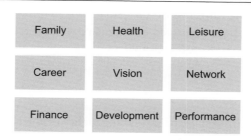

This tool can then be used for coachees to describe their current reality and aspirations. It also acts as a diagnostic aid to evaluate issues such as work–life balance, time management and personal fulfilment, providing information to assess where the most valuable focus can be applied. Over time coachees may want to add to or refine the way they have compartmentalized the different areas of their work and life.

Perceptual positions

Many coaching issues have their roots in relationship dilemmas. Perceptual positions (see Figure 5.7) illustrate three standpoints in a relationship: first position, self (how you see the world); second position, other (their perspective); and third position, observer (a neutral, objective viewpoint). By taking the position of other and observer, coachees are able to heighten their awareness of a situation and bring valuable insight back into their own reality, which may alter their perception and behaviour.

FIGURE 5.7   Perceptual positions

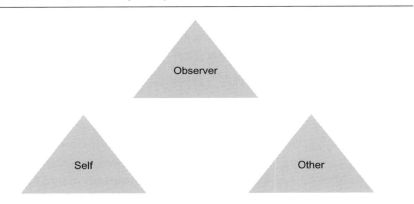

A coach can keep moving the coachee around the three positions until they have clarity about what the real issue is and what might constitute a way forward. In the third position it can also be helpful for the coachee to imagine a mentor, boss, respected colleague or partner giving advice to add another dimension to the reflective process.

FLOW model

It is important for the coach to assess the quality of the coaching session as it proceeds. With this in mind I developed the FLOW model (see Figure 5.8). This plays on the idea of 'being in flow' within a conversation and as an acronym it stands for 'Fast, Linked, Outcome and Worthwhile'.

FIGURE 5.8   FLOW model

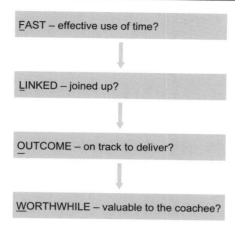

I suggest that coaches use it as a checklist with their coachees, enabling them to know whether they are being effective. Over time it can be internalized and used implicitly to monitor interactions as they unfold.

Ten key questions to guide your way

It would be a mistake to think that there is an ultimate list of 'killer questions'. Coaching interactions always need to be appropriate to the individual in their unique position, and thus a coach who falls back on a predictable set of tried and trusted questions is likely to be mechanical and out of tune with the coachee. Having said this, the following list of questions (Alexander and Renshaw, 2005), based on thousands of hours of coaching, have a high probability of value to the coachee, particularly if coached in language that fits for both the coach and coachee.

1. What is your purpose in your life and your career?

This question helps coachees clarify their vision, mission and values. The outcome can be that coachees develop an effective and potent mission statement that captures their unique and enduring reason for being.

Typically I start by asking a coachee the purpose of their work and life. Given that many coachees have a variety of options for what they could be doing, the question helps to discover a person's drivers and motivations.

2. What would be the most valuable topic to focus on?

It's important at the outset of a coaching session to help coachees gain clarity about what they really want to focus on. In some cases gaining this insight plays a part in resolving it.

3. When you get up out of your chair, what outcome would be most valuable for you?

Having established the topic it is vital for a coachee to clarify what they really want out of a coaching session and what would be the 'takeaways' at the end of the session.

4. What is the current situation?

It is vital for coachees to describe all aspects of their current reality in relation to the topic of the coaching session before moving on to resolution.

5. What could you do?

Having described current reality in rich detail, the coach then helps the coachee to identify options for moving forward in relation to the topic of the coaching session.

6. If you could do anything, what would you do?

On occasion it's appropriate for coachees to consider radical concepts that challenge their habitual frame of reference. The purpose of this type of questioning technique is to generate as many options (however unlikely, impractical or zany) as possible. This type of question facilitates a more 'outside the box' phase in the coaching process, and can be added to with the use of other creative thinking techniques.

7. If you could only take the one option that you believe would add the most value, what would it be?

Once the coachee has a comprehensive list of options the coach asks more open questions in order to pin down the best option.

8. What are the implications of taking this action?

The coachee arrives at one final option that they are ready to break down into specific action steps, but prior to this further probing is necessary.

9. What will you do, when?

Assuming the appropriateness of the option chosen, the coach now pins the coachee down to commit to action.

10. Is this an effective use of time?

A coach needs to check if a coaching session has moved too fast or too slowly. This type of question at the end of a session provides permission for feedback and space for a conversation on what is working and what is not working in the coaching relationship.

References

Alexander, G and Renshaw, B (2005) *Super Coaching: The missing ingredient for high performance*, Random House Business Books, London

Chartered Institute of Personnel and Development (CIPD) (2004) *Coaching and Buying Coaching Services*, CIPD, London

Goleman, D (2002) *The New Leaders: Transforming the art of leadership into the science of results*, Little, Brown, Boston, MA

Howell, W and Fleishman, E (eds) (1982) *Human Performance and Productivity: Volume 2: Information processing and decision making*, Erlbaum, Hillsdale, NJ

Solution-focused coaching

06

ANTHONY M GRANT

The solution-focused coaching model explained

Coaching is necessarily a solution-focused activity. Coaching focuses on where people want to go, how they are going to get there, and how they are going to achieve outstanding results. Rather than where they have been or what has happened to them in the past. Coaching can be defined as a collaborative, solution-focused, results-orientated and systematic process, in which the coach facilitates the enhancement of performance, life experience, self-directed learning and personal growth of individuals and organizations. Coaching is more about asking the right questions than telling coachees what to do. Coaches work with their coachee to help them identify and construct possible solutions, delineate a range of goals and options, and then facilitate the development and enactment of action plans to achieve those goals.

The solution-focused approach to coaching, like many coaching models, comes originally from the therapeutic world. Solution-focused approaches have their roots in Milton H Erickson's approach to strategic therapy. Brief solution-focused therapy was developed by therapists such as Insoo Kim Berg, and Steve de Shazer (1988) at the Brief Family Therapy Centre in Milwaukee, which was founded in 1982 (see Berg and Szabo, 2005 for further information).

These therapists had become disenchanted with the diagnostic medical approach. Rather than trying to analyse problems, develop diagnoses, uncover root causes, and prescribe treatment plans based on an *a priori* theoretical model of the issue, they began to simply ask questions that focused their clients' attention on building solutions. They found that, in many cases, this could be a very effective methodology. Indeed, there is a body of research that shows that solution-focused therapy can be effective for a range of problems including couple counselling (Murray and Murray, 2004), child and adolescent counselling (Corcoran and Stephenson, 2000; Lethem, 2002) and depression (Dahl, Bathel and Carreon, 2000), and there is research that supports the use of solution-focused coaching in both personal coaching (Green, Oades and Grant, 2006) and workplace coaching contexts (Barrett, 2004; Theeboom, Beersma, and van Vianen, 2013).

There has also been research which has directly compared the relative effectiveness of solution-focused coaching with that of problem-focused coaching approaches (Grant and O'Connor, 2010; Grant, 2012). This research found that both the problem-focused and the solution-focused coaching approaches were in fact effective at enhancing goal attainment. However, the people in the solution-focused coaching group had significantly greater increases in goal attainment compared to the problem-focused group. Interestingly problem-focused coaching questions did not change the way that people felt – there was no change in positive or negative effect or self-efficacy. In contrast the solution-focused approach significantly increased positive effect, decreased negative effect, and increased self-efficacy, as well as increasing goal attainment. In addition, the solution-focused group generated significantly more action steps to help them reach their goal. Not surprisingly, the authors suggested that agents of change should aim for a solution-focused theme if they wish to conduct effective coaching sessions.

Core characteristics of solution-focused coaching

Coaching emerged during the mid-1990s as an important tool for personal and organizational change. Looking for fast and user-friendly ways to facilitate change, coaches began to use the techniques and principles of solution-focused therapy. Drawing on the work of O'Connell (1998), the following are central characteristics of solution-focused approaches, and the key principles underpinning the solution-focused approach to coaching:

- Use of a non-pathological framework: problems are not indications of pathology or dysfunctionality, rather they stem from a limited repertoire of behaviour.

- A focus on constructing solutions: the coach primarily facilitates the construction of solutions rather than trying to understand the aetiology of the problem.

- Coachee-based expertise: the idea is that the coachee is the expert in his or her own life rather than the coach.

- Learning from the coachee: each coaching session is an opportunity for the coach to learn more about coaching *from the coachee*. This is a useful attitude that helps prevent the solution-focused coach slipping into an 'I'm the expert' mindset. At the beginning of each session, ask yourself, 'What can I learn from this coachee?'

- Use of client resources: the coach helps the coachee recognize and utilize existing resources.

- Action-orientation: there is a fundamental expectation on the coach's part that positive change will occur, and the coach expects the coachee to do the work of change outside of the coaching session.

- Clear, specific goal setting: setting of stretching but attainable goals within a specific time frame.

- Assumption that change can happen in a short period of time: this stands in contrast to the assumption that change must be worked on over a long period of time.

- Strategic: coaching interventions are designed specifically for each coachee.

- Future-orientation: the emphasis is more on the future (what the coachee wants to have happen) than the present or the past.

- Attraction: the coaching process is designed and conducted in a way that is attractive and engaging for the coachee.

- Active and influential coaching: the coach is openly influential and challenges the coachee to think in a new way.

The emphasis on solution construction in preference to problem analysis, as well as the use of positive, non-pathological language is important in coaching. The use of pathological or medical terminology can be unhelpful (de Shazer, 1984) and may even create or maintain problem behaviours (Walter and Peller, 1996). This is not to say that a solution-focused approach ignores the existence of problems. As Insoo Kim Berg has said – just because we are solution-focused, it does not mean that we are problem-phobic! Many coachees want to talk about their problems, and stopping them from doing so can alienate them. Having the time and space to talk about problems can be cathartic. Indeed, in doing so coachees often develop significant clarity and insight, and such conversations can build rapport between coachee and coach.

The point here is that the solution-focused coach's skills lie in helping the coachee tell his or her problem story in a way that reframes the presenting problem as being solvable. The talk needs to move from a problem-focused discourse towards a discourse that emphasizes self-directed learning, the coachee's resources and his or her own personal ability to define and then move towards a solution.

In essence then, the foundations of a solution-focused conversation consist of three core facets (Grant *et al*, 2012):

- Goal-orientation: An orientation toward solution construction through the articulating and use of approach goals and active self-regulation.

- Problem disengagement: This facet involves an explicit disengagement from presenting problems. Although the ability to disengage from a problem is conceptually independent of one's ability to be orientated towards a solution, problem disengagement is vital for full engagement in the goal pursuit process central to the solution-focused endeavour.

- Resource activation: This is a focus on acknowledging, identifying and activating a wide range of personal and contextual resources and personal strengths.

The skilful coach can do this at quite a fast conversational pace while at the same time building a collaborative and motivating relationship.

Self-directed learning

Self-regulation and self-directed learning lie at the heart of the solution-focused approach. The principles of self-directed learning include a self-reliance on discovering solutions to problems, seeking and accepting feedback on progress and reflecting on such feedback, taking responsibility for creating change, the use of structured learning activities, and the integration of the learning experience into other aspects of one's life (Zachary, 2005). Self-directed learning and self-regulation go hand in hand in coaching.

Self-regulation is essentially about the ability to set and work towards goals. The cycle of self-regulation is an important part of the solution-focused approach. The cycle is a simple process of setting a goal, developing an action plan, acting, monitoring, evaluating, and then changing what does not work and doing more of what does (see Figure 6.1). The coach's role is to facilitate the coachee's journey through this cycle while holding the coachee's focus on his or her goal(s).

FIGURE 6.1   The cycle of self-regulation

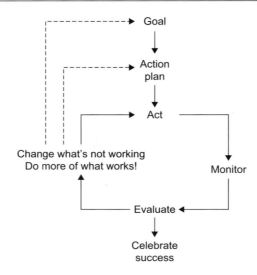

Philosophical issues

There are some controversial philosophical issues related to the solution-focused approach that have important implications for both theory and coaching practice. It has been argued that solution-focused approaches are theory-free methodologies in which the coach does not need any expert knowledge about the coachee's problems, and only needs to ask the right questions in order to help the coachee develop appropriate solutions (eg de Shazer, 1988).

However, this cannot truly be the case. For the coach to ask the right questions, the coach must have a theory about the issue, and a theory about what kind of question will best help the coachee articulate a solution. Furthermore, the coach needs to have solid well-developed skills in rapport building and process facilitation, and these involve the use of expert knowledge and the application of theory to practice. If the coach really had no expert knowledge or skills, or no theory about how best to help the coachee, then it is hard to understand why the coachee would employ the coach in the first place (see Held, 1996, for a detailed discussion of these issues).

Coaching is a process of facilitation in which the coach helps the coachee uncover solutions. This process requires a fine balance between asking questions that foster self-discovery and self-directed learning, and giving the coachee information or advice. The use of questions thus lie on a dimension, from being very non-directive, for example, asking 'What is the most useful thing you could do next?', to a more directive approach such as, 'Other people have found X and Y to be very helpful, because of Z. Which might work best for you?'

Asking the right questions and steering the coaching conversation towards solution-construction requires that the coach is constantly developing working hypotheses about what the presenting issues are and what the possible solutions could be. This kind of conceptualization is the theory that underpins any solution-focused coaching intervention. Although the coach is constantly developing ideas about the nature of the issue, and the factors that maintain the problem, in solution-focused coaching this information is not normally overtly brought into the conversation by the coach. Rather the emphasis is on what might work. Coaches need to be able to draw on their knowledge of human change, and their understanding of the coachee's specific context in order to ask the right questions and move the conversation forward at just the right pace. Too fast and the coachee will be left fumbling in the dark reaching for answers that will not appear; too slow and the coachee will overly focus on the problem.

Used well, the solution-focused approach enables people to access and use their own wealth of personal experience, skills, expertise and intuition to set goals and develop action plans. It allows coachees to find individualized and creative solutions to the issues and concerns that face them, and does so in a way that builds their skills, knowledge and well-being.

When does the solution-focused approach work best?

What is needed for the solution-focused approach to be effective? Let's consider the coach's beliefs, feelings and behaviours.

First, the coach needs to *believe* in the solution-focused approach, to be engaged in a solution-focused mindset and be able to see the coachee as being resourceful, creative and able to construct possible solutions. Holding the coachee in such unconditional positive regard is not always easy, but it is vital because the quality of the working alliance significantly contributes to success (Horvath and Symonds, 1991). There will be many times when the coach will not know what to say, or how to handle a particular situation. Having the faith to fall back on basic solution-focused principles and techniques and apply these without knowing how the conversation will develop is challenging, particularly for coaches whose previous training has centred on the delivery of expert knowledge as therapists or business consultants.

Second, the coach needs to be able to generate the *feelings* that will best help coachees reach their goal. The coach works on multiple levels simultaneously with the coachee. As the conversation develops, the coach uses the basic communication skills of open or closed questioning, reflection, paraphrasing and summarizing to help raise the coachee's awareness of the *facts* of the issue, and in doing so, helps him or her articulate possible solutions. But the coach also needs to be working on an *emotional* level, recognizing emotions as they are expressed in the conversation, and then amplifying or moderating them through conversation in order to develop the coachee's levels of motivation and enthusiasm. This aspect of the coaching conversation is rarely discussed in the coaching literature, but it is a vital part of coaching. This is not about excessive emotional hyperbole; rather it is about judiciously recognizing when the coachee has a useful emotional response and then reflecting and amplifying that in order to enhance engagement and motivation.

Third, the coach needs a sophisticated set of *behavioural* skills: coaching is as much about *doing* as *being*. In addition to core communication skills, the coach needs the skills to work with a range of different coachees and issues and to be able to manage the coaching process. Such management skills include effectively structuring the individual coaching sessions and helping the coachee design action plans and action steps. In addition, skilful management of the processes and procedures involved in the coaching engagement is particularly important when providing external coaching for organizations, and many coaching engagements fail because the boundaries of the coaching engagement and its relationship to the sponsoring organization have not been skilfully defined (Jay, 2003).

The coachee's characteristics also impact on whether a solution-focused approach will be successful. Broadly speaking there are three factors. There needs to be *discontent with the present*. If there is no recognition that the situation could be better, then there is no motivation to change. The coach may need to work to amplify existing levels of discontent. Such discontent could come from a recognition of missed opportunities, unfulfilled dreams or some type of self-examination or from feedback from others.

The coachee also needs to have a *vision of the future*. This vision needs to incorporate both a vague 'fuzzy vision' of the distant future, and more specific immediately attainable goals. Clearly these need to be inspirational and motivational and be based on values and beliefs that are congruent with the coachee. Much of the solution-focused conversation will be about getting the coachee to articulate his or her preferred future vision and, in doing so, pathways to goal attainment will become clear.

Last, the coachee needs to have the *skills to do the work of change*. He or she needs the ability to form a plan of action, to enact the plan, to maintain action, and also to celebrate success. This process often involves developing an understanding of his or her personal responses to change and examining a range of assumptions about themselves and the world, and this can be personally quite challenging, particularly if the coachee is heavily problem-saturated.

Proud to be superficial?

The solution-focused approach avoids delving deeply into examinations of coachees' problems, their psychological profile, or in-depth explorations of other issues that may have been influential in the past. Is this a superficial, surface approach?

Solution-focused approaches have been criticized for being superficial (eg Ellis, 1997), and it has been claimed that, for coaching to be truly effective, a 'deeper' approach is necessary (eg Kilburg, 2004). Of course, there are times when the solution-focused approach is not appropriate, for example, when coachees have both long-standing problems and an entrenched need to explore aetiology, or the coachee comes to coaching with a strong commitment to a specific philosophical framework that is not congruent with the principles of solution-focused coaching. In these cases the coachees may already have embedded causal stories about how the problem arose, and such stories may well be an important and central part of their world view. For such coachees, the solution-focused approach may pose significant challenges, and here the solution-focused coach needs to make informed choices about whether to refer on, or work with the coachee. Indeed, to force a solution-focused perspective onto an unwilling coachee runs counter to the core principle of respecting the coachee's personal world view, although experience shows that giving coachees a solid rationale for the use of a solution-focused approach can significantly help foster a shift towards acceptance of such an approach.

It is interesting to note that the notion of any specific approach being 'surface' or 'deep' is really a subjective value judgement about the worth of different approaches, rather than an objective measurement of how much any specific approach strikes to the heart of an individual's sense of self. Further, it has been my experience when using solution-focused coaching approaches that if an issue is really important, it will become apparent in time, and then it can be addressed. There is no need to go looking for 'deeper' underlying issues. There is a real discipline in staying solution-focused, working with what is presented, working on the 'surface', and in this sense, solution-focused coaches should indeed be proud to be superficial!

Tools and techniques

A very useful tool to help coaches develop solution-focused skills is the ask–tell matrix (see Figure 6.2). The questions we ask as coaches lie on two intersecting dimensions: 'telling to asking', and 'why to how'. Observe yourself when you are coaching. Which quadrant are you in at any specific moment? Do you spend most of your time telling the coachee how to do things, or in asking how to? Or maybe you spend a lot of time telling them or asking them why? Of course, it is not wrong to ask coachees a 'why' question, or to *give* advice. The point is that a skilful solution-focused coach will emphasize asking 'how to questions' rather than 'telling or why'.

FIGURE 6.2   The ask–tell matrix

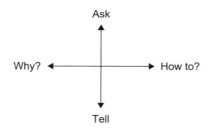

Change the viewing to change the doing!

There are two key factors involved in solution-focused work: 1) *changing the viewing* – that is, helping the coachee to see the situation anew; and 2) *changing the doing* – that is, helping the coachee to develop new behaviours.

Changing the viewing is about acknowledging the progress made so far, identifying exceptions to the problem, detailing the preferred outcome, amplifying existing resources, and building coachee self-efficacy.

Changing the doing is about recognizing possibilities by turning presenting problems into springboards for solution construction, asking 'how' questions instead of 'why' questions, generating coachee-centred multiple options, using small specific achievable action steps, and finding ways to leverage systems to facilitate individual change.

This is a non-exhaustive list of solution-focused tools and techniques to help change the viewing and the doing:

- A refusal to purchase the problem. In every conversation there is a buyer and a seller. One person 'sells' his or her explanatory story of the situation to the other, and the other person 'buys' it. Successful solution-focused coaches refuse to buy into problem stories. Rather, they keep listening until they hear the glimmer of a solution. Maintaining an attitude of intelligent curiosity, service and facilitation allows the coach to respectfully, but firmly, hold the conversation on solution construction.

- Compliments. Appropriately praising the coachee and paying them compliments builds self-confidence.

- Exceptions to the problem. Highlighting when the problem does not exist gives clues as to what to do to make those exception times more frequent.

- Doing more of what works. Once you have uncovered when the problem does not exist, the coachee can plan to do more of whatever it is that is making the difference.

- Do less of what doesn't work. This sounds obvious, but we frequently keep trying to solve problems by using the same (failed) solutions. Insanity, as they say, is doing the same thing but expecting different results!

- Scaling. This is a versatile way of subjectively measuring experience and can be used in many different ways; for example, ask coachees to rate on a 1 to 10 scale how close to their goal they are, and then ask them what would take them to the next point on the scale.

- Small steps. Have coachees take small, easily achievable steps that build in time to overall stretching goals, rather than overwhelm them with large initial actions.

- Highlighting resources. Listen out for hidden and unacknowledged resources. It is amazing how often a presenting problem holds unrecognized strengths and resources. It is a cliché, but true, that every problem is the seed of its solution.

- Possibility language. This involves communicating with the coachee in a way that fosters discovery of potential solutions. A well-known technique is the 'magic question' in which the coach asks something like, 'Imagine that you went to bed tonight, and when you woke up the problem had somehow magically disappeared, and the solution was present ... but you didn't know that the solution had arrived ... what is the first thing that you'd notice that would tell you that the solution was present?' Sometimes this kind of language is not congruent with the coachee, and this kind of mismatch can make it quite difficult for the coachee to answer the question. A useful variation is the 'what if' question – 'If things were going a bit better, what would be different?'

- Reframing. Reframing is a vital tool. The coach needs to be able to reflect and reframe the coachee's statements in a way that creates new ways of viewing and doing.

Reframing draws on the tools and techniques above. Following are some examples of solution-focused reframing:

- Reframing that uses compliments. *Coachee*: 'It's far too expensive.' *Coach*: 'It's great that you are concerned about keeping on budget. How can we make it more affordable?'

- Reframing that highlights exceptions. *Coachee*: 'I really loathe my work.' *Coach*: 'It sounds very unpleasant ... tell me, which parts of your job are less unpleasant for you?'

- Reframing that acknowledges possibilities. *Coachee*: 'I just can't relate to those people.' *Coach*: 'So, up till now you haven't found a way to communicate with them. I wonder what might help to begin to develop good communication?'

- Reframing that clarifies goals. *Coachee*: 'I really want to improve my parenting skills.' *Coach*: 'So, what does good parenting mean to you?'

- Reframing that moves them forward and creates options. *Coachee*: 'I feel completely overwhelmed with this situation ... I feel so lost.' *Coach*: 'So, you'd like to get back a sense of direction and control? What would give you that?'

- Reframing that rolls with resistance. *Coachee*: 'But I couldn't do all of that ...' *Coach*: 'So which bits could you do?'

- Reframing that fosters a shift to a systems perspective. *Coachee*: 'I really don't think I can handle this.' *Coach*: 'I wonder who would be most surprised to hear you say that?'

Strategic overview of a solution-focused coaching intervention

So, how are the ideas expressed so far actually applied in typical coaching engagement? The coaching process starts with the very first contact between the coachee and the coach. This is often a short phone call in which an appointment is made and a brief overview of the issues is normally presented by the coachee. Rather than wait for the first coaching session to begin, the solution-focused coach may ask the coachee to keep a lookout for any signs that things are getting better, and to be ready in the first coaching session to talk about any changes that he or she notices.

A useful initial task is for the coachee to keep a lookout for any 'nuggets' that might appear. Nuggets are those moments when things go really well, or events that are particularly good. It really is amazing how many nuggets there are in each day, yet oftentimes we simply are not on the lookout for them and we fail to notice the simple but great things that happen in our day-to-day lives. The coach should follow-up on the results of this experiment: any successes can form a useful beginning point for the coaching session.

The coaching agreement

The first coaching session would probably start with a brief explanation of what coaching is, and what it is not, and would explain that the coach's role is to ask questions that challenge coachees to find their own solutions rather than telling them what to do. This initial part of the coaching relationship is vital in setting expectations. Here the coach asks for permission to challenge and stretch the coachee. The coach might say something like, 'During our coaching, I will probably sometimes ask you questions that will be quite difficult or challenging. Is that OK with you?' Many professional coaches will have some kind of printed handout with such details. Experience shows that most of the problems in coaching can be circumvented by having a clear upfront coaching agreement.

The coach might then ask the coachee what he or she would like to get out of the coaching relationship, and also what he or she would like to get out of the present session. Sometimes coachees can clearly articulate exactly what they want to achieve. Sometimes coachees want to engage in problem talk, and explain the problem in great depth, but are much less clear about their goals.

The coach will try to shift from a problem-focused conversation to a solution-focused one as quickly as is possible without alienating the coachee. This shift can occur quite soon, within a few minutes. However, with some heavily problem-saturated coachees the coach will have to be patient. It is not unknown for coachees to take a number of sessions before they can start to adopt a solution-focused mindset.

Oscillating process

A typical process is for the coachee to start with problem talk, and then shift to solution talk, but then loop back again to problem talk, and then back to solution talk again. This kind of oscillation can be frustrating for the inexperienced coach. The tip here is for the coach to simply stay with the process: allow coachees to explore their thinking, and act as a facilitator rather than the expert who has to deliver a solution. Taking a 'not the expert consultant' position is one of the most powerful tools in the solution-focused coach's toolbox because it allows the coach to relax and enjoy the creative process of coaching without being fixated on delivering a specific outcome. It is the ability to sit with the uncertainty and ambiguity that marks creativity which differentiates the effective coach from the novice.

As the coaching conversation unfolds, the coach is working to build up a picture of the coachee's preferred future through reflection and reframing. Scaling can be used to help the coachee judge his or her progress in relation to specific goals. Scaling is nearly always an opportunity for the coach to give a compliment. Even if the coachees say that they are at a 3 on a 10-point scale, the coach can respond, 'Well done – one-third of the way there already.' Although this comment is meant in all seriousness, this kind of technique clearly requires that the coach has a fairly robust and well-grounded sense of humour, while at the same time holding the coachee in genuine unconditional positive regard.

The miracle question

It might be useful during the above process to start asking direct possibility questions, such as the miracle question, once the coachee has shifted from a deliberative mindset to an implementational mindset (Gollwitzer, 1996; Heckhausen and Gollwitzer, 1987). The deliberative mindset is quite problem-focused and is characterized by a careful weighing of the pros and cons of action (Carver and Scheier, 1998). The implementational mindset is more solution-focused and is engaged once the decision to act has been made.

This mindset has a determined, focused quality, and is biased in favour of thinking about success rather than failure. To ask the miracle question before the coachee has moved into an implementational mindset can result in confusion, a lack of engagement, and even anger or resentment.

The timing of these questions is vital. To ask a big picture miracle question, before the coachee has had a chance to move on from any problem talk about his or her current situation, will almost certainly not be effective and could well result in the response from the coachee along the lines of, 'Well – that's what I'm paying you for ... to tell me what to do ...'. In such a case the coach has to make a choice. The coach could explain that, 'I understand ... and as we discussed in the first session, sometimes my role is to ask difficult questions ... this is one of those times ... is that OK?' The coach could then either ask a more concrete variation of the magic question, such as the 'two videos' question. Here the coach asks the coachee to picture two videos in his or her mind's eye. One video shows the problem as it is; the other video shows the preferred outcome. The coachee's role is to simply describe the difference between the two. Most people can do this. Failing this the coach can ask, 'If you had a friend in the same situation, what would you advise them to do?' The point of these questions is to get coachees to take a meta-cognitive position, to stand outside of themselves and take a different perspective – to change the viewing to change the doing!

Such resistance from the coachee is often a sign that he or she has not spent enough time talking about the problem. So, when faced with resistance, the coach could just roll with it, move on, and change the topic by possibly revisiting some of the problem talk, and then come back to possibility talk later. When all fails, a useful question is to ask the coachee, 'What would be the most useful question I could ask you right now?' Such techniques can be very effective, but of course it is better to pace the session so that rapport is maintained.

One way to purposefully pace the coaching conversation is to give the session a clear structure. Structured sessions can be extremely powerful ways of holding the conversation on track, and depending on which models are used, can provide an invaluable road map of the coaching conversation. What is a structured coaching conversation? And why should the solution-focused coach use them?

Structuring the coaching session

A structured coaching session is one where there are clearly differentiated sections within a single coaching session, and each section has a particular function (for example, setting goals, uncovering barriers to change, or developing action plans), and within each section the coach tries to focus the conversation on those specific factors. This allows the conversation to be highly focused, and session structure has been shown to be positively related to outcomes (Howard *et al*, 1986). Skilful coaches are able to track the coaching process and know at any time which section they are in and where they are aiming to go next.

Coaching sessions are typically quite structured, although there should always be flexibility in the way structures are applied. Session structures tend to fall into one of two camps: those that have outcomes or goal setting as the very first activity in the session; and those that focus on the current situation, problem or issue before moving on to goal setting.

You can read elsewhere, such as in Chapter 4, about ways in which you could structure the session. GROW offers a useful structure in which the solution-focused approach can work, moving the coachee from objective (goals) to action planning (way forward).

Ten key questions to guide your way

1. If our coaching sessions work out, what will be different for you?

This question could be asked at the beginning of the coaching relationship and would be asked to get the coachee to begin to articulate, from his or her *own personal perspective*, the key hallmarks of success. The coachee's ability (or inability) to give a coherent well-thought-out response to this will give the coach useful insights about the extent to which the coachee is ready for change, what is important to him or her and how the coachee thinks about himself or herself and the world. If the coachee has a lot of trouble answering this question, as many will, it may be best not to push for a specific response because that can make the coachee feel as if he or she has 'failed'. Instead, elicit a broad vague response and then try the next question.

2. How would other people be able to tell if our coaching had been successful?

The point of this question is to help the coachee look at the situation from other people's perspectives. This is a way of fostering a meta-cognitive viewpoint and can be very useful for coachees who are very bound up in their own personal experience, and who see themselves as being the total centre of the universe. Sometimes you will get a quite astonished reaction, almost as if the coachee had never thought about how other people might perceive them. This is a great question for exploring the system in which the coachee lives or works.

3. What do you want to take away from this session?

Use this question at the start of a session to set a goal for the session. Try to make the goal as specific as possible. Coachees will not always be able to articulate what they specifically want to get out of the session. If that is the case, then take time to visit and re-visit the goal over the course of the session. Beware of rushing to set the goal. Take your time. It will be important that the coachee is aware that each session will start with explicitly setting a goal, otherwise they may experience the goal-directed nature of these questions as invasive or intrusive.

4. What would you really like to do?

Emphasize the *really* and this question becomes a great tool for getting to the heart of what they *actually* want, as opposed to what they *think* they should want. You can use this question when you sense ambiguity or lack of commitment to a goal or action plan. The key to this question is to be comfortable with silence and uncertainty. Ask the question and then let it hang there.

5. Is it x or y that we need to focus on?

This question is a closed, double-bind question that encourages the coachee to make a decision. Use this question when both choices have been discussed and there is uncertainty in the coachee's mind, or the coaching conversation is going around in circles. Using this question at the wrong time, before adequate discussion has taken place, may result in increased resistance to making a choice.

6. What personal strengths do you bring to this?

This question can be asked once the goal has been articulated. This is a useful question when exploring options and action plans where the coachee seems to be hesitant in committing to action steps or seems to lack confidence. Used well this question can really build coachees' self-efficacy through helping them to list all the resources they have. The coach may need to be very encouraging, as some people find it hard to list their personal strengths. Judicious (and genuine) use of compliments and praise may be useful here.

7. What are you committed to actually doing?

Asked well, this question cuts to the heart of the coachee's commitment to action. The coach will need to pace this question well, and emphasize the *actually doing*. This question gives the coachee permission to select some actions over others. Make sure that you ask this question from an attitude of facilitation, curiosity and service, rather than judgement. This can be quite a challenging, confrontational question so only ask it when there is good rapport with the coachee.

8. How confident are you, on a scale of 1 to 10, that you can do this?

This is a straightforward scaling question to help coachees self-assess their ability to actually do the action steps. The word 'confident' is important here as it is less threatening for many people than a word such as 'committed'. Unless they respond with '10' always ask, 'What would it take to take you to (the next point on the scale)?' This question should be asked at the end of all coaching sessions once action steps have been outlined. This question can act as a check to ensure that the action plans are truly congruent for the coachee. On occasion, despite apparent rapport and motivation during the session, a coachee will report quite low confidence. In that case spend some time to uncover what would make the difference. The coach should also learn from this how he or she could have improved his or her coaching technique.

9. How can you keep track of your successes?

This question should be asked in the wrap-up stage of the coaching session, during the action planning process. This question presupposes success and links the coaching action plans explicitly to the cycle of self-regulation: monitor, evaluate, change what's not working and do more of what works. The coachees need to be able to keep track of their successes in concrete measurable ways, and this will help keep the coaching grounded.

10. Tell me some more about that ...?

This is one of the most useful questions in the coach's toolbox and is an open question that invites the coachee to elaborate on previous comments. In addition to eliciting more detail from the coachee, this is also very useful for the times when the coach does not know what to say next!

Summary

The solution-focused approach to coaching is about asking the right questions, about keeping coachees focused on what they want to achieve, not what has happened in the past. It is about stretching coachees so they can be the best they can be. Its primary focus on outcomes over analysis may seem simplistic to some, but the solution-focused approach takes pride in keeping it simple. Staying focused on solutions is the essence of great coaching.

References

Barrett, F (2004) Coaching for resilience, *Organization Development Journal*, **22** (1), pp 93–96

Berg, I K and Szabó, P (2005) *Brief Coaching for Lasting Solutions*, W W Norton, New York

Carver, C S and Scheier, M F (1998) *On the Self-regulation of Behavior*, Cambridge University Press, Cambridge

Corcoran, J and Stephenson, M (2000) The effectiveness of solution-focused therapy with child behavior problems: a preliminary report, *Families in Society*, **81** (5), pp 468–74

Dahl, R, Bathel, D and Carreon, C (2000) The use of solution-focused therapy with an elderly population, *Journal of Systemic Therapies*, **19** (4), pp 45–55

de Shazer, S (1984) The imaginary pill technique, *Journal of Strategic and Systemic Therapies*, **3** (1), pp 30–34

de Shazer, S (1988) *Clues: Investigating solutions in brief therapy*, Norton and Co, New York

Ellis, A (1997) Response to Jeffrey T. Guterman's response to my critique of his article 'A social constructionist position for mental health counseling', *Journal of Mental Health Counseling*, **19** (1), pp 57–63

Gollwitzer, P M (1996) The volitional benefits of planning, in *The Psychology of Action*, ed P M Gollwitzer and J A Bargh, pp 287–312, Guilford, New York

Grant, A M, and O'Connor, S A (2010) The differential effects of solution-focused and problem-focused coaching questions: A pilot study with implications for practice, *Industrial and Commercial Training*, **42** (2), pp 102–111

Grant, A M (2012) Making positive change: A randomized study comparing solution-focused vs problem-focused coaching questions, *Journal of Systemic Therapies*, **31** (2), pp 18–31

Grant, A M, Cavanagh, M J, Kleitman, S, Spence, G, Lakota, M and Yu, N (2012) Development and validation of the solution-focused inventory, *Journal of Positive Psychology*, **7** (4), pp 334–348

Green, L S, Oades, L G and Grant, A M (2006) Cognitive-behavioural, solution-focused life coaching: enhancing goal striving, well-being and hope, *Journal of Positive Psychology*, **1** (3), pp 142–49

Heckhausen, H and Gollwitzer, P M (1987) Thought contents and cognitive functioning in motivational versus volitional states of mind, *Motivation and Emotion*, **11**, pp 101–20

Held, B S (1996) Solution-focused therapy and the postmodern: a critical analysis, in *Handbook of Solution-focused Brief Therapy*, ed S D Miller, M A Hubble and B L Duncan, pp 27–43, Jossey-Bass, San Francisco, CA

Horvath, A O and Symonds, B (1991) Relation between working alliance and outcome in psychotherapy: a meta-analysis, *Journal of Counseling Psychology*, **38** (2), pp 139–49

Howard, K I, Kopta, S, Krause, M S and Orlinsky, D E (1986) The dose-effect relationship in psychotherapy, *American Psychologist*, **41** (2), pp 159–64

Jay, M (2003) Understanding how to leverage executive coaching, *Organization Development Journal*, **21** (2), pp 6–19

Kilburg, R R (2004) When shadows fall: using psychodynamic approaches in executive coaching, *Consulting Psychology Journal: Practice and research*, **56** (4), pp 246–68

Lethem, J (2002) Brief solution-focused therapy, *Child and Adolescent Mental Health*, **7** (4), pp 189–92

Murray, C E and Murray, T L, Jr (2004) Solution-focused premarital counseling: helping couples build a vision for their marriage, *Journal of Marital and Family Therapy*, **30** (3), pp 349–58

O'Connell, B (1998) *Solution-focused Therapy*, Sage, London

Theeboom, T, Beersma, B and van Vianen, A E M (2013) Does coaching work? A meta-analysis on the effects of coaching on individual level outcomes in an organizational context, *The Journal of Positive Psychology*, **9** (1), pp 1–18

Walter, J L and Peller, J E (1996) Rethinking our assumptions: assuming anew in a postmodern world, in *Handbook of Solution-focused Brief Therapy*, ed S C Miller, M A Hubble and B L Duncan, pp 9–27, Jossey-Bass, San Francisco, CA

Zachary, L J (2005) Raising the bar in a mentoring culture, *Training & Development*, **59** (6), pp 26–27

Cognitive behavioural coaching

07

MICHAEL NEENAN

The cognitive behavioural coaching model explained

Coaching helps individuals to get the best out of themselves in order to achieve their important work/life goals. While this may be an inspirational message for a coachee to hear, simply following a goal-orientated action plan is usually insufficient to bring about this end. What often blocks the way to change are the coachee's self-limiting/defeating thoughts and beliefs (eg 'I'm not good enough'), counterproductive behaviours (eg procrastination) and troublesome emotions (eg prolonged anxiety). Cognitive behavioural coaching (CBC) helps coachees to identify, examine and change such thoughts and beliefs, develop more productive behaviours and become more skilled at emotional management – all of which leads to coachees demonstrating greater resilience in tackling their present and future difficulties (Neenan, 2009). The ultimate goal of CBC is for the coachee to become his or her own coach.

CBC derives from the work of two leading cognitive behavioural theorists, researchers and therapists, Aaron Beck (1976) and Albert Ellis (1962): Beck's model is known as cognitive therapy while Ellis's is called rational emotive behaviour therapy – the similarities and differences between the two models are beyond the scope of this chapter. The origins of cognitive behavioural therapy (CBT) can be traced back to the Stoic philosophers, Epictetus and Marcus Aurelius. Epictetus stated a profound truth that is at the heart of CBT: 'People are disturbed not by things, but by the views which they take of them.' In other words, the viewpoint we choose determines our reaction to 'things'. The idea of choosing a viewpoint can trigger a range of responses in coachees, from revelation and receptivity to resistance. With the first group, coachees are eager to discover new problem-solving perspectives; the second group are willing to engage with CBC and expect a successful outcome; the last group may insist that their views are determined, not chosen, by past or present events or are too ingrained to change but, reluctantly, give CBC the benefit of the doubt for a trial period.

By helping coachees to recognize their idiosyncratic styles of problem-perpetuating thinking and using reason and reality testing to modify them, they learn to think about their concerns in more helpful, balanced and adaptive ways. The philosopher Simon Blackburn describes self-reflection thus:

> Human beings are relentlessly capable of reflecting on themselves ... We can habitually think things, and then reflect on what we are thinking. We can ask ourselves (or sometimes we get asked by other people) whether we know what we are talking about. To answer that we need to reflect on our own positions, our own understanding of what we are saying, our own sources of authority ... We might start to wonder whether what we say is 'objectively' true, or merely the outcome of our own perspective, or our own 'take' on a situation.
>
> (Blackburn, 1999: 4)

CBT does not say that problems are created solely by one's thinking: adverse events do occur but how we think about these events can increase our difficulties in dealing with them (eg accused of being the 'weak link' on a project, the person dwells on the unfairness of the accusation instead of dealing directly with it, and falls behind with his work on the project thereby justifying the original accusation). CBT might suggest by its name that emotion is ignored, but this is untrue as it does explore upsetting feelings but not endlessly so, as this can actually strengthen these feelings and the beliefs underpinning them (Grieger and Boyd, 1980). The route to emotional change is through cognitive and behavioural change, as with a coachee who thinks her 'boss is a bully' and gets angry every time she sees or thinks about him; by developing an assertive outlook, the coachee is able to 'coach upwards' and moderate her boss's abrasive interpersonal style as well as her own anger.

CBT can sometimes be misconstrued as positive thinking: the therapist being a 'cheerleader' for always looking on the bright side of life (Leahy, 2003). Rather, CBT emphasizes realistic thinking, ie trying to ascertain how things actually are, free from distortions in our thinking such as accepting that we live in a world of probability and chance rather than insisting on guarantees that our endeavours will never backfire. Positive thinking should not be confused with a positive attitude: the first outlook relies on mindless optimism while the second one seeks to find constructive ways of handling difficulty and distress with the expectation that things will eventually turn out well.

Beck and Ellis have been eager to move CBT out of the counsellor's office to reach a wider audience with their psychological problem-solving approaches. With this aim in mind, turning CBT into CBC has been growing apace in both personal and workplace coaching (Anderson, 2002; Grant and Greene, 2001; Kodish, 2002; Neenan and Dryden, 2014; Peltier, 2001; Reivich and Shatté, 2002).

Research

CBT, or more particularly Beck's cognitive therapy, has become the 'single most important and best validated psychotherapeutic approach. It is the psychological treatment of choice for a wide range of psychological problems' (Salkovskis, 1996: xiii). Moreover, 'there are indications that they [CBT approaches] may produce an enduring effect rarely shared by other approaches' (Hollon and Beck, 2004: 482). The current guidelines of the National Institute for Health and Clinical Excellence (NICE, 2005) make CBT the first line treatment for a range of clinical disorders.

Does the success of CBT in treating clinical problems translate into similar success in coaching with coachees who are striving for personal and professional satisfaction? Research into CBC is limited. Grant (2001) found that combined cognitive and behavioural approaches with trainee accountants 'was associated with an increase in academic performance, deep and achieving approaches to learning, enhanced self-concepts related to academic performance, and a reduction in test anxiety'. Other studies that use evidence-based cognitive behavioural, solution-focused (CB-SF) techniques in life coaching have found significant increases in coachees' goal-striving, well-being and hope (Green, Oades and Grant, 2006) and coaching outcomes are enhanced when coaching is provided by a professional life coach rather than someone from one's peer group acting as a coach (Spence and Grant, 2007). Grant and Greene (2001) have developed manualized CB-SF coaching programmes. Cognitive coaching, which is taught in educational and other settings, uses meta-cognition (thinking about your thinking) to enhance self-directed learning and improve decision-making skills and problem-solving capacities. Research in cognitive coaching has linked its implementation to increased student achievement, greater teacher efficacy and satisfaction, higher levels of conceptual thinking among teachers and more professional, collaborative cultures (Edwards, 2001).

Many coaching texts make great claims for the effectiveness of coaching but, presently, lack great empirical data to support such claims (though, of course, lack of adequate testing does not mean lack of effectiveness). However, as various authors observe, research into coaching is in its early stages but 'it is growing and the empirical foundations of the profession are strengthening' (Skiffington and Zeus, 2003: 5). Furnham (2004) states that to determine if coaching works it should be subjected to the 'gold standard' of scientific evaluation – randomized controlled trials (RCTs). An RCT provides the highest grade of evidence for an intervention's effectiveness because the evidence produced from the trial is the least likely to be contaminated by bias (Wessely, 2001).

CBC practice

The usual structure of each session is to discuss and clarify the coachee's issues, establish goals (clear, specific, measurable and within the coachee's control to achieve), develop action plans, confirm the coachee's responsibility for implementing these plans and, at the end of the session, gain feedback to determine what was helpful and unhelpful about the session in order to customize coaching to the coachee's preferences. At the next session, progress with the action plans is reviewed. This is the smooth-running view of coaching, which sometimes occurs.

More often than not, psychological difficulties intrude at the outset (eg the coachee believes he or she has been 'sent' for coaching or is ambivalent about the benefits of change) and/or during its course (eg the coachee becomes demoralized as the hard work of change kicks in). Cognitive behavioural coaching is therefore a twin-track approach to goal achievement: the psychological and the practical (Neenan and Dryden, 2014). The psychological track helps to remove the stumbling blocks to change such as procrastination, excessive self-doubt, indecisiveness and self-deprecation, while the practical track assists coachees to develop an orderly sequence of goal-directed action steps (sometimes coachees articulate clear and exciting goals but are vague about the steps that are required to get them there).

However, the practical side of coaching can be neglected because, in my experience, some coaches, particularly from counselling backgrounds, are too eager to 'dig deep' into psychological issues, overly focusing on them before there is evidence to warrant such an investigation or before they have been given permission from the coachee to do so. Such behaviour is likely to lead to a poor coaching relationship punctuated by frequent ruptures. It is important to point out to these coaches that understanding and removing psychological blocks is necessary but not necessarily sufficient to bring about change: following an action plan leads to self-actualization and achieving the satisfactions that the coachee has been seeking. Therefore, dealing with the practical aspects of goal-achievement is equally as important as the psychological blocks that impede it.

The ABCDE model

A framework for understanding and dealing with psychological blocks in coaching is the ABCDE model (Dryden and Neenan, 2004; Ellis and MacLaren, 1998).

Situational A (activating event)

The coachee's objective description of the situation – giving a presentation to colleagues in two weeks' time.

Critical A (activating event)

The coachee's subjective account of the most troubling aspect of the situation – 'I might not be able to answer some of the questions.'

B = self-limiting/defeating beliefs

These are triggered by the critical A – 'I must be able to answer all the questions otherwise I'll be exposed as a phoney, derided as the so-called expert.'

C = consequences

Emotional	rising anxiety.
Behavioural	frantic over-preparation, sleep disturbance, reduced work performance.
Physical	continual tension, headaches.
Interpersonal	irritation with family and work colleagues.
Cognitive	catastrophic thoughts and images about the aftermath of being exposed as a 'phoney'.

D = disputing or examining these self-defeating beliefs

- Is this belief rigid or flexible: does it allow for outcomes other than the one demanded – answering all the questions?
- Is this belief extreme or non-extreme: is it excessive for the person to call himself a 'phoney' because he may be unable to answer a question or two?

- Does this belief make sense: because he wants an outcome to occur (answering all the questions), does it follow logically that this outcome must occur?

- Is this belief realistic: where is the evidence that he must be able to answer all the questions rather than do the best he can on the day? If he was a phoney rather than an imagined one, would his boss have asked him to give the presentation?

- Is keeping this belief helpful: are the costs greater than the benefits?

E = new and effective outlook

(Adaptive, compassionate, balanced, and self- and performance-enhancing.) 'I now realize that my standards are rigid and harsh. A true phoney would be attempting to deceive his audience, which I'm definitely not trying to do. On the other hand, an expert is very, not completely, knowledgeable. If I can't answer a question I will ask someone in the audience or find out myself. Gaps in my knowledge are to be filled, not condemned. I expect to give a competent performance with a strong preference for improvement over time. If one or two people do think I'm a phoney, then I can choose whether or not to agree with them.'

The coachee's new outlook is lengthy and elaborate because it takes a rounded view of the situation, in stark contrast to the all-or-nothing quality of his original self-defeating beliefs. He is now able to view the forthcoming presentation with 'excited curiosity' instead of as a potential catastrophe. In order to internalize his new outlook, the coachee made regular presentations, as a one-off presentation is unlikely to dislodge his old ideas.

When teaching the ABCDE model, the coach needs to emphasize that A (events – past, present or future) does not cause C (but contributes to it); B (beliefs) largely determines C (consequences). This is an empowering view of how change occurs because it allows us to develop different beliefs (D→E) about A and, consequently, modify our reactions at C; if A really did cause C then we would be dependent on others or situations changing first before we could.

When does CBC work best?

CBC works best with coachees who are psychologically minded and are keen to detect, examine and change their maladaptive thinking because they see its adverse effects upon their performance. With coachees who are less psychologically adept at introspection, the presentation of the CBC model linked to examples of their current problematic behaviour can quickly help them to 'tune' into which aspects of their thinking need modifying, which, in turn, can produce quickly observable performance improvements. Just as one swallow does not make a summer, initial gains from CBC need to be maintained over the longer term to demonstrate that substantial change has occurred. Maintenance of gains, including the ability to deal with setbacks by pinpointing the reactivation of former self-defeating beliefs and behaviours, shows that coachees have made optimal use of CBC.

CBC might not work well with people who find it difficult to engage in introspection, see it as an 'intimate' process they feel uncomfortable with, are not prepared to expend the effort to become aware of, examine and modify their problematic thinking, are worried about a stranger 'poking about in my head', or see action as the answer to their current concerns, not 'navel-gazing' (navel-gazing is self-absorption or profitless introspection whereas developing realistic thinking is goal-orientated). In my experience, the real problem is not usually outright rejection of the CBC model but how it is presented and implemented by the coach.

Tools and techniques

Tools and techniques are used to help coachees understand and implement the ABCDE model that is at the heart of CBC.

Teaching the cognitive model

This demonstrates how our thoughts are congruent with our mood and behaviour. For example, a coachee comes to coaching irritable and restless ('Coaching is just another bloody fad! All it's really about is how to get more work out of you'). The coach addresses the coachee's perceptions of coaching without dodging the issue of improved performance as an organizational goal; additionally, the coachee's personal needs are elicited ('I want to get these long hours under control'). By focusing on the organizational and personal, the coachee begins to feel hopeful and relaxed in the session ('Maybe there is something in it for me. I'm prepared to give it a go'). The coach then reviews the two different viewpoints that the coachee has expressed and their impact on her mood and behaviour, to demonstrate the cognitive model in action. The coach would also want to know if the coachee has any reservations about, objections to or criticisms of the model so they can discuss them.

Other ways of teaching the model (and tweaking it for business purposes) would be to couple self-defeating beliefs to reductions in performance, productivity and profit such as a person believing that completing important paperwork is 'dull and boring', procrastinates over doing it and thereby misses deadlines and reduces sales.

Inference chaining

This involves asking your coachee a series of assumption-driven questions to tease out his or her personally significant inferences about a situation in order to pinpoint its most troubling aspect, called the critical A. In this example, a manager is anxious about confronting one of her staff about his poor performance and the coach follows the logical implications of each coachee thought:

Coach:	What's anxiety-provoking in your mind about doing that?
Coachee:	He probably won't like it.
Coach:	And if he doesn't?
Coachee:	He'll probably get angry.
Coach:	And if he does respond like that?
Coachee:	Then I'll be placed in an awkward position.
Coach:	How so? (This is a clarifying question before resuming inference chaining.)
Coachee:	I don't like dealing with angry people. I avoid it whenever I can.
Coach:	And if you don't avoid it and try to deal with him?
Coachee:	Then I'll become all tongue-tied, red-faced, my mind will go blank, and I'll probably crumble.
Coach:	And if you do crumble?
Coachee:	Then I'll have lost my credibility as a manager. It will be all round the office. Him smirking and strutting around like he's won.
Coach:	So is losing your credibility as a manager the most troubling aspect of this situation?
Coachee:	Losing my credibility. That's it. (The coachee's critical A has been located.)

The critical A triggered the coachee's rigid key belief: 'I must not lose my credibility as a manager in dealing with this man otherwise I will be seen as weak and pathetic.' Through discussion and cognitive restructuring (ie belief change), the coachee was able to see that she was taking one aspect of her role, dealing with interpersonal conflict, as the cornerstone of her credibility as a manager and forgetting or minimizing her managerial strengths (most of her staff respected her). By stepping back from this belief she was able to formulate a new one: 'The evidence shows I'm a competent manager but I do need to toughen-up in dealing with this man. I don't like confrontation and probably never will but it's something I want to try to get to grips with because it's likely to happen again.'

It is important that the coach does not push the coachee for radical restructuring of her beliefs ('learn to embrace confrontation'), because this strategy is likely to be met with understandable resistance as she sees these beliefs being undermined through forced, false and fast change. Coachees are more likely to modify their beliefs when change is gradual and stays within their value system (Dowd, 1996).

Common cognitive distortions (CCDs)

CCDs are also known as 'thinking traps', which result from coachees processing information in a consistently biased way thereby helping to maintain their troublesome feelings and problematic behaviours. Typical distortions include:

- All-or-nothing thinking: viewing events as either black or white. 'Either you're for me or against me.'

- Overgeneralization: drawing sweeping conclusions on the basis of a single incident or insufficient evidence. 'As I wasn't given the lead on this project, I'll never lead another one.'

- Mental filter: only the negative aspects of a situation are noticed. 'Look at all the things that have gone wrong this week.'

- Catastrophizing: assuming the worst and, if it occurs, your inability to deal with it. 'It will be terrible if I don't get the promotion. I'll be stuck at this level for ever and vegetate.'

- Musts and shoulds: rigid rules that you impose on yourself and others. 'I must never show any weaknesses to my colleagues'; 'Everyone should work as long and as hard as I do.'

- Fallacy of fairness: believing in a just world. 'Bad things won't happen to you if you're a good, hard-working, honest person.'

- Perfectionism: striving for standards that are beyond reach or reason (Burns, 1980). 'I must do everything perfectly or else I'm no good. A competent performance equals failure.'

Coachees can learn to identify the distortions in their thinking and determine the accuracy of them: 'There's that all-or-nothing thinking again about people being for or against me. Based on the evidence, people have a range of reactions to me, not simply for or against. I want to develop more balanced thinking about this issue and stop this extremist nonsense.'

Experiments

Thoughts are viewed as hypotheses, not facts (unless they can be verified). Carrying out experiments allows coachees to test the validity of their predictions. For example, a coachee thought that if she presented her ideas at a meeting they would be rejected or ridiculed. While her ideas were neither rejected nor ridiculed, they were considered to be 'insufficiently robust at the present time and need more work' (guidelines for improvement were suggested). While the coachee was not overly pleased with this outcome, at least it pointed the way to possible eventual acceptance of some of her ideas if she acted on the new information generated by the experiment.

Self-acceptance

This is a way of being, not a technique. Self-acceptance means rating aspects of oneself but never judging oneself on the basis of these aspects: 'My performance was poor in that situation based on the feedback. I want to learn from the feedback in order to improve my performance, but my performance can never define me.' A person is too complex to be given a global evaluation like 'useless' or 'worthless'; in other words, such evaluations are meaningless. Self-acceptance also involves looking at oneself in the round by acknowledging one's strengths and weaknesses and attempting to change the latter if desired, and frequently reminding oneself that human fallibility cannot be eradicated (so do not waste time trying!) but the incidence of fallible behaviour can be reduced by learning from one's mistakes thereby making fewer of them.

Self-condemnation adds nothing of value or clarity to problem solving. If coachees doubt this, they can spend a week, for example, noting how much time they waste on self-condemnation and feeling frustrated when things go wrong instead of focusing on immediate problem solving. Self-acceptance can be difficult to learn but its practical effects can be seen and felt through higher levels of performance and motivation.

Task assignment record

This is filled in near the end of every session and helps to keep coachees focused on their goal-directed action steps:

- What is the task you are going to complete before the next session? ('Make three contacts as part of my marketing strategy to launch my coaching practice.')

- What is the purpose of doing this? ('To stop procrastinating over setting myself up as a coach and to keep reminding myself that my confidence and competence as a coach develops over time, not straight away, so get on with it!')

- Any anticipated obstacles in completing the task and what solutions will you use to overcome them? ('I may start procrastinating again so I will make all three contacts in the next 48 hours rather than leaving them until the end of the week.')

It is important that the tasks are reviewed in every session to discover what the coachee did or did not do. Task review is based on learning, not success or failure. Whatever is learnt provides valuable information on your progress or lack of it towards goal achievement.

Three key insights

These can act as an *aide-mémoire* for present and future problem solving:

1 You largely feel the way you think ('largely' because you are influenced, but not controlled, by other factors). You can control your emotional reactions to an extent you may never have realized by paying close attention to how you think when you get upset.

2 No matter how you acquired your unhelpful beliefs, you still choose to subscribe to them today ('I didn't go to university so I have to keep proving I'm not stupid') and act in ways that strengthen these beliefs, such as trying to impress graduate colleagues with how smart you are.

3 The way to get rid of or weaken these beliefs is to continually think and act against them by adopting a more helpful viewpoint, 'I know I'm an intelligent person because I now look at a wide range of factors connected to the question of intelligence instead of my previous black or white view of university or stupidity', and stop trying to impress the graduates and let them make up their own minds about how smart you are.

Ten key questions to guide your way

1. What thoughts are going through your mind in that situation?

This helps the coachee to become aware of and identify negative thoughts linked to counterproductive behaviours, unpleasant feelings and bodily sensations. A possibly reply from the coachee is, 'I don't know.' This often results from the coach not helping the coachee to imagine the situation as clearly as possible. Once this is done, thoughts and feelings are usually activated.

2. What stops you from . . . (following a particular course of action)?

This is an assessment question to uncover blocks to change and discover what the maintaining factors are in holding back the coachee, such as low frustration tolerance ('It's too hard or boring') or perfectionism. The coachee might say, 'I'm not sure.' A way round this is to ask the coachee to imagine not being stuck and what would have changed in order for him or her to move on. Even if the blocks are practical ones like skills deficits or lack of knowledge, there is often a psychological block impeding remediation of these practical difficulties, so the same tactic can be used.

3. What are the short- and long-term costs and benefits of change?

Some coachees might reply, 'Lots of benefits', yet little change is occurring. This might be because these coachees are dwelling on the unarticulated costs of change ('I'm worried that it all could go wrong') while publicly espousing the benefits. What is 'hidden' needs to be uncovered and examined.

4. What is the clear and specific goal you want to achieve?

This is to clarify the coachee's thinking about goal selection and counter the vagueness of 'I want to be happier' or 'I want to be more confident'. In what specific contexts does the coachee want to be more confident and what does more confident actually look like?

5. What's the problem with making mistakes or experiencing failure?

'Because I don't like it' comes the standard reply. On further investigation, coachees are often coupling their self-worth to performance failure, which has a much deeper and more unpleasant resonance than simply not liking it.

6. What advice would you give to someone else struggling with the same issue as yourself?

This encourages the coachee to step back from the issue to gain more objectivity in thinking about it. However, coachees often say, 'But I wouldn't follow my own advice.' This response reveals a double standard, which usually involves showing compassion and understanding to others ('If you miss a few performance targets it's not the end of the world'), but being harsh and unforgiving towards oneself ('Missing my targets shows how utterly incompetent I am. It does feel like the end of the world'), which would then require further examination.

7. What would be the first concrete steps towards reaching your goal?

Once the coachee's concerns have been clarified and goals agreed, specific action is now required rather than a general statement of intent: 'I'd better start getting into gear on this issue.'

8. How will you know you are making progress towards your goals?

A usual reply is, 'I'll feel better.' The coachee is informed that specific behavioural evidence is required to evaluate progress, not just subjective responses.

9. What are the most valuable ideas and techniques you have got from coaching?

If the coachee says, 'I got a lot from it', the coach needs to encourage him or her to be specific.

10. Acting as a self-coach, how will you maintain and strengthen your gains from coaching?

'Keep at it, I suppose' might be the doubtful reply. Developing an idiosyncratic and detailed blueprint for the future reminds the coachee that self-coaching needs to become a way of life if his or her gains are not to decay.

Conclusion

CBC is a powerful way to help coachees reach their potential with its focus on both the psychological and practical aspects of goal achievement. Coachees can learn that many obstacles to change are psychologically constructed rather than stand as immutable facts and that by trying out new ways of thinking and behaving, obstacles dissolve and exciting possibilities beckon.

References

Anderson, J P (2002) Executive coaching and REBT: some comments from the field, *Journal of Rational-Emotive and Cognitive-Behavior Therapy*, **20** (3/4), pp 223–33

Beck, A T (1976) *Cognitive Therapy and the Emotional Disorders*, International Universities Press, New York

Blackburn, S (1999) *Think*, Oxford University Press, Oxford

Burns, D D (1980) The perfectionist's script for self-defeat, *Psychology Today*, November, pp 34–51

Dowd, E T (1996) Resistance and reactance in cognitive therapy, *International Cognitive Therapy Newsletter*, **10** (3), pp 3–5

Dryden, W and Neenan, M (2004) *Rational Emotive Behavioural Counselling in Action*, 3rd edn, Sage, London

Edwards, J (2001) *Cognitive Coaching SM: A synthesis of the research*, Center for Cognitive Coaching, Highlands Ranch, CO

Ellis, A (1962) *Reason and Emotion in Psychotherapy*, Citadel, Secaucus, NJ (rev edn Birch Lane Press, New York, 1994)

Ellis, A and MacLaren, C (1998) *Rational Emotive Behavior Therapy: A therapist's guide*, Impact Publishers, Atascadero, CA

Furnham, A (2004) *Management and Myths: Challenging business fads, fallacies and fashions*, Palgrave Macmillan, Basingstoke

Grant, A M (2001) *Coaching for enhanced performance: Comparing cognitive and behavioral approaches to coaching*, Paper presented at the 3rd International Spearman Seminar: Extending Intelligence: Enhancement and New Constructs, Sydney

Grant, A M and Greene, J (2001) *Coach Yourself: Make real change in your life*, Momentum, London

Green, L S Oades, L G and Grant, A M (2006) Cognitive-behavioral, solution-focused life coaching: enhancing goal-striving, well-being, and hope, *Journal of Positive Psychology*, **1** (3), pp 142–49

Grieger, R and Boyd, J (1980) *Rational-Emotive Therapy: A skills-based approach*, Van Nostrand Reinhold, New York

Hollon, S D and Beck, A T (2004) Cognitive and cognitive behavioral therapies, in *Bergin and Garfield's Handbook of Psychotherapy and Behavior Change*, 5th edn, ed M J Lambert, Wiley, New York

Kodish, S P (2002) Rational emotive behaviour coaching, *Journal of Rational-Emotive and Cognitive-Behavior Therapy*, **20** (3/4), pp 235–46

Leahy, R L (2003) *Cognitive Therapy Techniques: A practitioner's guide*, Guilford Press, New York

National Institute for Health and Clinical Excellence (2005) *Clinical Guidelines for Treating Mental Health Problems*, NICE, London

Neenan, M (2009) *Developing Resilience: A cognitive behavioural approach*, Routledge, Hove

Neenan, M and Dryden, W (2014) *Life Coaching: A cognitive-behavioural approach*, second edition, Routledge, Hove

Peltier, B (2001) *The Psychology of Executive Coaching*, Brunner-Routledge, New York

Reivich, K and Shatté, A (2002) *The Resilience Factor: Seven essential skills for overcoming life's inevitable obstacles*, Broadway Books, New York

Salkovskis, P M (1996) Preface, in *Frontiers of Cognitive Therapy*, ed P M Salkovskis, Guilford Press, New York

Skiffington, S and Zeus, P (2003) *Behavioral Coaching: How to build sustainable personal and organizational strength*, McGraw-Hill, Sydney

Spence, G B and Grant, A M (2007) Professional and peer life coaching and the enhancement of goal-striving and well-being: an exploratory study, *Journal of Positive Psychology*, **2** (3) pp 185–94

Wessely, S (2001) Randomised controlled trials: the gold standard?, in *Evidence in the Psychological Therapies: A critical guide for practitioners*, ed C Mace S Moorey and B Roberts, Brunner-Routledge, Hove

NLP coaching

08

IAN MCDERMOTT

The NLP coaching model explained

Originating in the USA in the mid-1970s, neuro-linguistic programming (NLP) has since spread around the world, primarily I suspect because it delivers practical tools that can greatly improve performance. But these are really just the fruits of a unique mindset that focuses on two things, the study and replication of excellence, and, the structure of subjective experience. Structure here refers not to the content of experience but to the way it is put together – not to the fact that a person feels overwhelmed but to exactly how that sensation and experience is put together internally. What we want to know are the building blocks of that experience.

The primary tool employed in NLP is modelling. A model is a simplified description of the key elements of a process. The value of any model is its usefulness. The title of the very first NLP book, *The Structure of Magic* (Bandler and Grinder, 1975), suggested that, though what certain therapists did seemed quite magical, there was in fact a structure to their way of working that could be discovered and organized into a working model. That model could then be taught to others.

In NLP the word 'model' is also used in another sense – one who is a model of excellence. NLP practitioners are interested in looking for models of excellence in just about any field of human endeavour and will be asking, 'How do they *do* that?' They seek to specify precisely what it is that makes this individual or organization outstanding. NLP has developed a range of tools and distinctions that aid this process. Another may be good but this one is outstanding. NLP is interested in what it is that makes the difference. Wouldn't you like to know just how an outstanding coach achieves such *consistent* excellence? Wouldn't you like to have the opportunity to achieve that level of excellence? That's what NLP aims to deliver.

In 1990 I proposed a four-fold typology of elements that represented the essence of an NLP approach. I called them the 'Four pillars of NLP'

(O'Connor and McDermott, 1996). These have now been widely adopted. They are: the capacity to establish and maintain rapport, an outcome orientation, heightened sensory acuity and great behavioural flexibility.

Both NLP and coaching presuppose that most coachees have within them the ability to determine what they want and how they might go about achieving it. Both presuppose that it is possible for coachees to shape their destiny if they are able to access the resources they need. Both therefore presuppose a vast reservoir of potential that it's possible for the coachee to tap. NLP coaching offers a way of realizing these assumptions at a very practical level for both coach and coachee.

All coach training programmes say that it is important to listen to the coachee. NLP actually teaches people *how* to do this by giving them the linguistic tools to understand the structure of what is being said (eg, the meta model, page 151). Again, all training schools exhort their students to notice what's going on with the coachee. NLP empowers the coach to do this by teaching *how* to notice what's happening so students acquire a whole new level of sensory acuity.

Over the last few years I have been interested to see bona fide coaches applying to take our NLP practitioner training. When I've asked them why, they tell me the speed of NLP means they can be more effective in the limited time of a coaching session. However, as a trainer of coaches, what I've actually observed is that coaches who learn NLP work with a much greater degree of precision.

When does NLP coaching work best?

To answer this question accurately it's important to consider not only the coachee but also the coach. As regards coachees, NLP coaching works best when they are unclear either about what they want or how to achieve it. As ever, a little motivation goes a long way, but an NLP approach is very well suited to working with ambivalence because it presupposes ambivalence to have a positive intention. (Specific techniques have been developed which allow all of the elements to be honoured.)

The tools developed make NLP coaching particularly valuable when coachees need to engage in belief change work, strategic thinking or learn the specific how-tos that are part of acquiring new capabilities. Whenever issues are multifactorial or require shifts in physiology NLP will have tools that make change easier.

The coaches most suited to an NLP approach are those who are naturally curious, ethical, willing to be flexible, able to address macro and micro issues, who don't need to know the answers and who are willing to work with issues at all logical levels (see page 149).

NLP coaching, however, is not for everybody. It is, of course, no substitute for therapy, not even NLP therapy (McDermott and Jago, 2001a). And it should be avoided when coachees are really seeking subject specialist input – eg financial planning. Because it is remarkably empowering NLP coaching makes it difficult to maintain the fiction that we are only on the receiving end of life: if you know how to change your internal experience you know how to change your life, and this may be more than some coachees are willing to take on. Similarly NLP coaching does not sit well with coaches who have a low tolerance for alternative maps of the world. Coaches who believe there is only one right way, who think they know what's best for the coachee, or who favour the relentless 'to do' list approach to coaching are unlikely to feel at ease with the NLP approach.

Tools and techniques

Over the last 30 years a remarkable array of NLP tools and techniques have been developed that offer specific intervention protocols that can be almost endlessly modified and enhanced to suit individual needs, requirements and circumstances. They provide a bridge between aspiration and realization by making new distinctions that can be operationalized and offer step-by-step how-to templates.

It is not possible here to do justice to such a range; a fuller account can be found in McDermott and Jago (2003). A book such as this is primarily a linguistic medium. I have therefore chosen to focus on linguistic tools as this medium can accommodate these most readily. Clearly this skews things. Even here, though, I want to start by highlighting the importance of states as they are central to NLP. Were this a DVD you'd be seeing a lot of this more limbic dimension of NLP as I'd probably be demonstrating how NLP works with physiology by showing you the remarkable changes that are possible.

States and physiology

Anyone who speaks more than one language fluently will know that the way you use your body is quite different depending on the language you are speaking. Each language has its own physiology. In the same way different activities – be they external behaviour or internal processing – have different physiologies. Arguably one of the most effective ways of increasing our choices is to extend the range of use of physiology that we are comfortable with. Getting into the right state can make all the difference. At one extreme it's the basis of 'fake it till you make it'; at the other it's what every world-class athlete does prior to the crucial event.

If coachees are to achieve the goals they aspire to they will need to be able to access the states that support what they're going for. But states are equally important for the coach. What's the optimal state for you to be in to coach at your best? Do you know how to access this at will? We owe it to our coachees to find out. NLP offers both coaches and coachees a range of specific techniques and protocols to establish and maintain an appropriate state – at will.

Logical levels

One of the primary ways we can achieve greater leverage in our lives is to make distinctions that clarify what kind of issues we are dealing with. Logical levels are a set of such distinctions which coaches and coachees find extraordinarily useful. They can both help identify what the 'real' issue is and the appropriate level at which to intervene.

Imagine that as a coach you hear the following six statements from six different coachees:

  1 I wish I was doing a job that served some higher purpose.
  2 I just don't feel I can be myself in this job.
  3 I don't believe in this job.
  4 I don't think I know how to do this job.
  5 I don't know what to do in this job.
  6 I don't think I can do this job in this kind of working environment.

Clearly these six coachees are talking about very different things:

  1 When someone says they can't do the job in this kind of working environment, they're not saying they can't do the job. The implication is that they could do the job if it were a different kind of working environment. So the issue is the *environment*.
  2 If you don't know what to do that's different again. This is about what you actually do. It's a matter of *behaviour*.

3 Not knowing *how* to do something means you lack certain skills at least at this time. These would give you the *capability*.

4 When someone doesn't believe in something they are obviously telling you about their beliefs and this will probably take you into their values as well. So here we are addressing *beliefs and values*.

5 If you don't feel you can be yourself doing a certain job you're talking about your sense of yourself – *your identity*.

6 Finally, if you wish your job served a higher purpose you have now gone beyond your own identity; you may be envisaging some larger system, purpose or being. We might call this spiritual but I tend to use the more value-neutral phrase that in some way you have gone *beyond identity*.

We can represent these levels either as a series of concentric circles or a vertical hierarchy:

- beyond identity;
- identity;
- beliefs and values;
- capabilities;
- behaviour;
- environment.

None are more important than the others. But it is fascinating to note the biases that people – and not least coaches – betray. I often find trainee coaches are surprised to find that they prefer to work with issues at particular logical levels. From an NLP point of view I want them to be flexible enough to honour and work at any logical level. Often when I am training I will pause during a demonstration session with a coachee to ask students at what logical level the issue as just stated is. As they get used to thinking in this way their diagnostic skills – and the kind of interventions they deem appropriate – improve dramatically.

Many coachees find logical levels an invaluable strategic thinking tool. It sensitizes them to how frequently messages are sent from one level (eg behaviour) but received at another (identity) – as in the annual review, a parent-child fracas or a lovers' quarrel. It also alerts them to incongruencies. Corporate clients, for instance, will often talk of the need to win hearts and minds. To achieve this they'll need to address the levels of beliefs and identity. Frequently, though, the proposed initiatives are at the behaviour level. Now they begin to understand why these are so ineffectual.

The value of the logical levels may also stem in part from how they seem to fit with idiomatic English where we sometimes make distinctions by referring to levels. As one of my coachees put it in a recent final review: 'On one level losing my major customer last year was a disaster, but on another it freed me up. It made me question whether I really wanted (beliefs and values) to keep doing (behaviour) the same kind of things. I had the skills (capabilities) to work in different corporate environments (environment). The question was, did I have the courage (beliefs and identity)? Over the past six months this coaching has given me faith in myself (identity), clarity about what to do next (behaviour) and why it really matters (beliefs and values) to *me* (identity).'

The meta model

The way we use language can be enormously informative for the coach. As ever, it ain't just what we say, it's the way that we say it. The linguistic distinctions that the meta model gives us enable us to examine the deeper structure of the language we use.

To make sense of our experience, NLP suggests we need to construct some kind of model of the world. The meta model postulates three primary processes we use to do this: deletion, generalization and distortion:

- *Deletion* – to avoid sensory overwhelm we ignore or don't notice a lot of information.
- *Generalization* – we devise rules that predict what is likely to happen and the way the world works.
- *Distortion* – we assign information – eg other's behaviour – meaning often on minimal evidence.

In using the meta model the first step is to recognize the patterns that you or others are using. Are you deleting, generalizing or distorting and is that helping or hindering? Each process will be reflected in your use of language. At the absolute minimum we can identify a dozen different language patterns. Once you have identified the pattern you may choose to intervene and change the language used. So often when you change the language you change the experience. This, of course, has enormous implications for coaching.

In dealing with generalizations, for instance, the coach's outcome is to explore and sometimes challenge their accuracy and efficacy. By so doing they can expand the limits of the coachee's model of the world. 'I've never been any good at this.' 'Never? Never, ever . . . ? There has not been a single moment in your life when you have ever been any good at this at all?' Generalizations are extraordinarily vulnerable: it only takes one counter-example to require some qualification of the original claim. When that starts to happen new boundaries of reality are being delineated. 'Well, maybe there have been times when I've been able to.' 'And if you could do it once, what might be possible now . . . ?' These are the obvious kind of generalizations.

However, there is a more subtle form. Technically they are known as 'modal operators'. These articulate the coachee's beliefs about what is possible and necessary given their model of the world. An example: a coachee says, 'I can't speak to my boss.' If the coach asks, 'What stops you?' he or she will learn something of the coachee's model of the world as regards the perceived cause of his or her problem. Alternatively, inquiring, 'What would happen if you did?' will help him or her come to understand the presumed effects. Just two questions, therefore, could provide an insight into how this coachee has cause and effect structured in his or her understanding of this issue. Teasing this information into consciousness is itself a powerful intervention.

Meta programmes

Meta programmes are largely unconscious sorting patterns that we use to filter our experience and determine what to pay attention to. They help us clarify what is important for us and are the means by which we organize our experience. Many have been identified in NLP. I shall touch on just one which coaches have repeatedly told me has been especially valuable in their work. It's called 'Moving away from – moving towards'.

Suppose your coachee says, 'I want to stop spending so much time at work and I'm fed up with feeling tired.' Clearly, he or she wishes to move away from the current experience. At this moment the coach has no idea what he or she might wish to move towards. The NLP coach will seek to pace the coachee so that he or she can move from avoidance towards something he or she deems desirable. Learning to do this can make a profound difference for a coachee who is used to focusing on what he or she doesn't want.

Successful institutions and group leaders need to be able to recognize and accommodate both meta programmes. One dazzling example would be the Christian Church, which has appealed both towards and away from meta programmes for centuries by offering believers both the carrot of heaven and the stick of hell.

If you know your predominant meta programmes you can play to your strengths. For instance, you'll know how to motivate yourself, but people often presume that what works for them will surely work for others. Many times I have seen team leaders who have a strong towards meta programme provide wonderful towards incentives. But some members of their team just don't seem to respond. This is not surprising given that in any group you'll probably have a mix of towards and away froms. Motivating the away froms means making clear the unpleasant consequences of not following a proposed course of action. What's needed is the acuity to determine the predominant meta programme and the flexibility to respond appropriately in real time.

Each pattern is valuable, each has its strengths and weaknesses. Maybe an away from mindset seems a bit negative? But a coach needs to know that towards coachees who tell you what they want and what they like are often less adept at recognizing what should be avoided. They may tend to minimize negative consequences and at the extreme can be oblivious to what is going wrong. That's a different meta programme. NLP coaching can redress such imbalances, first interpersonally by providing a savvy coach, and second intra-psychically by helping the coachee internalize an additional way of thinking.

Ten key questions to guide your way

When I first read the brief from the editor for this chapter I was puzzled by this heading. When I am working with a coachee there most certainly is not a set of questions that I am working through. But as I thought about it more there certainly are considerations that I will probably address as I come to understand what it is that the coachee and I are focusing upon. They come from an orientation. In what follows I have coded this orientation in question format. A health warning: this list is neither comprehensive nor definitive.

1. What do you want?

This is one question that every NLP coach will ask explicitly of a coachee and often repeat over time. It presupposes that the coachee knows or can find out through exploration. Even in its simplest form it has extraordinary power. If you have been grappling with some problem this question will take you from the present state to the desired state. As you begin detailing what it is that you want, you make it more vivid. This has neurophysiological consequences. So often when coachees begin to focus on what they're really going for their state changes in palpably observable ways.

One of the more subtle effects of this basic question is the reorientation in time that it frequently achieves. It is not uncommon for it to move a coachee from the present to a hoped for future. However, it is not only a question for the coachee. A good coach will be asking this of him- or herself in their own life as well as when working with a particular coachee.

2. How would you know if you got it?

'I just want to feel like I'm doing something worthwhile with my life.' But how will this coachee know when he or she is? This is a fundamental, epistemological question: how do we know what we know? And how will the coach know that this coachee has achieved his or her outcome? Both coach and coachee need to have some kind of evidence procedure. It could take many forms but to be most useful it will need to be sensory specific. So, what will you see, hear and feel (maybe even taste and smell) that will demonstrate to you that the outcome has been achieved? I find that paying attention to these specifics early on saves an awful lot of time later. In answering this inquiry coachees frequently get much clearer about what it is they do and don't want at the outset.

3. What is being presupposed here?

A coachee says, 'I wish I was more confident. Then I could meet somebody and settle down and be really happy'. Another, who has been referred by his manager for coaching says, 'But I'm really good at my job.' In both cases there's a lot that's being presupposed – for instance, more confidence will make new behaviour possible that could lead to romance, or that if you're good at your job you don't need a coach.

While it is important to understand how coachees' presuppositions are structuring their world it is just as important for the coach to be aware of his or her own. This is true moment by moment in any coaching session. Every question has built into it a number of presuppositions – not least that of all the questions one could ask, this particular question merits asking right now. These presuppositions frame our perception. So what will the coach be presupposing in the next question he or she asks? And will this be useful to the coachee?

4. What resources are needed?

One useful way of thinking about pretty much any issue that an individual or a corporate client might raise is that they come with a present state. We then determine what would be a desired state. The challenge is how to move from the former to the latter. In NLP coaching we will be looking for what resources are needed which, if applied, will make this transition possible. So many of the tools and techniques that have been developed in NLP are designed to provide the how-tos that make it possible to fully access these resources and incorporate them.

A resource can be almost anything. On occasion it may be some obvious external tangible asset, such as financial backing. More often though, the resources that can make all the difference are decidedly intangible: a change in attitude, an improved relationship sometimes with another, sometimes with oneself, a finding of purpose or the acquisition of a new skill set. We can formulate this way of thinking very simply:

Present State + Resources = Desired State.

5. How am I right now?

So often my own internal state is an invaluable barometer to what is actually going on. There have been times when, after a good night's sleep, feeling refreshed and alert I am with a coachee and I notice a change in my own state. Maybe I have become suddenly uneasy, restless, tired or bored. On one occasion I found myself starting to feel bored and I couldn't think why. So I said to the coachee, 'You know it's a funny thing, up until a few minutes ago I was right with you but then my mind starting wandering, my energy's gone down and I now just feel a bit bored.' And the coachee's response? 'Me too … I think I was just trying to convince myself but it's a con really. I just don't believe what I was saying anymore.'

6. What is the structure of this subjective experience?

How we put our internal experience together can make our world heaven or hell. Our senses provide the building blocks of our experience. Our internal world is ultimately comprised of sensory data – ie what we see, hear, feel, taste and smell – which we represent to ourselves in endlessly varied ways. If you want to know just how powerful these representations can be, consider this. For anyone who has a phobia it is quite unnecessary to be physically in the presence of what they're phobic about for them to have a phobic response. Talk about it in enough detail and they'll start having that phobic response. From an NLP point of view this is very good news! You are generating the response so potentially it could come under your control. If you understand the *structure* of the subjective experience that you have created internally you can change it and produce an equally dramatic but beneficial change in your physiology.

All internal experience has a structure. When you know how something is put together you can effectively rearrange it if you choose. By exploring with coachees how they (usually unconsciously) manipulate images, sounds, feelings, tastes and smells to help or hinder their experience and aspirations, the NLP coach is often able to help a coachee design new ways of thinking, quite literally.

7. What is an appropriate state and physiology?

The state you are in at any given moment has an enormous impact on what you are capable of at that time. Imagine having to make most of your life's major decisions when in the state that goes with having flu! A person's physiology and internal state are critical. For the NLP coach a recurring question is going to be, what state is the coachee in and what state does he or she need to be in to achieve and sustain the changes he or she seeks?

While many elements can influence our state – for instance, the kind of thoughts we're having – one that is frequently focused on in NLP is our use of physiology. Just how we are standing, sitting and moving generally (or not) will have a profound impact on our state. Many times I have encouraged a coachee to get up and walk around so that they may energize themselves and their thinking.

Suppose you needed to be at your best on a particular day because you were going to be making a presentation or going for an interview. How would you prepare? So often coachees attempt to resource themselves by acquiring information. But being able to be in the right state can make all the difference. NLP coaching can give coachees – and coaches – the tools to access at will the state they need to be in to give of their best.

8. What are the systemic implications?

Any proposed change has systemic implications (O'Connor and McDermott, 1997). After all, no man – or indeed woman – is an island. It's important to me to understand what the potential consequences of change could be for the larger system in which this individual operates. I think of that larger system as having three dimensions: the intra-psychic, the interpersonal, and the organizational. If we want the change to be real and sustainable we will need to take into account all three dimensions. The intra-psychic – if the coachee is at odds with him- or herself this does not bode well: 'Well, part of me really wants to start a new life, but part of me says it's too late.' Clearly we have work to do. The interpersonal – you may have decided to become self-employed but how does your spouse feel about this? The organizational – even if you are the head of the organization you would be well advised to take into account the likely perceptions and implications of any change programme before you implement it.

9. What are the positive by-products of the present status quo?

In my experience coachees rarely seek coaching because everything is wonderful and they wish to make it even more so. Usually there is a strong desire to effect change that will, they believe, result in some kind of improvement. Sometimes this can produce an impatience and dissatisfaction with the way things are now. They want to get on, make the changes and be finished with the old.

However, in order that this can be achieved I often find myself in the somewhat paradoxical position, at least temporarily, of being an 'advocate' for the status quo. I'll be asking coachees, be they private individuals or employees, questions like, 'So, what do you get out of what you do now?' or, 'What might you be in danger of losing?' Many times I have asked someone who wanted to quit smoking what they get out of smoking. A Danish coachee who found smoking gave her 32 specific benefits holds the record. It was, for instance, the primary way she would 'give time to myself'. For her this was a revelation and finally explained why it had been so difficult to give up previously. We prioritized these benefits and looked at how she could find alternative ways of achieving them.

Too often when we seek change both individuals and organizations are in danger of throwing out the baby with the bath water. When we do so we make it hard to sustain the change because we are violating our own internal ecology. So often this could be avoided if someone had known and taken the trouble to ask: what do we get out of what we do now?

10. How do you do that?

Really this is a modelling question. The perseverance and attention to detail that modelling requires means you've really got to want to know! You need to be really curious. Curiosity is non-judgemental and can be applied not only to excellence but also to understanding how we mess up. It can be of enormous value in coaching.

Many times I have found that my own curiosity about just how clients manage to consistently achieve a result they do not want has been sufficient to enable them also, perhaps for the first time, to become genuinely curious about just how do they do that? Even as they pay closer attention than usual they actually step back and see things with a fresh eye. They can take a dispassionate interest in how they do what they do.

Summary

I've sometimes been struck by how, when NLP coaches encounter coaches from different backgrounds, they are always curious about that alternative approach and want to know more. Equally striking, this curiosity is often not reciprocated. But such curiosity is invaluable not just for coachees but also for the coach's own development. If we want to be the best we can be more of the time, it's probably going to be useful to model our own best practice. So, when you've done a really good job you too might want to ask, 'Just how did I *do* that?'

References

Bandler, R and Grinder, J (1975) *The Structure of Magic*, Science and Behaviour Books, Palo Alto, CA

McDermott, I and Jago, W (2001a) *Brief NLP Therapy*, Sage, London

McDermott, I and Jago, W (2001b) *The NLP Coach*, Piatkus, London

McDermott, I and Jago, W (2003) *Your Inner Coach*, Piatkus, London

O'Connor, J and McDermott, I (1996) *Way of NLP*, Thorsons, London

O'Connor, J and McDermott, I (1997) *The Art of Systems Thinking*, Thorsons, London

Transpersonal coaching

09

JOHN WHITMORE and HETTY EINZIG

The transpersonal coaching model explained

Transpersonal coaching has its origins in the wider transpersonal psychology movement. Transpersonal goes beyond the personal to include the universal and beyond the psyche to include the spiritual. Just as family therapy sees the child as part of a system, the family, so the transpersonal perspective takes a systems approach, recognizing the interconnectedness of individuals, families, communities and organizations and actively engages our deeper awareness of this (McBeath and Wynne, 1985). It also recognizes and works with the yearning, ingrained in the human psyche, for something *beyond the personal*, beyond the material and the everyday. This may be expressed in many different ways, through spiritual or ethical practice, through creativity within and outside the workplace, through volunteering, community work and other forms of service.

The key distinguishing feature of transpersonal psychology is that it does not draw a line between personal and spiritual development but sees them as stages on a continuum. In the West we still tend to equate the spiritual with religious practice, and, as this declined with the rise of the consumer society from the 1960s onwards, spiritual ideas or practices were relegated to the private domain. This is now changing. There has always been in the West a solid interest in eastern spirituality and mysticism and many have turned to Buddhism or more esoteric religions for guidance and solace (The Dalai Lama and Cutler, 1998; Hardy 1987). In recent decades a number of factors have brought the spiritual back into the mainstream. Advances in physics and the neurosciences have stimulated a revival of debates about mind and consciousness, the economic and banking debacles of the early 2000s have heightened disenchantment with consumerism, and rising awareness of the climate and social justice crises have led to both acute criticism of the destructiveness of the market economy (see Pope Francis's encyclical *Laudato Si'*, May 2015) and a resurgence of interest in values and spiritually rich lifestyles – witness, for example, the rise in popularity of mindfulness practices and meditation. Many leaders and coaching writers overtly talk now of the spiritual dimension of their work (Senge *et al*, 2004; Dehnugara and Breeze, 2011; Long, 2012). Here is how one of the fathers of the transpersonal defines the spiritual:

> [the spiritual includes] not only the specific religious experience, but all the states of awareness, all the functions and activities which have as common denominator the possessing of values higher than the average, values such as the ethical, the aesthetic, the heroic, the humanitarian and the altruistic. (Assagioli, 1965)

It is this dimension that gives a uniquely human shape to our lives:

> That which gives … unique definition … to our humanity is our need to place our enterprises in a frame of wider meaning and purpose. The spiritual in human beings makes us ask why we are doing what we are doing and makes us seek some fundamentally better way of doing it. It makes us want our lives … to make a difference. (Zohar and Marshall, 2004)

Just as the introduction of the concept of emotional intelligence – EQ (Goleman, 1995) – changed forever our reliance on IQ as the key measure of intelligence, so current reference to spiritual intelligence (SQ), is demanding a further shift in understanding (Zohar and Marshall, 2004; Long, 2012). SQ requires us to access our sense of deeper purpose, a purpose aligned with our own potential and with wider, even global, needs – or to reinvent the triple bottom line, it demands we seek a win–win–win: for self, organization and planet. The pressures from the world of work fuelling the reintegration of the spiritual are threefold: increased global competition, highly fluid and insecure markets, and the demands for meaning and purpose at work from a rising Generation Y (born around the millennium they will make up 75 per cent of the global workforce by 2020). Those who seek the edge of high performance in business are being challenged to identify what really matters to them, where their passion lies, where they stand as regards ethical practice and how they can best serve the organization as a whole to serve its customers and society. This is the domain of the transpersonal work that is now being done in leadership training within the corporate sector.

Individuals express their spirituality in two principal ways: transcendent or immanent. 'Transcenders' are people who find the everyday world lacking and humdrum. They focus instead on big ideas and higher ideals and, if action-orientated, are often driven to change things. People who express their spirituality in an immanent way are more focused on 'right living', behaving ethically, with care and consideration, within everyday life. Most of us have both these orientations but a stronger tendency towards one or the other. Both expressions contain some element of service, of being more focused on the good of others than one's own gain.

Psychosynthesis is the most well-known and robust of the transpersonal psychologies in that it not only provides elegantly effective tools to raise awareness and promote development but embeds these in a complete and coherent ethical philosophy. This is important as coaching develops beyond its early roots in sport and behavioural sciences. To flourish and serve out there in the real world coaching must be more than a clever toolkit. It must be rooted in a positive world view that sustains and empowers both coach and coachee to engage with the complex problems we all, leaders and followers alike, face in the world today. As well as supporting an underpinning spiritual, ethical and systemic approach to coaching, psychosynthesis offers accessible maps and models that can be used creatively and flexibly in all coaching interventions.

When does transpersonal coaching work best?

Here is a sample list of the types of issues coaches are asked to address:

- solve a problem;
- perform a task better – well;
- learn a new skill;
- become a more effective manager;
- plan a career path;
- develop oneself personally and professionally;
- live a more balanced life;
- become more creative;
- address a crisis;
- find meaning and purpose in life;
- develop a career path of service.

The further down the list we go the more essential transpersonal coaching becomes. The last five issues can barely be addressed at all without recognition of the spiritual for they are largely spiritual issues; but what of the others?

Whereas trained coaches will follow the agenda and the direction that the coachee takes in a session, they also, consciously or unconsciously, via their own attitudes and beliefs, prescribe the frame of the coaching sessions. So let us for a moment consider three ways in which a coach might perceive the coachee and thus set the frame:

1 If the coachee has a history of bringing problems to the table, the coach might no longer see a person coming through the door but, with sinking heart, feel, 'Here comes trouble! Yet another problem.'

2 An alternative view – and probably a healthier one for coachee and coach – is to see the coachee as 'a person who *has* a problem'.

3 A transpersonal coach is likely to have a very different frame for most situations, however great or small. It would be something like this: 'Here is a person who is full of potential and has all the skills and qualities needed to tackle his problems', or: 'Here is an individual spirit who has challenges and obstacles to overcome on her journey through the university of life. This is another such learning opportunity.'

A coach adopting these transpersonal points of view will have far more compassion and positive regard for the coachee and for the coachee's problem. We suggest therefore that even if coaches are dealing with more mundane issues most of the time, they and their coachees would gain much if the coach were transpersonally-orientated.

The traditional or behavioural way to teach a new skill is to use demonstration, instruction and correction. The typical coaching approach is to facilitate the learner to discover 'how to do it' from the coachee's own experience through coaching enhanced awareness, and possibly adding a few hints and tips where discovery is not bearing fruit.

However, this too falls short. Gallwey (1974) identified this issue: 'you begin to play the Inner Game when you recognize that the opponent within your own head is more formidable than the one the other side of the net'. The object of the 'Inner Game' is to eliminate the internal obstacles to learning, performance and enjoyment. Once those obstacles, of which fear of failure is the most common, are alleviated, a person is able to learn or to play at his or her best. This leads to the next stage of coaching which is around the core question of 'what for?'. Transpersonal coaching is about developing a purpose-led approach to work; it helps the client understand what work means to them and what their unique contribution can be.

Tools and techniques

Psychosynthesis brings us many techniques, maps and models, all highly practical, and many of which have been subsequently adopted by NLP and other schools of coaching. We briefly outline the main ones here. However, a word of caution. Transpersonal coaching is not a matter of simply expanding the coach's toolkit with some clever new tricks. While deceptively simple in themselves they are also powerful in opening doors to deeper areas not reached by conventional cognitive methods. This may be daunting for the coach if he or she is not familiar or trained to go beyond the surface. We advise anyone guiding someone on a journey to have been on or be currently travelling their own journey of discovery.

The 'egg' model, devised by Assagioli (1974) – see Figure 9.1 – is a major contribution to psychological thinking in a number of ways. As all practitioners and writers on psychosynthesis stress, it is a map, not the territory: it is not the truth. Every individual discovers the territory for themselves: the individual's personal experience verifies the model, not the other way round.

FIGURE 9.1   The 'egg' model

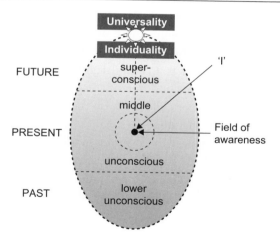

Significantly the diagram gives equal weight to the superconscious as to the lower unconscious. This means that focusing on our future and the development of our potential, on accessing more of our intuition and inspiration, and our higher feelings (eg altruism, care, service) is every bit as important as examining our past or feelings and events we may have repressed. While it is generally agreed that the realm of the lower unconscious belongs to those trained in counselling and psychotherapy, the superconscious is very much the domain of transpersonal coaching.

At the centre of our psyche is the 'I' or 'self'. This is linked to and reflects the higher Self. The Self (capital S) lives on the border of the egg, which itself has a dotted line around it to indicate the permeable nature of the psyche, with energy flowing both ways.

Around the 'I' is the field of awareness accessible to us, and beyond this are aspects of ourselves, others, our environment, of which we are more or less conscious. Most current coaching takes place in this realm, helping the coachee to become more aware of their current reality. As their awareness broadens to include an understanding of the deeper organizational dynamics, of the marketplace, of the social and global context in which the company operates, the coachee and coach will draw increasingly on the field of the superconscious.

Within the field of awareness will be what Ferrucci (1982) calls 'a disordered collection of clashing tendencies'. Often the first work of transpersonal coaching is to help the coachee meaningfully harmonize these 'clashing tendencies' or sub-personalities around the centre, the 'I', to become effective and resilient.

Sub-personalities

The concept that we are both unified and multiple – both one person and many within one skin – is not new: all philosophies, religions and psychologies present this paradox. It is a central feature of psychosynthesis, and enables us to work with clients in different creative ways. Sub-personalities include the inner critic or inner child, but also the many and varied parts of ourselves, each with its distinct mini-personality. They can form around our identification with stereotypical roles (father, worker, boss), with job titles (accountant, doctor), with personality characteristics (being clever, angry or always happy), with psychological formations (the winner, the victim), or with cultural, racial and social alliances. We all have a cast of characters within us (eg the victim, nice guy, perfectionist, joker, stern father, fair manager, the charmer, control freak, tower of strength) each with its own beliefs and behaviours. Each has a certain quality, tone and triggers. The best analogy is with instruments in an orchestra: the French horn is very different from the violin and again quite distinct from the flute. But together they make up a whole: an orchestra.

The trouble is that we have a tendency to identify with whichever sub-personality is dominant or triggered by the situation. We forget that there are other perspectives on current reality, or that we have other skills and qualities that we might bring to bear. So the orchestra often sounds like it's tuning up – a cacophony of 'clashing tendencies', opposing arguments repeating in our heads, or arbitrarily different notes as we bounce from one sub-personality to another.

The sub-personality concept is an excellent awareness-raising and inner conflict resolution tool. When a coachee reveals an issue of conflicting desires, the coach might ask some of these questions: 'What part of you wants to do this and what part wants something else? What else does that part want? What need is that "character" in you seeking to meet? How else could you meet that need? Let us imagine a negotiation between these two parts of you. What gift does this part bring and how does it block you?' Most often the consequent understanding is sufficient to dissolve the internal conflict in the short term. As awareness of this sub-personality and its needs increases, its power to disrupt and undermine will dissipate.

The technique works well in both individual and group coaching. People easily identify many sub-personalities and the situations in which each comes to the fore. Much coaching work could focus on sub-personalities, since as the coachee recognizes, accepts and harmonizes them – as with a troupe of actors or an orchestra – they begin to 'play music together' more effectively. We live our lives through our sub-personalities; however, they are not who we really are.

Dis-identification and the I

The transpersonal perspective asserts that we are all 'spiritual beings', that our core is pure spirit. We have a body, we have emotions, we have a mind and an intellect, but in essence we are a soul (or spirit, light, energy). This gives coaches a broader perspective of our clients and allows us to help them gain a measure of distance from themselves and their problems. As coachees become more familiar with and accepting of their orchestra of sub-personalities, they start to see them more clearly, to be less driven by them, and to feel less identified with them.

It may seem paradoxical but the process of dis-identifying gives us a stronger sense of self. Using a variety of techniques we can help the coachee to move closer to a sense of their essential 'I', to that sense of 'I am'. This is also described as one's core, centre or essence. Identifying with the 'I' is immensely freeing. It does not mean abandoning all the colour and interest of sub-personalities, but it does mean gaining a vantage point above the hurly burly and gaining some choice over one's actions. The 'I' is the conductor of the orchestra: it is the conductor who directs the various instruments and helps them create together a piece of music that is greater than the sum of the parts.

The 'I' is at the centre of the psyche, at the core of our being. Empty of content, it can be described as a place of pure consciousness and pure will. This is a familiar state to those who meditate. Qualities we associate with the 'I' are:

- consciousness (awareness);
- will (responsibility);
- self-managing, self-directing, choice;
- free from distortion, restriction;
- individuality, identity;
- non-judgemental;
- stillness, constancy, continuity.

The will

In psychosynthesis the will is accorded a central place in the psyche paired with its counterpoint energy, love (expressed as awareness, consideration, empathy, care for others, tolerance, etc). Like yin and yang together they form the 'I'. Assagioli (1974) contributed this new understanding of will to counteract the Victorian notion of will-power, associated with duty and 'pulling yourself up by your bootstraps' which was rejected by the anti-authoritarian youth culture of the 1960s. This era saw the first widespread social rebellions against the continued abuse of state power (for example, large demonstrations against the Vietnam War). Love was the rallying cry, and emphasis on our need to 'make love not war' was everywhere.

However, will is essential if we are going to act in the world. It is our source of power, providing motive force, a sense of direction and energy to make things happen. Will and love *together* underpin our ability to live our lives with purpose. At a pragmatic level, will is expressed through responsibility – the choice to take ownership for one's actions; then through the purposeful life and, at the highest level, through a sense of being part of a purposeful universe. The source of the core coaching concepts of aware-ness and responsibility (Whitmore J, 2009) is in the understanding that love and will are the two essential drives at the very heart of the human being (see also Kahane, 2010).

Two dimensions of development

Transpersonal coaching sees life as a journey. Figure 9.2 shows how, in our society, we largely develop along the lateral axis, maturing psychologically, gaining success in our careers and personal lives. However, many of us will at some point hit a crisis of meaning. This may be triggered by a dramatic event (a redundancy, a personal shock) or a creeping sense of meaninglessness, or by a sense of alienation from the values we once took for granted. This crisis was typically associated with mid-life, but we are now seeing it among younger people too. It manifests in a myriad different ways: as depression, a sense of losing one's grip, fits of anger, uncontrollable stress, workaholism, dependency on escapist drugs and activities. The crisis may be sudden or last for years. Helping coachees realize the nature of this crisis, that they are not weak, useless or going mad, and that this is a stage in their life journey is a keynote of transpersonal coaching: it involves helping the coachee find a sense of purpose (Scouller, 2005; Whitmore J, 2009; Einzig 2011). Their crisis represents an opportunity for coachees to make a step change in their life and work. We find that working with crises of this nature may precede the individual taking on significant leadership roles.

FIGURE 9.2   Developmental journey

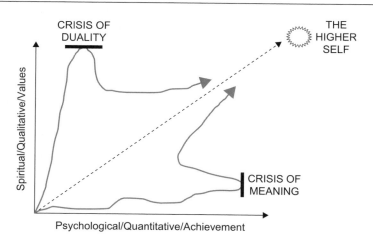

The vertical axis represents the spiritual development path. This may not look overtly 'spiritual'. You may recognize it in those who, for example, love the creative side of business but hate the compromises and sheer grind often needed to bring projects to fruition; in those who are full of integrity, whose values are admirable, but who are unable to actualize or pay the bills; or the 'space cadets' full of marvellous plans but who can't organize their everyday lives. Those who are 'higher sidelining', as we call it, may at some point hit the crisis of duality. Essentially this is where the gap between a person's idealized vision of how the world could be and the realities of damage, injustice and failure becomes so wide and so painful that a crisis ensues.

One application of this model is to present coachees with a sheet of paper with the two axes drawn on it. Give them some time to draw their own journey to date as they see it. This awareness-raising process will throw up questions such as, 'What triggered this change in direction of your life line?', 'How did this change affect x?', 'What direction do you wish to go in now, and what would you have to do to achieve that?' It will soon become clear to the coachee that steering towards the middle path, effectively gaining balance between manifesting love and will, brings many benefits.

Emerging purpose: pain, crisis and failure

Coaching tends to be viewed as an action-orientated way of addressing problems. However, the traditional coaching focus on problem solving is based on a deficit model of work as a succession of problems to be dealt with. It presupposes an ideal that we are always trying, unsuccessfully, to reach – the glass is always half-empty. Furthermore it is a very limited model of the human being as destined to just fix what has gone wrong. This can become ultimately dispiriting and energy draining.

As a popular organizational development model, Appreciative Inquiry has done much to raise understanding that what we give attention, or oxygen, to will grow. Put simply, if we focus on problems, then we will get more of them. If we look for where the positive energy is, the vitality and spirit, and explore and build on this, then we are more likely to promote positive growth, in the individual and in the company.

Transpersonal coaching takes this deeper and proposes that every problem, crisis or moment of failure harbours within it an emergent purpose: a clue to the next step on our journey. This is in no way to make light of the very real distress that people suffer, but on the contrary to experience and move through the situation with a sense of meaning and intention.

Our usual reactions when we hit a problem or crisis include the following: denial, anger, blaming, bargaining, self-pity, resistance, rebellion, paralysis or depression. The transpersonal coach helps her coachees through their crisis by guiding a different process. She asks the coachee to consider these questions:

- What does this mean for me, for us, for the organization?
- What is trying to emerge or unfold?
- What needs to transform here?
- What is the next step?
- What is the bigger picture?

All writers on the transpersonal, since the earliest times, talk about these moments of despair and crisis – at its most extreme, the 'dark night of the soul'. Leadership writer Warren Bennis sees what he terms 'crucible experiences' as the defining moments for stepping into leadership (Bennis and Thomas, 2002). It is the individual's ability to live through and be transformed by the crisis (from base metal to gold as in the alchemist's crucible) that differentiates the leader.

The key to coming through a time of crisis is how one chooses to perceive the situation: we cannot always change outer circumstances, but we can change our inner response. Acceptance is the point that needs to be reached before transformation can take place (Frankl, 1987; Kübler-Ross, 1969). This is not resignation but a true spiritual act of will, a choice to be in the present with no further striving to change circumstances: eliminating the 'useless acts of rebellion' and 'collaborating with the inevitable', as Assagioli put it. Paradoxically, this is when deep change can occur because we cease to be a victim. Energy is channelled, new insights are released and a sense of unity or wholeness is achieved. This imparts a new depth to the individual's character; perhaps a new gravitas, a stronger focus and sense of purpose resulting in a step-change rise in performance.

Guided imagery

Use of imagery is central to transpersonal coaching. More than a technique, transpersonal work holds that without imagination there is no empathy and no future: it is only our capacity to imagine the other and to imagine change that creates these. The Israeli novelist, Amos Oz, reflecting on the need for understanding in the world today, said 'imagining the other is a powerful antidote to fanaticism and hatred ... It is also, in my view, a major moral imperative' (*The Guardian*, 3 September 2005).

Working with imagery (whether visual, auditory or embodied) directly reflects the language of the unconscious: this is non-rational, weaves stories and pictures, pays little heed to the rules of the 'real' world, relies strongly on intuition, instinct and insight, and experiences time differently from clock time. Using imagery, whether through guided visualizations, drawing, producing a symbol for a goal or idea, accesses and cultivates the skills and qualities of the unconscious and superconscious, the myth-making, story-telling parts of ourselves, thereby developing EQ, SQ and general creativity (Whitmore D, 2004).

The decision to use guided imagery must be based on the coach's assessment of the coachee's inner experience and behaviour. A contraindication for using imagery work would be, for example, where the coachee appears ungrounded or talks in the abstract much of the time without giving specific examples, tends to 'higher sidelining', has an overactive imagination with little or no actualization or will to action. This coachee may have a shaky sense of identity and an underdeveloped 'I' (Whitmore J, 2004). He may need grounding in very practical, action-orientated coaching steps.

There are two principal ways we work with imagery: *evocative* and *directive*. Evocative is the drawing out from the coachees' own unconscious an image or symbol to represent and deepen their understanding of a situation and themselves. Working with closed eyes to direct attention inwards, coachees might be asked to evoke the situation or problem they have just been talking about, see it clearly again in their mind's eye and at a certain point to allow an image or symbol to emerge for the problem, the other person or for a resolution – whatever is most useful to move the coachee's awareness of the issue forwards.

In directive imagery work we draw on archetypal images to help cultivate a skill, quality or behaviour that the coachee most wants or needs to enhance at this point in their journey. Often this is done via a guided visualization.

Imagery always expands awareness; it creates new understanding and meaning. The coachee's new awareness will need balancing with a focus on responsibility: the coach will help the coachee integrate the new insights and ground them in action and in the coachee's life. This might look similar to the kind of coaching done in the will section of the GROW model.

Ten key questions to guide your way

1. What makes your heart sing? What are you passionate about outside work? What brings you joy?

We often use this type of question very early on in the coaching. It helps evoke the positive, enlivening energy of the client, which will feed the work ahead by sparking the superconscious. It sets the tone for the style of coaching, letting coachees know that the coach is interested in their potential and the life-enhancing aspects of their inner world, not just their problems. The choice of out-of-ordinary words such as 'passion', 'joy', 'heart', 'sing' is deliberate and helps the client move out of the limits of intellectual, workplace language.

2. What does this sub-personality want? What does he or she need? What benefits or 'gifts' do they bring?

This group of three questions, asked one by one, is always asked when working with sub-personalities. The first brings awareness of the most accessible drive of the sub-personality, the second asks the coachee to understand what the underlying need might be, and the third encourages an appreciation of qualities and skills this sub-personality gives the coachee. This last question is especially important as we often identify our most troublesome and least likeable sub-personalities. The urge is to get rid of them, but they will keep sabotaging our best intentions until we understand and value their gifts.

3. How could these two parts of you come to an accommodation with or even cooperate with one another?

Usually a difficult sub-personality is clashing with another, equally insistent character – hence the circular conversations we have in our heads. This question is asked when the work above has taken place, to encourage the coachee to harmonize and integrate the two within the overall personality. This, like all sub-personality work, is excellent for raising the coachee's awareness of, and skill in dealing with, conflict in his or her team and wider workplace.

4. What do you see when you step back and view the whole?

The coachee is encouraged to adopt the observer position, perhaps after sub-personality work or talking through a complex situation involving others in the workplace. This provides fresh insight, and is the first step in dis-identification and towards the 'I'. The coachee will start to experience the stillness, compassion, non-judgemental quality of the 'I' as he becomes skilled at 'un-hooking' himself from his warring sub-personalities or the passions of workplace conflict.

5. What direction do you wish to go in now, and how does it serve your journey?

As coachees begin to conceive of their life as a journey, they realize (through sub-personality and other coaching work) that they have ultimate control over steering their life course. Seeing each choice as serving a longer vision strengthens it and galvanizes intention. It stimulates will and creativity to look at different routes to achieve purpose.

6. What does this mean for me, for us, for the organization, for society?

With transpersonal work we look behind a problem for its meaning and wider implications. This question also fosters the coachee's ability to be aware of the interface and impacts across three key domains: the self, the immediate environment (team, department, function), and the wider environment (whole organization) and beyond. It also provokes a return to fundamental values.

7. What needs to change here and what is your contribution to this change?

These questions stimulate the coachee's will, their sense of responsibility, their sense of agency and their active creativity. This is key to shifting seemingly intractable situations and polarized, antagonistic or victim positions. It can evoke a sense of service in the coachee.

8. What is trying to emerge or unfold?

A quintessentially transpersonal question, this moves the coachee on from a solution-focused stance to understanding deeper patterns and meaning. The coachee is encouraged to see the current situation in the context of her life journey, or to the organization's growth. It brings hope and a sense of rebirth and possibility.

9. What is an image or symbol for x?

This question aims to bring insights from the unconscious to consciousness so they can enrich the coachee's understanding. Images have an essential force, they are universal and they have longevity. People can remember scenes, objects and faces from their earliest past quite vividly – and the emotions associated with that time, place or person come flooding back just as sharply; similarly with new images and symbols. These can provide the coachee with a kind of personal talisman that they can subsequently evoke at will when needed, and draw on the required feeling, energy, thoughts and physical sensations encapsulated by the symbol.

10. What is the bigger picture?

Finally, the transpersonal sees the individual as part of the whole, the micro reflecting the macro, the interconnectedness of everything. This question encourages expanded thinking at all levels. It asks the coachee to imagine beyond his or her issue or problem to what this might reflect of the team, of the organization and the wider marketplace, both national and global and beyond. It encourages the coachee to tap into his or her higher self and thereby into the collective unconscious.

Summary

From the egg diagram you will recognize that most regular coaching takes place in the middle unconscious realm, where the coach takes coachees deeper than their normal field of awareness into their partially unconscious mind, but generally using rational, cognitive methods.

A transpersonal perspective of the coachee and the issue might give better results even at this level of coaching. It is clear however that there is an expanded realm that the coachee can explore with the help of a transpersonal coach – the area known as the superconscious, where access to our higher qualities, values, creativity, aspirations, inspiration, peak experience and our sense of purpose can be found.

Transpersonal work favours meaning and direction. It works with what the Greeks called 'entelechy': the dynamic propulsion to be all that we can be. Coaching in this wider context is highly rewarding for both parties and may give the coach a deep sense of fulfilment through assisting another person on their journey.

References

Assagioli, R (1974) *The Act of Will: A guide to self-actualisation and self-realisation*, Turnstone Press, Wellingborough

Bennis, W and Thomas, R (2002) *Geeks and Geezers: How era, values and defining moments shape leaders*, Harvard Business School Press, Harvard

Dalai Lama, His Holiness and Cutler, H (1998) *The Art of Happiness: A handbook for living*, Hodder and Stoughton, London

Dehnugara, K and Breeze, C G (2011) *The Challenger Spirit*, LID Publishing Ltd, London

Einzig, H (2011) The Beast Within – coaching the dark and light, in *Coaching at Work*, vol 6, Issue 3

Ferrucci, P (1982) *What We May Be: The visions and techniques of psychosynthesis*, Turnstone Press, Wellingborough

Pope Francis (2015) encyclical letter, *Laudato Si'*, of the Holy Father Francis on Care for our Common Home, Vatican Press, Rome

Frankl, V (1987) *Man's Search for Meaning*, Hodder and Stoughton, London

Gallwey, T (1974) *The Inner Game of Tennis*, Random House, New York

Goleman, D (1995) *Emotional Intelligence*, Bloomsbury Press, London

Hardy, J (1987) *A Psychology with a Soul: Psychosynthesis in evolutionary context*, Routledge and Kegan Paul, London

Kahane, A (2010) *Power and Love: A theory and practice of social change*, Berrett-Koehler Publishers, Oakland

Kübler-Ross, E (1969) *On Death and Dying*, Scribner, New York

Long, K (2012) The 'S' Factor: Exploring the Spiritual Dimension to our Work as Coaches, *The International Journal of Mentoring and Coaching*, vol X, Issue 1, April 2012, EMCC

McBeath, B and Wynne, D (1985) Integrating Systems in Psychosynthesis: Applications to work with families, groups and organisations, in *Readings in Psychosynthesis: Theory, process and practice*, ed J Weiser and T Yeomans, Department of Applied Psychology, The Ontario Institute for Studies in Education, Toronto

Oz, A (2005) The Devil's Progress, *The Guardian newspaper*, 3 August 2005, Manchester and London

Scouller, J (2005) The challenge of coaching to evoke a sense of purpose, MSc Paper, Coaching and Development, Department of Business Studies, University of Portsmouth

Senge, P, Scharmer, C O, Jaworski, J and Flowers, B S (2004) *Presence: Human purpose and the field of the future*, SoL publishing, Cambridge, MA

Whitmore, D (2004) *Psychosynthesis Counselling in Action*, 3rd edn, Sage Publications, London

Whitmore, J (2009, 2010) *Coaching for Performance*, 4th edn, Nicholas Brealey Publishing, London

Zohar, D and Marshall, I (2004) *Spiritual Capital: Wealth we can live by*, Bloomsbury, London

Appreciative coaching: pathway to flourishing

10

ANN L CLANCY and JACQUELINE BINKERT

Introduction

The Appreciative Coaching® approach is based on the Appreciative Inquiry (AI) model of change, which is a highly successful organizational change methodology recognized around the world. It is a generative approach to change focusing on strengths and on growing the aspirations and visions of people in organizations. The model of Appreciative Coaching® also draws on other positive approaches to change including Positive Organizational Scholarship, Positive Psychology and Solution-Focused Brief Therapy. All of these methodologies share a core belief that organizations and individuals are capable of generating life paths to flourishing. We will explore how Appreciative Coaching incorporates the best of these positive approaches to change – from a sound theoretical foundation to offering the reader appreciative principles and tools.

Shifting to the positive

In seeking to make the most of our own lives and as Appreciative coaches striving to help others get the most out of theirs, we have, over time, gradually broadened our view of what is possible in life. Personally and professionally, we've made our own journeys from a limited perspective of life (satisfied with surviving and recovering from hardships and thwarted dreams) to a belief that we as humans intrinsically have the capacity to be not only resilient in life but also to thrive and flourish. Keyes (2003) describes flourishing as being filled with positive emotion and to be functioning well both psychologically and socially. We are happy to report that we now live in this state for the most part, as do many of our clients. Perhaps this capacity to flourish can be best understood in light of some very illuminating discoveries made in neuroscience around the brain's negativity bias for survival and in the overall movement across disciplines towards a more balanced perspective of human change and potential (Rozin and Royzman, 2001; Baumeister *et al*, 2001). A shift has occurred in the field of human sciences from focusing primarily on human deficits and limitations to studying the positive in human evolution. From neuroscience, for example, we now know that our conscious mind can be directed to look for and take in positive experiences to not only address the brain's negative memory bias but also actually change the physiology of the brain (Hanson, 2009; Amen, 1998).

The field of Positive Psychology has been instrumental in bringing to light a view of human potential that is integral to the theory and practice of Appreciative Coaching. Seligman, founder of Positive Psychology, explained in his foreword written for Keyes and Haidt's (2003) textbook on *Flourishing* that three beliefs underlie the new discipline. First, one of the best ways to help people in need is to focus on positive aspects of life. Second, experiences that lead to positive emotion cause negative emotion to dissipate rapidly. Third, a person's strengths and virtues act as buffers against the impact of misfortune or psychological disorders and are keys to building a person's resilience. It appears that at the core of a person's sense of well-being is the presence of positive feelings.

In 2000, Martin Seligman and Mihaly Csikszentmihalyi wrote a seminal article on Positive Psychology stating, 'The exclusive focus on pathology that has dominated so much of our discipline results in a model of the human being lacking the positive features that make life worth living.' They challenged their field to look beyond how people survive and endure adversity to understand and build the positive qualities that allow people to flourish. Appreciative Coaching is a further step in the movement that considers joy, hope, wisdom, spirituality, perseverance and the like to be unique characteristics of human beings that allow us not only to deal with negative circumstances but to thrive.

Moving towards 'what's right'

The core belief in the power of positive feelings was implicit in the original article describing Appreciative Inquiry by David Cooperrider and Suresh Srivastva in 1987. It presaged a radical new approach to organizational change. In their seminal article, Cooperrider and Srivastva offered AI as a conceptual reconfiguration of action-research, a tool for problem solving which, they asserted, largely failed to transform organizations in fundamental ways. Little did they anticipate that they had started a groundbreaking movement, shifting attention away from what is wrong and what needs to be fixed to what is right and positive and what can be created.

At the time of the article, the belief in the power of problem solving was considered the primary approach for change in organizations. This was due in part to the prevailing view of organizations-as-machines; that is, organizations were seen as problems to be fixed by applying rational change processes. Inherent in the problem-solving approach (still a predominant practice) is the logic-based conviction that with the right information all problems can be fixed. This, coupled with the tendency to categorize every issue, challenge or opportunity as a problem, has resulted in problem solving as a default mode (Lewis, Passmore and Cantore, 2008). This methodology works well for 'tame' problems that can be clearly formulated or written down so any knowledgeable person can apply a logic-based process. The difficulty arises in that issues in the human realm are rarely tame; they are, instead, as Rittel (1972) describes, 'wicked problems' which have the following characteristics:

- A wicked problem has no definitive formulation.
- How a wicked problem is formulated indicates the solution, so that every reformulation suggests a different solution.
- There is no stopping rule; that is, you can always do better in describing a wicked problem.
- A solution to a wicked problem cannot be tested to be proven right or wrong.
- Every wicked problem is essentially unique.

With the traditional problem-solving approach, action is considered to be linearly sequenced; that is, one action must precede another. This belief that action only occurs in a linear sequence is a legacy of the Newtonian world view which defines us as living in an objective, predictable and controllable universe – the universe-as-machine. In such a universe, time proceeds along a fixed line from past through present to future. Cause always precedes effect and the two are forever separated in time. In organizations, therefore, the belief has been first to investigate an issue before taking action and then develop a plan to fix the problem. Implicit in this understanding is a second belief, identified by Lewis *et al*, that this first phase of investigation does not really change anything. This approach does not recognize that organizations are actually 'living human systems' that when prodded (asked questions) will react. In other words, just the act of inquiring about or investigating an issue in the organization will produce some change (Lewis *et al*, 2008).

While the Newtonian static view of the world has held sway over our concepts of human change, a 'new science' paradigm has emerged that accounts for the dynamic nature of the universe. It explains the complexity, chaos, subjectivity and interconnectedness of human life as well as the use of language to create social reality. In this new paradigm of change it is understood that inquiring into an aspect of organizational life is not con-sequence-free; rather, the more inquiry into a particular area, the more information will be generated and the more that area will grow. According to Lewis *et al*, this leads to two important points about change in human beings. 'First, there is recognition that to inquire is not a precursor to doing something – it is doing something. And second, that since we are likely to produce more of what we ask about, we should take care selecting that into which we choose to inquire, as it will change our lives.'

Given the nature of wicked problems and a new understanding about human change, it is not surprising that Cooperrider and Srivastva found problem solving to be inadequate in dealing with organizational problems and searched for an alternative method for change:

> Used in place of the traditional problem-solving approach – finding what is wrong and forging solutions to fix the problems – Appreciative Inquiry seeks what is 'right' in an organization and uses these as a force for change (Passmore and Hain, 2005). It is a habit of mind, heart, and imagination that searches for the success, the life-giving force, the incidence of joy. It moves toward what the organization is doing right and provides a frame for creating an imagined future that builds on and expands the joyful and life-giving realities as the metaphor and organizing principle of the organization.
>
> (Watkins and Cooperrider, 2000)

It is not that AI ignores problems or difficulties in life; rather it shifts atten-tion to what is the desired future. For that future to be created, problems are resolved or become inconsequential.

Developing the Appreciative Coaching model

We were intrigued by the idea of applying the highly successful organizational model and principles of AI to the one-on-one methodology of coaching. We launched a two-year research project to explore its application, which culminated in the development of our model (see Figure 10.1). This model is based on the four stages of AI as seen in Figure 10.1: Discovery (reflecting on and discovering one's strengths and abilities), Dream (articulating potential and one's future), Design (directing attention and action to create that future), and Destiny (seeing and living the dream in the present). Not evident in the model is the interplay of five clearly defined principles from AI that are part of the philosophy of Appreciative Coaching and which come into play through all four stages: the Constructionist, Positive, Simultaneity, Poetic and Anticipatory Principles.

FIGURE 10.1   The Appreciative Coaching® model

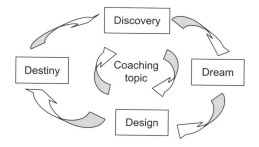

Our model is also based on the discipline of Positive Organizational Scholarship (Cameron *et al*, 2003) developed at the University of Michigan Ross Business School which, like AI, investigates the positive, asking us to imagine organizations that are characterized by trustworthiness, resilience, wisdom, humility and high levels of positive energy. As already mentioned, Positive Psychology, with its shift to studying flourishing or optimal functioning of individuals, has provided Appreciative Coaching with direction in how to support our clients in their growth, both when they are in a state of positive expectations and when they are not. Positive Psychology helps us understand as coaches what happiness is and how we can guide our clients to use their strengths to achieve their deepest desires.

Finally, Solution-Focused Brief Therapy (SFBT), which emerged from family psychotherapy (Berg and Miller, 1992), also underlies our methodology. Like the disciplines mentioned above, this model offers a non-problem-solving approach to individual change. A core premise of SFBT is that the future is created and negotiated. Therefore, individuals are not considered slaves of past experiences, not even of traumatic events, but can learn to negotiate and implement many useful steps leading to a more satisfying life. In addition, SFBT rests on the belief that a small change can lead to big differences in the future. Change in one part of the system can effect change in the whole system. All these positive methods underlie and contribute significantly to the appreciative tools, techniques and processes of our coaching approach (Orem, Binkert and Clancy, 2007).

Adopting an appreciative stance

To become a practitioner of Appreciative Coaching is to accept a core belief about our clients and how they change: individuals are mysteries to be appreciated. We do not see our clients as problems to be solved or as deficient in some way. Our job is not to fix them. Our job is to partner with them in a positive, generative approach in which they are agents of their own change. At times, our clients will have problems to resolve, but the clients themselves are not problems. This is a profound distinction for us that we have grown to respect as a result of our appreciative research and experiences. We discovered early in our research process that beliefs in the deficiencies of humans (especially when it comes to our own frailties) are deep-seated.

Acknowledging the core belief that individuals are mysteries to be appreciated is the first step in ensuring the effective application of Appreciative Coaching. It requires a shift in perception on the part of the coach away from looking at the world and oneself through the dull and incomplete lens of problems and deficits to seeing the fullness of life through appreciative and positive eyes. Yes, there are problems in life but there are also infinite possibilities for hope, joy and excitement in our present and future. Our lives are made up of endless solutions, not problems. To truly support others in generative change, we believe coaches need to adopt what we call an 'appreciative stance'.

There are a number of key ways that Appreciative Coaching has been applied in the field of coaching:

- embracing it as the primary coaching model and approach in a coaching practice;
- applying selectively such elements as appreciative language, questions, and tools to enhance other coaching methods;

- training managers and supervisors in appreciative skills;

- presenting the underlying theory, principles and stages of Appreciative Coaching in an educational or training context.

We have been coaching executives, business owners, professionals and authors using this approach. We have also been teaching Appreciative Coaching in online courses, workshops and seminars in countries around the world.

Weaving together the principles and tools

Powerful shifts of perception and energy have come about for our clients through the steady application of the five appreciative principles. They form the foundation of a world view that with practice helps make us resilient and inspires us to be our best selves. To understand the role of the five principles, imagine the craft involved in weaving beautiful handmade rugs. The foundation of each hand-woven rug is made up of threads that run the length (warp) of the loom. They form the base on which the horizontal threads (wefts) are then interwoven. For the weaver to move the weft threads across the loom, the warp threads must be strong and resilient enough to hold the weft in place. The five principles are like the warp threads on the loom: they are philosophically resilient enough to form the base on which the appreciative stages unfold, and they inspire the processes and tools that guide us to maintain the integrity of the appreciative approach. They also help identify the distinctions between Appreciative Coaching and other coaching methodologies.

Based on these principles, we identify five tools we consistently use with our clients to help them take that next step towards building flourishing lives. These tools are the power of vision (Anticipatory Principle), appreciative stance (Constructionist Principle), art of the question (Simultaneity Principle), pivoting (Poetic Principle) and genuine affirmation (Positive Principle). We have included Ian's[1] story below to exemplify how the Appreciative Coaching principles and techniques can lead to significant shifts of perception and energy for clients.

The Anticipatory Principle relates to our innate human capacity for anticipating the future. This ability to anticipate or imagine our future is one of the most important resources we have for individual change. Our images of the future not only guide our current behaviour in the direction of that future, they also create a tension within us that compels us to act towards that future. It is no surprise that research demonstrates a relationship between positive imagery and positive action. Individuals with strong positive beliefs about themselves will take on more serious challenges, relinquish difficult tasks less easily, and see themselves as capable and successful, even when they experience failure. By using the power of vision, we can help clients identify a positive future by soliciting and listening for phrases that paint images of, and express longings for, their desires. A common misperception is that the Appreciative approach means ignoring difficulties. Rather, we acknowledge problems while at the same time understanding the powerful creative force the positive images and expectations of our clients have in influencing what is to come for them. We encourage them to be proactive about their future.

> When his coach was introduced to Ian, he was the head of a hospital. He was young, enthusiastic and a high-potential leader in the medical system. In the first meeting with his mentor and coach, Ian expressed his desire to apply for a Regional President position in the system where an external search was under way. While his mentor was his advocate and a strong supporter, he was not sure the timing was right for Ian to take on the larger responsibility. Ian, however, came to coaching with a clear vision of his future, one where he saw himself as leader of a large complex system. His coach sensed the creative tension within him between his present situation and his strong longing for his desired future. His coach supported Ian in building on that powerful creative force to take action towards that vision. By being courageous in first expressing that vision for himself, Ian was then able, with the support of his coach, to proactively express it to others.

The Constructionist Principle, as the name implies, expresses the view that how we see the world constructs or creates our world. That is, what we pay attention to and are curious about forms the foundation for how we take action in creating our future. This means that the stance from which we see the world will impact how we will react and interact with it. Because a person's self-awareness and destiny are interwoven, choosing to take an appreciative stance will influence how we view ourselves, and that, in turn, will influence the actions we decide to take and the circumstances we bring about. By taking an appreciative stance, it is possible to make desired changes through conscious choices. An important part of Appreciative Coaching is the examination of who the client is now and how he or she talks about him- or herself in the past, present and future. Choosing to take an appreciative stance through this process of self-examination is a liberating act.

As is typical with many executive coaching engagements, the coaching process with Ian began with 360° interviews and, with the support of his coach, Ian decided that he wanted to be assessed in comparison to senior executives. While risky, this positive stance encouraged him to hear high-level feedback about actions and behaviours he would need to grow into. He was coached on how to appreciate his current strengths and successes and on how he could apply them in his future arena. He also discovered some talents and capabilities that showed him ways in which he was already living part of his vision. Just by taking an appreciative stance, Ian created opportunities for himself to move forward. By putting energy and vision into where he wanted to be in the future, he began to grow his future in the present.

The Simultaneity Principle underscores the power of the present in effecting change. Inquiry and change are not really separate moments in time (as implied in traditional problem solving) but happen simultaneously. As we change the present through our questions and dialogue, so do the meanings of the past and future change, and as the past and future change, so do the meanings of the present – simultaneously. The questions we ask 'laser' attention in a certain direction, intended or not, and sow the seeds of change. What we discover through our questions becomes the linguistic material for the stories we use to conceive, talk about and construct our future. As questions literally create the path of inquiry and change, developing the art of asking questions is a key tool for Appreciative coaches. These are not just any questions, but questions that are carefully crafted to create a joyfully focused state of mind as our clients consider and answer them.

Ian and his coach were not only careful in selecting questions that would give him the information he sought – they were also strategic in the persons they invited into the interview process. The system CEO, COO and a board member were among the respondents. The coach's questioning of these members sent vibrations throughout the system. Asking these individuals about Ian's capabilities, his successes and his abilities as compared to those of a senior executive caused them to visualize Ian as a real candidate. Their assessment of him shifted and he was invited to apply for the Regional President position.

The Poetic Principle affirms that we are continually writing and rewriting the stories of our lives. Through the choices we make, we find that the experiences of our past, present and future are endless sources of learning and interpretation, just like reading a good poem. When our life journey does not take a straight path and new situations arise to challenge us, we can apply this principle to help us shift our perspective and find new possibilities. Pivoting as a tool is the conscious act of turning attention from what we do not want or what is wrong to what we do want or what is good. It is like a basketball player making a quick turn or pivot on the gymnasium floor to move past an obstacle towards a more favourable direction. Pivoting can help us turn our attention from what we do not like in a situation or what makes us uncomfortable to discovering what is already good there or what we want in place of the discomfort. Implicit in the negative statements is a desire for something better. When we find ourselves or others talking about the negative aspects of a situation, we can ask, 'What you don't want is x, so what do you want instead?' or the question can take the form, 'What you don't like is x, so what is good in the situation?'

> When Ian first viewed the results of his 360° interviews, he did what many of us do – he focused on the perceived gaps and deficiencies. He focused on 'lack of' rather than on what he might do 'more of'. With the help of his coach, he began to see the areas where he was already demonstrating his strategic abilities and other executive talents that the feedback was encouraging him to expand and build on. The feedback was filled with what he was doing right and on areas he would need to grow into. Ian realized, with a shift of focus (a pivot), that the 360° respondents were seeing his strengths and providing him with encouraging feedback for growth into an expanded role. Immediately, he felt more grounded. He acknowledged that he did not need to change himself so much as demonstrate more of who he already was.

The Positive Principle is an expression of all the concrete ways we can focus on the power of the positive. Research has shown that momentum for change requires large amounts of positive affect and social bonding in order to succeed. Positive emotions are contagious; positive inquiry moves us towards what we most desire. When we are in a positive mode, we act more effectively. To gain and maintain this positive mode, people need lots of positive feeling and positive social bonding to make lasting changes in their lives. A person's positive core expands as it is affirmed and appreciated by others. This positive emotion not only affects how we are today but also influences our ability to change and move towards a new future. The principal tool related to the Positive Principle is genuine affirmation from people who encourage us to use our best abilities, stay focused and keep heart. They represent the Positive Principle in action.

> Throughout the process, Ian's coach consistently reminded him to consider how his successes, abilities and desires made him a strong candidate for an executive position. He was encouraged to take a balanced view of himself and to stretch into his dream. Ian not only applied for the Regional President position; he also went through the interview process and actually secured the position. While this achievement is all Ian's, he insists that his coach's genuine affirmation and positive support of his capabilities increased his confidence and belief that he indeed possessed the talent to carry him into the new role.

Conclusion

Ian's story is about an individual who went from thriving in his career to flourishing. When coaching began, he was successful in his career as a hospital administrator and he was grateful to his mentor for supporting him in becoming an outstanding leader in that role. With the help of his mentor, he knew the areas where he needed development and was looking forward to working with his coach. But his coach soon discovered that Ian had a grander dream – a dream of becoming the CEO of a large system. Following the Appreciative Coaching model, his coach shifted the focus of coaching from the areas that needed to be developed to a clearer picture of his dream and how he could begin creating that dream in the present. His development would still need to occur, but in the more exciting context of his dream.

In a short amount of time, Ian went from being seen as a valued leader of the hospital to being seen as an executive leader in the system. In fact, Ian expressed surprise at how quickly this change came about and how at times it seemed almost magical. While he had always held a clear vision for his future, he had not seen himself stepping into the role in the circumstances presented to him. But with the support of his coach, he began paying more attention to his strengths and abilities and thereby steadily increasing the possibilities and momentum for change. His coach reminded him many times that it was his shifts in perception about himself and his situation that allowed him to see opportunities and take new, bold action. While it may have seemed almost magical at times, the creation of his desired future in a short time span was all his own doing. He chose to create his pathway to flourishing.

Clients like Ian are living examples that flourishing in work and life is indeed possible. Our clients are truly mysteries to be appreciated and viewing them from a problem-solving perspective cannot begin to tap into the generative power for change that they possess. What is exciting to realize is that we as coaches now have the tools and knowledge to lead ourselves and others along the appreciative path to flourishing.

Note

1 We have changed the name of this client for confidentiality purposes.

References

Baumeister, R F, Bratslavsky, E, Finkenauer, C and Vohs, K D (2001) Bad is stronger than good, *Review of General Psychology*, **5** (4), pp 323–70

Berg, I K and Miller, S D (1992) *Working with the Problem Drinker: A solution-focused approach*, W W Norton, New York

Cameron, K S, Dutton, J E and Quinn, R E (2003) *Positive Organizational Scholarship: Foundations of a new discipline*, Berrett-Koehler, San Francisco

Cooperrider, D L and Srivastva, S (1987) Appreciative inquiry in organizational life, in *Research in Organization Change and Development*, vol 1, ed W Passmore and R W Woodman, pp 129–69, JAI Press, Greenwich, CT

Keyes, C (2003) The Mental Health Continuum: from languishing to flourishing in life, *Journal of Health and Social Research*, **43** (2), pp 207–22

Lewis, S, Passmore, J and Cantore, S (2008) *Appreciative Inquiry for Change Management: Using AI to facilitate organizational development*, Kogan Page, Philadelphia

Orem, S L, Binkert, J and Clancy, A L (2007) *Appreciative Coaching: A positive process for change*, Jossey-Bass, San Francisco

Passmore, J and Hain, D (2005) Appreciative inquiry: positive psychology for organizational change, *Selection and Development Review*, **21** (5), pp 13–17

Rittel, H (1972) On the planning crisis: systems analysis of the 'first and second generations', *Bedriftsokonomen*, NR8, pp 390–96

Rozin P and Royzman, E (2001) Negativity bias, negativity dominance and contagion, *Personality and Social Psychology Review*, 5 (4), pp 296–320

Seligman, M E P (2003) Forward: The past and future of positive psychology in *Flourishing Positive Psychology and the life well lived*, ed C Keyes and J Haidt, pp xi–xx, American Psychological Association, Washington DC

Seligman, M E P and Csikszentmihalyi, M (2000) Positive psychology, *American Psychologist*, 55 (1), pp 5–14

Watkins, J M and Cooperrider, D (2000) Appreciative inquiry: a transformative paradigm, *OD Practitioner*, 32 (1), pp 6–12

Integrative coaching

11

JONATHAN PASSMORE

The integrative coaching model explained

Previous chapters in this book have offered frameworks based on single models. These models are often derived from psychological schools of thinking such as behaviourism (GROW) and cognitive psychology (cognitive behavioural coaching) or from theories of human behaviour and behavioural change (NLP and solution-focused). The integrative model seeks to depart from this approach. It offers a model that has been designed exclusively for executive coaching.

The integrative model consists of six streams that flow together to form an integrated model for use by the coach. The first two streams are concerned with the formation and maintenance of the relationship between the coach and coachee. The next three streams are the focus of the work between the coach and coachee. They are concerned with the coachee's behaviour, his or her conscious thought and unconscious thoughts. While working in each of these three streams, the coach maintains attention on the relationship and works to sustain the relationship without which progress cannot be made. The final stream is systemic. An overview of the model is provided in Figure 11.1.

Streams 1 and 2: The coaching partnership

Before any coaching to enhance performance or develop personal insights can begin, the coach needs to build a working relationship with the coachee. The coach-coachee relationship is the foundation stone of effective coaching. Without a firm foundation, progress cannot be achieved, as the coach is less likely to be open, trusting or willing to take the cognitive risks

FIGURE 11.1 Integrative coaching model

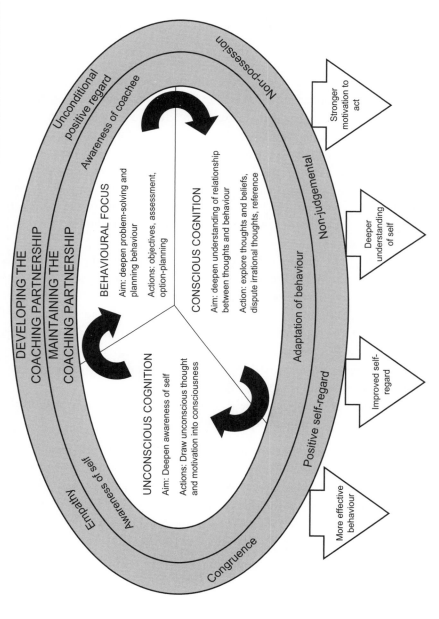

DEVELOPING THE COACHING PARTNERSHIP

MAINTAINING THE COACHING PARTNERSHIP

Unconditional positive regard

Awareness of coachee

Non-possession

BEHAVIOURAL FOCUS

Aim: deepen problem-solving and planning behaviour

Actions: objectives, assessment, option-planning

CONSCIOUS COGNITION

Aim: deepen understanding of relationship between thoughts and behaviour

Action: explore thoughts and beliefs, dispute irrational thoughts, reference

UNCONSCIOUS COGNITION

Aim: Deepen awareness of self

Actions: Draw unconscious thought and motivation into consciousness

Empathy

Awareness of self

Congruence

Positive self-regard

Adaptation of behaviour

Non-judgemental

More effective behaviour

Improved self-regard

Deeper understanding of self

Stronger motivation to act

Improved performance at work

© Passmore 2005

which help coaching to be the effective intervention which is it (see Grant *et al*, 2010, and Passmore and Theeboom, 2016, for a review of coaching research).

It is this work in building the relationship that I have called Stream 1 (developing the relationship). The potentially close and affirming relationship of coaching demands mutual respect and trust. To create these, the coach needs to invest in the relationship. However, once established this work on the relationship cannot stop, although less effort may be needed. It is at this point the coach moves into Stream 2 (maintaining the relationship).

What are the key ingredients to create an effective working relationship? This question has in part already been answered by writers within the counselling tradition, such as Carl Rogers (1961). Rogers suggested that a series of elements need to be in place for a successful 'therapeutic alliance' to be formed. These relationship elements are of importance to any work with individuals in the consulting world. However, the one-to-one nature of coaching demands a stronger investment in the relationship by the coach than training or consulting.

During the first, and possibly the second, coaching session the coachee is evaluating the coach: Do I trust him or her? Do I like him or her? Do I value what he or she is offering me? If the coachee reaches a conclusion that he or she does trust, like and value the coach, the real work can start. However, if coachees reach the conclusion that they do not trust or value the coach, it is unlikely they will reveal much during coaching, even though coaching may continue, at least over an initially agreed set of sessions. If they don't like the coach, the relationship is most likely to come to an end.

Rogers' six conditions provide an excellent starting point to help in the formation of a coaching partnership:

1 The first of these six elements Rogers called 'positive self-regard'. This is the coach's belief that he or she is able to work constructively in an adult relationship with another person. This may be typified by the 'I'm OK' part of the transactional analysis (TA) model (I'm OK, you're OK) – a belief that he or she, the coach, is a worthwhile and valuable person.

2 The second feature is 'unconditional positive regard' of the coachee by the coach. It is an acceptance of him or her as a whole person. This can be regarded as the 'you're OK' part of transactional analysis. It is a belief that the coachee is a good person, even if the coach may disagree with or dislike aspects of the coachee's behaviour or values.

3 The third element is 'empathy'. This is the ability of the coach to show understanding of the coachee's situation; 'to see their world, as if it was our own'.

4 The fourth element is the establishment and maintenance of a 'non-judgemental mind'. This means the coach is slow to judge. If judgements are made, these are restricted to behaviours outside of society's norms; an extreme example is murder, but in a work context it may be financial fraud or deception for personal gain. However, the person is never judged and categorized as the behaviour which they may have displayed at a specific time or in a specific situation. That is, the person remains Jane or Jim, rather than becoming a murderer or fraudster. In a work-based situation the coach may challenge the behaviour, helping the coach to understand the potential consequences for themself and others, while continuing to value the person as a human being.

5 The fifth element is congruence. This is the idea that the coach should express what he or she feels. The coach, if angry, should appropriately express this anger with the coachee, in a way that is helpful to the coachee, rather than pretend he or she is always happy. The key aspect in this is to reveal material for the benefit of the coachee, rather than to satisfy the needs or desire of the coach, and to remain non-judgemental and empathetic.

6 The final element that supports the development of a coaching partnership is non-possessive warmth. This is the idea that the coach views the coachee as a capable person, who knows the solution to his or her own problem. The role of the coach is to act as a guide, helping the coachee along a path until he or she discovers this solution for themself. This ability to maintain a non-possessive relationship means the coach can be free from responsibility for the coachee's actions. The coach is neither a 'super-hero' if the coachee succeeds, nor a 'villain' if the coachee fails.

The result of these elements is the development of an appropriate, warm, trusting and open relationship. A relationship in which the coachee is able to share the full truth of his or her perception and feels accepted rather than judged. It is a relationship where coachees accept responsibility for their success. It is also a relationship in which the coach is able to gradually increase the level of personal challenge without devaluing the affirming nature of the relationship.

Once a relationship has been formed, the role of the coach is to maintain this relationship. The maintenance of the relationship is the second stream, and flows on directly from the work of building the relationship.

To maintain the relationship an effective coach needs to pay attention to three further aspects: his or her own emotions and behaviours, the emotions and behaviours of the coachee, and adapting his or her own behavioural responses appropriately to remain professionally detached while offering personal intimacy. These components make up the building blocks of emotional intelligence (Caruso and Salovey, 2004; Stein and Book, 2000).

In addition to emotional intelligence, the highly effective coach also needs to consider and manage transference and counter-transference issues. These aspects are of particular importance in the executive boardroom where power and role modelling are key features. However, these aspects can be relevant to the close working relationship between any coach and coachee.

These two aspects, building and maintaining the relationship, form a ring around the three remaining streams. Without this coaching partnership the coach is unable to begin to work in the three streams that will facilitate change and enable the development of fresh insights.

Stream 3: Behavioural focus

The third and most popular stream in which the coach works is that of behavioural coaching. Whatever the coach's theoretical orientation, a focus on external behaviour and how this is developed is a central feature of almost all coaching relationships.

The popularity of behaviourism is rooted in the 1920s, with the work of Pavlov (1927). Pavlov uncovered the concept of conditioned reflex: a response to a situation that is an adaptation to environmental conditions. While human motivation is more complex and broader than that of other species, the use of appropriate rewards or punishments is still a common feature within the workplace.

This view informed much of subsequent management writing during the pre- and post-war period, with a belief that, with an appropriate stimulus, behavioural change could be brought about. Much of management writing has not acknowledged its behavioural basis, but in management today, performance-related pay, performance management, goal setting and the use of competency frameworks all have links back to behavioural thinking.

In the 1970s, the work of Bandura (1969) took thinking into a new arena by adding social learning to the mix of stimulus–response models. Bandura argued that learning can take place not only in person, but also by observing others' successes and failures. The use of role models in organizations, as well as mentoring schemes, provides further support for the extent of behaviourist thinking.

Perhaps the most interesting concept identified by Bandura was self-efficacy: a person's belief in their own abilities. The concept is based on a self-perception: how well the individual believes they perform a task. Bandura (1977) argued that people with high self-efficacy perform better, as they are able to persevere longer without corresponding increases in stress. Subsequent research (Gist and Mitchell, 1992; Locke and Latham, 1990) has shown a strong relationship between high self-efficacy and high work performance. Also key to performance is the use of goals as a focus for measuring behavioural output and for rewarding success.

The development of these behavioural concepts has contributed considerably to our thinking and practice in management, human learning and, more recently, executive coaching. The most popular example is the ubiquitous GROW model. The model initially developed by John Whitmore and Graham Alexander (Alexander and Renshaw, 2005) has been popularized by many coaching writers (Whitmore, 2009), and is used in many of the blue-chip institutions as their own in-house coaching model.

GROW is a four-step coaching model, and has traditionally been viewed as a non-psychological model, suitable for coaches without psychological training. The coach adopts a Socratic learning style, using open questions to help the coachee move through the four steps. It aims to help coachees achieve enhanced performance or a stated goal.

The first of the steps is the identification of a goal. The second is a review of the current reality, the third a consideration of options, and the fourth a conclusion and the agreement on a way forward. There is considerable debate about the nature of goals, and this is covered in more detail elsewhere (Passmore, 2003).

While rejected by some coaching psychologists, GROW is a simple and useful tool that can easily be taught to new coachees to structure their coaching conversations. More sophisticated behavioural models have been developed that complement the essence of GROW (Passmore, 2005; Skiffington and Zeus, 2003). These add elements such as explicit statements about contracting, the ground rules of the coach–coachee relationship and the more legal contractor aspects of times and fees, or have been developed for the coaching manager.

The behavioural approach is of greatest value at the start of a relationship. However, adopting a single methodology limits the coach's ability to facilitate change involving emotions or faulty cognition. Around half of coaching interventions may stay in this stream, once a 'coaching partnership' has been established. As experience grows, either through participation in training events or through intuitive awareness, the more experienced coach broadens his or her approach to begin working with both emotions and cognitions.

Stream 4: Conscious cognition

The effective coach, having established the relationship and explored behaviours, is able to explore the cognitive patterns that sit behind the visible behaviours. In this stream the coach will typically draw upon cognitive behavioural techniques, initially developed by Beck (1991) and Ellis (1998) but refined by coaches (Neenan and Dryden, 2001; Peltier, 2001) to make them more suitable for the work of the coach than the counsellor.

Cognitive-based counselling interventions have grown significantly in popularity in the UK, and are now the most popular approach within government-funded counselling services. While this popularity has yet to extend to coaching, the growth in coaching training suggests that cognitive behavioural approaches will become the most popular approach used by experienced coaches.

In the integrative model, coaches would typically begin to explore thought patterns when they judged that the coachee was displaying or holding irrational thoughts that might inhibit successful performance, and they have already explored behaviourally-based solutions. Such irrational thoughts might be harsh judgements about themselves as coachee or judgements of their current or future abilities. The key feature is that the judgement is irrational, that is, it is not substantiated by facts. One danger is that irrational is confused with 'negative'. So the coach seeks to help the coachee challenge all negative views or perspectives. This is not CBC. Such an approach, if always looking on the sunny side, is naïve and lacks any evidence of being an effective intervention.

Working in this stream shares many of the principles that are applied to the other four streams: a dynamic process where both the coach and the coachee are constantly changing, a collaborative process between the coach and coachee, a focus on solutions and particularly on an agreed goal, an emphasis on the present, and a desire to use the process to give the coachee the ability to act independently in the future. Each of these principles is important to maintaining the working relationship and using coaching in a way that builds the coachee's ability to become a self-sustaining learner rather than increasing his or her dependence on the coach.

The central concept within this stream is encouraging coachees to identify the irrational beliefs and then helping them to challenge these. This two-stage process is supported through the diverse range of cognitive behavioural and rational emotive behavioural techniques used within counselling. However, these need to be grounded within the appropriate context or focus of the coaching relationship. Michael Neenan provides some excellent examples of tools in his chapter, and a few of these are described below in 'Tools and techniques'. It is recognized that many of these techniques can be used equally successfully in the fourth stream.

Stream 5: Unconscious cognition

For some people the fifth stream has echoes of the psychodynamic tradition because of its explicit 'unconscious' label. This is deliberate, and reflects a belief that unconscious thoughts influence our daily lives and behaviours, and that elements of the psychodynamic tradition can help the coach address these issues. However, this positive start also carries with it a warning. While many of the psychodynamic techniques may work well in the counselling room, they lack face validity for work with coachees, particularly with executives, and are less appropriate for the short and more focused work of coaching.

A second technique that can be drawn upon is EMDR (Eye Movement Desensitization and Reprocessing), which can be a valuable intervention to explore unconscious thoughts, particularly involving traumatic stress (Passmore and Pena, 2005). EMDR has to date been primarily used in the treatment of post-traumatic stress disorder, although there are limited references to its use in coaching (Foster and Lendl, 1996). Given the limited space in this chapter, the focus is on exploring unconscious aspects of motivation, drawing on motivational interviewing (Miller and Rollnick, 2002).

Motivational interview (MI) is a technique that has been developed in addiction counselling to help address low motivation to change. The approach helps the counselling client bring into conscious awareness the consequences of his or her behaviours and thus stimulates a stronger motivation to act. For coaches, MI offers an additional tool that is particularly useful where the coachee is resistant to change, but is unclear why initial efforts to change stall before they take off (Passmore, 2007).

As with humanistic, behavioural and cognitive streams within the integrative coaching model, MI has a track record of evidence-based application. This ranges from alcohol and substance abuse counselling (Burke, Arkowitz and Menchola, 2003; Miller and Moyers, 2002; Solomon and Fioritti, 2002) through management of chronic illness (Channon, Smith and Gregory 2003;

Prochaska and Zinman, 2003) to working with teenage contraception counselling (Cowley, Farley and Beamis, 2002). Despite this track record, the use
of MI in the coaching sphere to date appears to be limited (Passmore and
Whybrow, 2007).

The MI approach requires the coach to recognize and understand
ambivalence as a natural part of the change process (Miller and Rollnick,
2002) and to move from using cognitive grounded questions to exploring
beliefs and thinking patterns. A starting point for the coach is identifying
which stage the coachee is at in his or her personal change journey. To identify
this, the coach could ask the coachee to rate his or her perceived readiness
to change on a scale of 0–10, with 10 being that he or she has already made
the change, and 0 being not at all interested in changing (see Figure 11.2).
These ideas, developed in therapy, have been developed as a set of useful
tools for coaches (see Anstiss and Passmore, 2012, and Passmore, 2011,
2012, 2013, 2014, for the application of MI techniques to coaching).

FIGURE 11.2   Change continuum

Change continuum

The coach then works with the coachee to help build arguments for change.
Traditionally, in managing change the coach might offer counter-arguments
that support change, effectively arguing against the coachee. MI takes a different perspective of change. It seeks to work alongside the person, to help
him or her to more fully understand the consequences and benefits of his or
her actions. In this sense it draws on aspects of rational thinking. One model
for doing this, the balance sheet, is included in the 'Tools and techniques'.

As fits the overall integrative coaching model, there is a strongly collaborative approach, with the coach being an ally of the coachee, rather than
being an expert into whose hands the coachee casts his or her troubles, or
an authority issuing advice.

I would most typically step into the unconscious cognition stream where
the coachee has been referred by others concerned about his or her work
performance, or when the behaviours are having a significant impact on

others and which the coachee feels pressure from others to address, although he or she may unconsciously be resistant to doing so.

Stream 6: Systemic

The last and final stream that the coach and coachee work within is the environment and cultural context. This stream surrounds, and influences, all of the preceding streams.

The coach may work simultaneously in this stream and in one of the three action streams of behavioural, conscious cognition or unconscious cognition. In this stream the task for the coach is to help coachees to understand the wider system within which they work, and how this system influences their behaviour and the behaviour of others they work with, including the coach. In this stream the coach seeks to bring these individuals into the coaching room. These may be individuals whom the coach works alongside, such as members of the team; it may be individuals from suppliers or customer organizations; it may include individuals and organizations from the wider environment that create legislation or influence the way work is conducted or people behave.

As well as helping the coachee to draw upon the influences of these individuals, the coach needs to make explicit his or her influence, as the coach too is part of this wider system.

When does integrative coaching work best?

It can be argued that the integrative model has almost universal application within the coaching environment. However, it is particularly suited to executive coaching and sports coaching. Its suitability for use in other areas of coaching such as health and life coaching is due largely to its use of a wide range of elements from other coaching traditions. The approach pays attention to the coachee's need to form a relationship. Without a relationship there is likely to be little progress in coaching.

Integrative coaching acknowledges that most people are, at least initially, drawn to coaching to be different. This difference may be being more successful at work or more successful in forming relationships. For some it may be about developing and refining a skill, or stopping a habit they have developed. In most cases this 'being different' involves behaving differently. The approach's use of behavioural elements enables it to contribute towards this behavioural goal.

Coachees, however, sometimes want something more. They recognize that their ineffective thinking or 'negative thoughts' get in the way of them succeeding. By addressing thinking styles, with a focus on developing more rational thinking, the model too can meet these needs.

For the most experienced coaches there is a recognition that addressing behaviour and thinking style is not always enough. To achieve the outcomes the coachee wants, the coach also needs to work at an unconscious level, sometimes with thinking styles, thoughts and beliefs that are outside of conscious awareness, and sometimes with motivation. In these cases the coach needs to help deepen self-awareness. The integrative model recognizes the role of the unconscious and seeks to integrate this into its pattern of working through drawing on elements from within the psychodynamic and motivational interviewing.

It may begin to feel as if integrative coaching is a magic bullet, a one-shot solution. The reality is that as an integrated approach it takes what works best for coaching from a series of previously evidence-based approaches and blends them together. Arguably most experienced coaches probably do this already, and the model simply describes what they are doing.

The integrative model has its areas of weakness. These are inherent in its development within the executive coaching arena. The first of these weaknesses is that the model lacks a spiritual dimension. The desire to deepen one's spiritual self is a healthy and arguably central aspect of life. Where this is an explicit goal of the coachee, the coach would be better advised to work with models such as the transpersonal model.

A second weakness of the model is that it assumes that behavioural change is what is being sought. Again, this is an outcome of its executive coaching focus. However, if the coachee is seeking a more general model to explore his or her experience of life and the future, a humanistic framework could arguably serve exclusively as a tool to achieve this objective.

Tools and techniques

The integrative model as described draws on tools and techniques from a range of approaches, including behavioural, cognitive behavioural, psychodynamic and motivational interviewing approaches. In this section some suggestions are made for each stream: building and maintaining the partnership, engaging in behavioural change, developing performance-enhancing thinking and deepening self-awareness.

In each case, the reader may wish to review the chapters on GROW (behavioural), cognitive behavioural coaching and stress coaching where more detailed examples illustrate the techniques within these models. This section provides more of an overview for each area.

The first of these is the process of developing and maintaining the relationship. A key tool at this stage is to set out the ground rules. In doing this the coach helps the coachee understand what is 'in' and what is 'outside' the coaching relationship. It sets out the conditions for confidentiality: largely everything is confidential with the exception of risk of self-harm and illegal activities where the coach has a duty to protect others. The ground rules also provide an opportunity for the coach to set out his or her credentials, providing reassurance to the coachee that the coach is a competent and reliable person. A second technique to help build the relationship is to provide space for the coachee to talk at length during the early period of the first session. This opportunity for the coachee to tell his or her story is not primarily to gather information, but to listen and show that the coach values what the coachee has to say. In listening, the coach may be summarizing and reflecting back to check understanding. Once the relationship has been built, the coach needs to continue to invest in it. However, the investment is contingent upon his or her coachee's needs. This draws the coach to deploy emotionally intelligent responses.

The second set of techniques is within the behavioural focus stream. While there is a range of models, the GROW model offers a four-stage process. The coach encourages the coachee to set a clear SMART goal, which can be more difficult than first thought (Passmore, 2003). Once established, the coach works to help gather evidence on current performance. A useful technique for doing this would be to ask the coachee to bring or review behaviour evidence from colleagues and peers. A 360° competency questionnaire is an excellent tool for doing this. Outside of the workplace, the coach may ask the coachee to go and talk to others about how he or she is perceived, either generally or in relationship to the skills or behaviour and its impact on others. This development of a holistic picture provides the coachee with stronger evidence of his or her current reality than a personal perspective.

Another technique in the behavioural focus stream is to help the coachee to get specific on his or her action plan. Typically the coachee offers a vague action plan, with little regard to when, how or what gets in the way. The use of effective and robust challenge at this stage will help the coachee to make the goal real.

The third set of techniques is within the cognitive stream. Typical techniques in this stream include reframing, emersion, visualization and the use of homework tasks to support activities within the coaching process. In reframing, the coach engages in a process of moving the coachee from a view of the world that lacks rational evidence to one that is based on evidence. Questions might include: 'How would your boss, mentor or colleague view this situation?', 'How might Gandhi tackle this problem if you asked him?', 'What other possible outcomes are there?', 'How likely is each of the possible outcomes?'

A second approach is the use of emersion. This technique is used in counselling as a way to gradually overcome irrational fears. This is in contrast to flooding, which is a rapid and immediate process of encounter. To illustrate the contrast between the two: emersion is gradually getting into the pool from the shallow end; flooding is jumping in the deep end. While flooding is generally to be avoided, emersion can help the coachee to test his or her new behaviours or skills gradually.

Visualization is a technique that is commonly used in sports coaching. References to it are pervasive throughout sport, such as Daley Thompson's visualization for a quick start, leaving the starting blocks at the 'b' of the bang. These examples help the coach to improve the face validity of this technique for the coachee. One area in which visualization can be of real value for the coach is helping coachees visualize the task they have set themselves, and particularly to identify potential barriers, and then overcoming these barriers.

The last example of techniques from the cognitive stream is the use of homework. While in other streams I would encourage the coachees to reflect on the session, and maybe to practise new behaviours, in this stream the homework task is a useful component. This may be encouraging coachees to monitor their automatic thoughts. An alternative is to ask coachees to practise the skill or activity in a controlled way, so using emersion, and at the next session reviewing its impact or the feedback that they have received.

The final selection of techniques is from the unconscious cognitive stream. In this stream the coach may encourage the coachee to examine patterns. This may involve patterns of working over many jobs, and even patterns of behaviour back to childhood. The assumption is that such patterns may reveal unconscious processes about beliefs or thoughts.

A second way within the unconscious cognitive stream is to explore these patterns and their meaning. One technique is to use a metaphor for exploring the mind, such as the technique of the old house. In this technique the coach may ask the coachee to visualize an old house in which he or she lives, and like most of us, stores stuff in the loft or cellar. In this house, however, there are a series of rooms in the loft. The idea is that the coach helps the coachee through the visualization to explore deeper into past events, stored in these rooms.

The third technique is drawn from motivational interviewing. This is the use of the balance sheet (see Figure 11.3). The balance sheet can help coachees explore their motivation for change by listing the benefits and costs of the two options they are evaluating. One option may be to stay as they are; a second option would be for change. The aim of the coach is to help coachees to build up stronger benefits for change, where the current behaviour is destructive or damaging to them or others. The coachee, when evaluating the costs and benefits, may only have identified the immediate benefits to him or her of the behaviour, and tends to ignore or minimize the impact of his or her behaviour on others. By bringing these elements into active consideration the coachee can begin to reflect consciously on a wider range of costs and benefits.

FIGURE 11.3   Coaching for change balance sheet

Benefits of activity	Costs of activity	Benefits of change	Costs of change

Ten key questions to guide your way

The first four questions are based within the behavioural focus stream, questions 5–7 are questions from the cognitive stream, and 8–10 from the unconscious cognitive stream.

1. What do you want to achieve?

This is a typical question for use within the behavioural GROW model. The aim of the question is to help the coachee to explicitly state his or her goal. Frequently, less experienced coaches take at face value the first statement and move on, and thus need to return to this at a later stage. More experienced coaches recognize that time spent at this stage, exploring the features of the goal, will save time later.

2. What is happening?

This question aims to help the coach and coachee gather evidence on what is the current situation. How close or far is the coachee to or from his or her goal? In gathering evidence, the less experienced coach can be tempted to accept at face value what the coachee provides as evidence. It is wise for the coach to challenge initial claims and seek third-party evidence for these. A 360° questionnaire, psychometric questionnaire and appraisal feedback all provide such evidence, and help ensure that the coach and coachee are working with a rounded view, not a single perspective, whether this is the coachee's or his or her manager's.

3. What options do you think there are?

Exploring options is a valuable process in all coaching, if there is a belief that the coachee already has the answer to his or her own question. Reviewing options is a two-part process. The coachee needs to be clear what criteria he or she is evaluating the options against. As a result the coachee needs to generate the criteria first, before he or she can start a process of generating or evaluating options.

4. Can you summarize what you are going to do and by when?

This question is concerned with action planning when working in the behavioural focus stream. The question encourages coachees to take responsibility for reviewing their process, summarizing what has been discussed and to formally state what they intend to do. This is a useful question to ask towards the end of a coaching session, even if the coach has been working with cognitive and unconscious cognitive aspects. The coach may then encourage the coachee to document this, and develop an action plan that includes a series of sub-goals or steps that take him or her to this goal over the coming week, month or year.

5. How would your boss, mentor or colleague see this situation?

This question encourages the coachee to begin to explore the issue or challenge that he or she faces from a number of different perspectives. Often an issue looks to be an insurmountable problem to us, but when considered from the perspective of another person, either solutions can be found or a deeper understanding of the issue gained. A parallel type of question is asking the coachee to consider the challenge as if he or she were a famous person. For a management issue, the coach may ask the coachee to consider how Richard Branson would deal with the problem, followed by a question on how Ronald Reagan would deal with the challenge. For a relationship issue, the coach might select two different characters offering different perspectives: Marilyn Monroe and Nelson Mandela. Initially the coachee typically provides a short or flippant remark, but the coach needs to focus on the coachee's response and ensure that he or she fully explores the issue and provides a what, where and when descriptive answer.

6. I would like you to close your eyes and describe to me what would happen if the event went perfectly

This visualization technique gets coachees to engage with a visualization and explore what they see and, with follow-up questions, what they feel, smell and think. Evidence has shown in the sports psychology arena that visualization not only builds self-confidence but also creates physical changes in the brain structure that aid subsequent muscle movement and thus enhance performance.

7. Can you summarize for me the task that you will try out before we meet again?

The summarizing task that has already been discussed is applied in this context to focus the attention of the coachee on a homework task. The use of the task provides an opportunity for emersion: gradual exposure to the challenging behaviour. Follow-up questions might be, 'What would stop you achieving this?', 'What could you do to overcome these barriers?' These questions enable the coachee to prepare for the real world of competing priorities and stakeholders who may need to be persuaded.

8. Tell me about a time when you have felt a similar feeling before

This may be a useful question to explore patterns. Preceding the question the coach will have encouraged coachees to talk about the current issue or problem, and in particular to draw out the feelings within their body which they experience. Using these bodily sensations the coach may then ask the pattern question that may help coachees to identify similar events, but to access these from bodily feelings rather than events.

9. How would others, such as your partner or family, be affected?

This question within motivational interview is drawn from work around the balance sheet. The coach may be exploring with coachees the costs and benefits of their behaviour. Coachees can underestimate the effect of their behaviour on others, and thus fail to include this in the calculation. The coach can focus the coachee's attention on this through the question and often build up the costs side of the equation for the coachee.

10. How ready do you feel you are to change on a scale of 1 to 10; where 10 is that you have already made the change, and 0 that you are not at all interested in changing?

This question refers to the motivational interviewing approach. This is a complex technique and suggests that the developing coach would benefit from training before making use of the technique. However, questions such as this provide clues to whether the coachee is likely to change, or if he or she needs more help to explore the benefits of changing. A low score of 1 to 7 would suggest that focusing on change tools would be a wasted effort; instead the coach needs to invest time exploring motivation and helping the coachee to develop the intrinsic motivation to change.

References

Alexander, G and Renshaw, B (2005) *Super Coaching: The missing ingredient for high performance*, Random House Business Books, London

Anstiss, T and Passmore, J (2012) Motivational Interview, in *Cognitive Behavioural Coaching in Practice: An evidence-based approach*, ed M Neenan and S Palmer, pp 33–52, Routledge, London

Bandura, A (1969) *Principles of Behaviour Modification*, Holt, Reinhart and Winston, New York

Bandura, A (1977) Self-efficacy: towards a unifying theory of behaviour change, *Psychological Review*, **84**, pp 191–215

Beck, A (1991) *Cognitive Therapy of Depression*, Guilford Press, New York

Burke, B L, Arkowitz, I I and Menchola, M (2003) The efficacy of motivational interviewing: a meta analysis of controlled clinical trials, *Journal of Consulting Clinical Psychology*, **71**, pp 843–61

Caruso, D and Salovey, P (2004) *The Emotionally Intelligent Manager: How to develop and use the four key emotional skills of leadership*, Jossey-Bass, San Francisco, CA

Channon, S, Smith, V J and Gregory, J W (2003) A pilot study of motivational interviewing in adolescents with diabetes, *Archives of Disease in Childhood*, **88** (8), pp 680–83

Cowley, C B, Farley, T and Beamis, K (2002) 'Well, maybe I'll try the pill for just a few months' ... Brief motivational and narrative-based interventions to encourage contraceptive use among adolescents at high risk for early childbearing, *Families, Systems and Health*, **20**, p 183

Ellis, A (1998) *The Practice of Rational Emotive Behavioural Therapy*, Free Association Books, London

Foster, S and Lendl, J (1996) Eye movement desensitization and reprocessing: four case studies of a new tool for executive coaching and restoring employee performance after setbacks, *Consulting Psychology Journal: Practice & Research*, **48** (3), pp 155–61

Gist, M and Mitchell, T (1992) Self-efficacy: a theoretical analysis of its determinism and malleability, *Academy of Management Review*, **17** (2), pp 183–211

Grant, A M, Passmore, J Cavanagh, M and Parker, H (2010) The state of play in coaching, *International Review of Industrial & Organizational Psychology*, **25**, pp 125–68

Locke, E and Latham, G (1990) *A Theory of Goal Setting and Task Performance*, Prentice Hall, Englewood Cliffs, NJ

Miller, W R and Rollnick, S (2002) *Motivational Interviewing: Preparing people for change*, 2nd edn, Guilford Press, New York

Miller, J H and Moyers, T (2002) Motivational interviewing in substance abuse: applications for occupational medicine, *Occupational Medicine*, **17** (1), pp 51–65

Neenan, M and Dryden, W (2001) *Life Coaching: A cognitive behavioural approach*, Brunner-Routledge, London

Passmore, J (2003) Goal-focused coaching, *The Occupational Psychologist*, August

Passmore, J (2005) The heart of coaching, *The Coaching Psychologist*, Winter

Passmore, J (2007) Addressing deficit performance through coaching: using motivational interviewing for performance improvement in coaching, *International Coaching Psychology Review*, **2** (3), pp 265–79

Passmore, J (2011) Motivational Interviewing – a model for coaching psychology practice, *The Coaching Psychologist*, **7** (1), pp 35–39

Passmore, J (2012) Motivational Interviewing Techniques – Typical day, *The Coaching Psychologist*, **8** (1), pp 50–52

Passmore, J (2013) MI techniques: Agenda Mapping, *The Coaching Psychologist*, **9** (1), pp 32–35

Passmore, J (2014) Motivational Interviewing, in *Mastery in Coaching: A complete psychological toolkit for advanced coaching*, ed J Passmore, Kogan Page, London

Passmore, J and Pena, A (2005) How to manage trauma, *People Management*, 28 July

Passmore, J and Theeboom, T (2016) Coaching Psychology: A journey of development in research, in *Coaching Psychology: Meta-theoretical perspectives and applications in multi-cultural contexts*, ed L E Van Zyl, M W Stander and A Oodendal, Springer, New York

Passmore, J and Whybrow, A (2007) Motivational interviewing: a specific approach for coaching psychologists, in *The Handbook of Coaching Psychology*, ed S Palmer and A Whybrow, pp 160–73, Brunner-Routledge, London

Pavlov, I (1927) *Conditioned Reflexes*, Oxford University Press, Oxford

Peltier, B (2001) *The Psychology of Executive Coaching: Theory and application*, Brunner-Routledge, London

Prochaska, J O and Zinman, B (2003) Changes in diabetes self care behaviours make a difference in glycemic control: the Diabetes Stages of Change (DISC) study, *Diabetes Care*, **26**, pp 732–37

Rogers, C (1961) *On Becoming a Person*, Houghton Mifflin, Boston, MA

Skiffington, S and Zeus, P (2003) *Behavioural Coaching: How to build sustainable personal and organizational strength*, McGraw-Hill, New York

Solomon, J and Fioritti, A (2002) Motivational intervention as applied to systems change: the case of dual diagnosis, *Substance Use and Misuse*, **37** (14), pp 1833–51

Stein, S and Book, H (2000) *The EQ Edge: Emotional intelligence and your success*, MHS, Toronto

Whitmore, J (2009) *Coaching for Performance: Growing people, performance and purpose*, 4th edn, Nicholas Brealey Publishing, London

PART THREE
Coaching issues

Intercultural coaching

12

PHILIPPE ROSINSKI and GEOFFREY ABBOTT

Integrating culture into coaching

We see culture as an important influence in all coaching relationships. Sometimes the influence is obvious, sometimes it is subtle – but it is always influential. By exploring the way culture might be influencing thoughts, feelings and behaviours in the different contexts of their coaching, coaches can utilize culture as a powerful force of change and development. We therefore see the consideration of culture as a virtual necessity in any high-impact coaching programme. Culture provides opportunity. We believe that coaching as a profession has not taken advantage of this opportunity. It is almost as though there is an underlying assumption that culture is an obstacle to be overcome, or that culture is not a factor.

Our experience is that a 'culture as opportunity' perspective can enhance the impact of any coaching intervention. We define coaching as the art of facilitating the unleashing of people's potential to reach meaningful, important objectives (Rosinski, 2003a). Intercultural coaching is the decision to recognize the possibilities of utilizing culture as a force of change to unleash coachee potential. Culture is always there as an influence; it is more a matter of how much attention we choose to give it. Intercultural coaching can bring to the surface issues and assumptions related to culture and harness them in unleashing coachee potential and facilitating positive change. This chapter highlights the benefits of leveraging differences that may be culturally based, rather than treating them as barriers, threats or irrelevancies.

Rosinski (2003a: 20) provides a working definition of culture as follows: 'A group's culture is the set of unique characteristics that distinguishes its members from another group.' Hall (1989: 17) describes culture as humankind's medium, and comments:

there is not one aspect of human life that is not touched and altered by culture. This means personality, how people express themselves (including shows of emotion), the way they think, how they move, how problems are solved, how their cities are planned and laid out, how transportation systems function and are organized, as well as how economic and government systems are put together and function.

We underestimate the influence of culture at our peril.

Our work in intercultural coaching is based on extensive research that reveals differences between people due to culture, which result in people seeing the world from different perspectives. Much of this research has been done at the level of national culture (eg Hofstede, 1980; Schwartz, 1999; Trompenaars and Hampden-Turner, 1998). However, groups of all kinds have cultures. Groups originate from various categories, including geography, religion, profession, organization, social life, gender, sexual orientation, etc. Our individual *identities* can be viewed as a personal and dynamic synthesis of the cultures of the multiple groups to which we belong.

Caution is required when making generalizations about culture. It is very easy to fall into unhelpful or negative stereotyping. The inherent paradox is that knowledge of cultural preferences and dimensions can provide invaluable insights about a group, yet careless use of such knowledge can be misleading and destructive. Wars, natural disasters, globalization, etc have meant that many societies are multicultural and multiracial. Cultural diversity (of many kinds) within national boundaries means that there is often considerable variation in style among people from one country. Australia, for example, is a culturally diverse society with many people exhibiting cultural characteristics more typical of their homeland than of any statistical norm for the country. At the same time, it is useful to know that there are certain ways that many Australian companies tend to do business. Generalization can provide insights, but we need to tread carefully. The same need for informed caution holds when considering work areas and organizational cultures where variation also occurs within groups as well as across them. There are individual personality differences that are based on genetic factors, and individuals are influenced by multiple cultural influences (such as when the parents are from different countries or religions).

Cultural influences are often subtle and operate beneath the surface, and people may have little awareness of the characteristics of various group cultures to which they are connected. They can therefore be oblivious of the influence culture may be having on their thoughts, behaviours and emotions. In organizations, often it is the outsider (such as the consultant, the coach, or the new employee) who can see the patterns and forces of culture at work. The people who are immersed in organizational culture, shape it, and are shaped by it may find it hard to define and virtually invisible. Trompenaars suggests that 'Culture is like gravity: you do not experience it until you jump six feet into the air' (Trompenaars and Hampden-Turner, 1998: 5).

To see how culture influences us, we need to create a little distance from our situation – to see ourselves 'in context' as others might see us. Similarly, to understand how others with whom we interact see the world, we need to make a mental shift out of our world and into theirs. This will provide rich material for leveraging cultural difference for personal, professional and societal growth. Intercultural coaching uses individual identity as the entry point to culture and provides an opportunity for people to work out into their worlds and to make use of the power of culture. Rosinski (2003a) has brought together diverse research on cultural difference into a cultural orientations framework (COF), which summarizes various orientations across which people differ. The COF is explained below, along with some ideas on how it might be used in coaching.

Traditional coaching has implicitly reflected particular norms, values and basic assumptions that reflect its originating culture – the USA. It is a well-researched fact that these do not necessarily hold true universally (see, for example, Nisbett, 2003). Intercultural coaching carries a Western assumption regarding our relationship to nature. We assume that our coachees have control over the direction of their lives, how they deploy their talents, and how they reach success. However, a wise coach also recognizes the relativity of the all-powerful control orientation. Simultaneously, we hold the assumption that many factors such as environment, genetic inheritance and luck can inhibit or enhance the degree of control we have at various times in our lives. The coach looks for balance and flow and understands the importance of timing. For the coachee, knowing your limits is not always obvious. But, humbly accepting them is paradoxically within your control. In the field of culture, contradictions and paradoxes are not uncommon and we encourage our coachees to roll with them and proceed on their journeys of positive change. We encourage coachees to consider the influence of culture through the process of reflective thought in the light of available evidence.

Intercultural coaching is a dynamic process that opens up possibilities for the client. Later in this chapter we describe a global coaching process (Rosinski, 2003a) that gives shape to the coaching approach. In the global coaching process, coaches and coachees connect their personal voyages with those of their families, friends, work colleagues, organizations, communities and society in general. Culture influences the direction of our individual journeys. If we travel with an attitude of curiosity and an eye for the potential of diversity, culture can enrich our experiences as we interact with others.

Intercultural coaching as we define it is a form of pragmatic humanism. It is pragmatic in that we draw on approaches and ideas that work in the context of the coachee. The measures of success are determined by the coachee. The approach is humanist in that we emphasize care of self and of others, quality of life and human growth. We will therefore work with coachees on approaches that are ethical and consistent with the humanist stance. Coaching from a cultural perspective is inconsistent, for example, with racial discrimination, or exploitative commercial practices.

Intercultural coaching – because it is pragmatic – makes sound business sense. The unleashing of individual potential and the leveraging of different approaches that are culturally based mean that companies receive sustainable benefits. Individuals become more productive, teams work better together, and solutions to issues become more creative and innovative. For example, joint venture companies (JVCs) across national boundaries are notoriously 'high risk'. A coaching approach that turns cultural differences into opportunities can increase the chances of JVC success. The need to consider and leverage cultural differences in business is growing. David Peterson (2015), Director of Executive Coaching and Leadership for Google, recently stressed the importance of coaches giving attention to diversity when working with leaders in the 'VUCA' world, one increasingly characterized by increasing volatility, uncertainty, complexity and ambiguity (Bernstein, 2014). The application of coaching to diverse international business contexts is explored in detail in other texts (Moral and Abbott, 2009; Passmore, 2009).

Embracing diversity

Cultural difference is potential. We lead towards and embrace diversity. Intercultural coaching requires that we value and explore differences rather than automatically impose our norms, values and beliefs. Considering alternative belief systems and ways of operating, as they are represented in different cultures, can help coachees to broaden their perspectives. As they explore their own cultural assumptions and practices through the interaction with others they may see opportunities for change. Intercultural coaching can expand cultural repertoires and achieve sustainable change. The end result for coachees is that they deal with their individual challenges, and have a deeper understanding of their own contexts and those of others with whom they interact. From a pragmatic perspective, they will be better equipped to achieve their aims and objectives. We embrace the idea of canvassing many different sources to find approaches that work in the context of the coachee. Intercultural coaching requires an appreciation that there are different views of the world – and each potentially has something to offer every person undertaking his or her unique journey.

Embracing diversity is easy at an intellectual level. However, intercultural coaching requires more. You need to become convinced in your heart and in your guts that a different truth or ideal is legitimate (though we do not of course propose that one should accept a cultural view that would promote intolerance, racism, xenophobia, or anti-Semitism). An emotional commitment is required. It is important that coaches learn as much as they can about the cultures that influence their clients. Books can help and there is an abundance of high-quality literature about culture. Experience informed by such knowledge is even better. Reflective interaction with the client is one way of experiencing his or her way of seeing the world. You can gain even more through extended onsite visits to a client's company, and talking to others there. Where national culture is a prominent influence, there are few better alternatives than travel.

People come to coaching with different approaches to dealing with cultural diversity. Interculturalist Milton Bennett (1993) describes six stages along a path towards enhanced cultural sensitivity. Coaches who operate with an awareness of these stages can assist their clients to follow their own journeys in productively exploring cultural diversity. In the early stages, Bennett describes approaches as 'ethnocentric pitfalls'. In stage 1, people ignore differences or deny they exist. In stage 2, there is recognition of differences but they are viewed negatively. Those who are different may be denigrated from a position of feeling superior. Stage 3 also sees recognition of differences, but they are trivialized. There is an assumption that regardless of small differences, we are all the same.

Beyond stage 3, there is a shift into what Bennett terms 'ethno relative approaches'. At stage 4, differences are recognized and acknowledged. At stage 5 there is a move out of the comfort zone. An empathetic perspective is possible where the person can take a temporary shift in perspective, but without adopting or assimilating that perspective. Bennett's stage 6 is one of integration. The person is able to hold different frames of reference and to analyse and evaluate situations from various cultural perspectives.

Intercultural coaching can assist coachees move through these stages, though the shifts are uneven and not easily measured. The coach encourages coachees to operate with ethno relative approaches. The coach supports coachees as they step outside their cultural comfort zones and accept alternative cultural views as valid. It requires a temporary suspension of one's own cultural viewpoint to genuinely take the view of another by imagining oneself to be the other person. This is a position of empathy, which is different from a position of sympathy where a person looks at another's view or situation still fixed in their own perspective. Bennett (1998) contrasts the golden rule of sympathy, 'Do unto others as you would have them do unto you' with the platinum rule of empathy, 'Do unto others as they themselves would have done unto them.' Bennett argues that the latter is more effective because people are different due to culture.

The common expression of seeking to put yourself into someone else's shoes illustrates the point. Getting into the shoes of someone very similar to ourselves is not much of an effort – same size, same style. However, it requires a leap of imagination to get into someone's shoes if that person is very different from you. The shift in thinking is to imagine yourself *as* the other person so that the shoes fit. The shift is temporary. Empathy does not mean permanently giving up your own cultural identity. The following case indicates the complexity:

> A Canadian client was having difficulty adjusting to her new position as a manager of local staff in Peru. Ellen was confused because her Spanish was perfect and she knew a lot about the local culture, yet she felt resistance from her staff. We talked about her approach. It turned out that Ellen was almost trying to *be* Peruvian by changing her dress style and attempting to speak with a local accent. It seemed likely that her staff did not feel comfortable with her because they perceived she had abandoned her own identity.

Stage 6 in cultural sensitivity incorporates the capacity to hold various perspectives and to able to move from one to the other – but with a sure sense of self-identity to which you always return. Nevertheless, empathetic immersion in new cultures or perspectives is likely to add new dimensions to one's identity as a natural part of personal and professional growth.

Embracing diversity is a way of respecting the identity of others. It also makes good sense. Being able to switch cultural perspectives enables us to see issues and problems in different ways and to come up with new and powerful approaches and solutions. Creative integration of this kind has a cost. It requires a high level of self-questioning. We encourage coachees to question things that they previously held as a fixed reality. This is more difficult than living with certainties, but it brings rewards. Once coachees and coaches begin on this path, they are not passive observers of their cultural environments. Cultures shapes us, but we shape culture – albeit more slowly. It is not for the fainthearted and there is a risk that we can become culturally disconnected and confused about our own values and identities. The coach can assist the coachee to remain grounded in reality, perhaps by recognizing a need for a client to withdraw a little back to the familiar and the comfortable before resuming the journey.

We believe there is potential for coachees to move beyond Bennett's stage 6 to another stage where they can leverage cultural differences. At this point coaches and coachees work together to strive for creative synergy. We look for gems in different cultures, to deal with paradox and contradiction, and to achieve unity through diversity.

Leveraging alternative cultural perspectives

The COF (see Table 12.1) is a useful tool for leveraging diversity. A common way of examining how values differ (or are similar) across cultures is to conceptualize them as to how people face universal challenges that confront them. Rosinski (2003a) has adapted the work of anthropologists, cross-cultural consultants and communications experts to identify challenges that are common across coaching situations. Different cultures choose different approaches in response to the challenges; these can be termed cultural orientations.

Our experience is that the COF is an effective tool when used with coaching. The COF online assessment is described in detail in Rosinski (2010). Use of the COF can help coachees to recognize cultural difference, thereby providing a potential for leveraging alternative perspectives. Clients are asked to identify their existing cultural orientations on the COF, and to examine other alternatives. Through experimentation and reflection, they then explore alternative orientations and work towards an approach that best suits their identities and contexts. This is an ongoing process of personal and professional growth and does not require letting go of original orientations, nor a surrendering of self. The approach is pragmatic in seeking to build on existing characteristics and strengths.

In using the COF the idea is not to select one approach or another, but to synthesize for maximum advantage. The approach is dialectical in working with the creative tension that exists between the different orientations. We look for contrast and for depth. New ideas, solutions and options emerge from the confrontation. The practice of deliberately accepting and building from apparently opposite approaches requires a certain comfort with paradox and complexity. One central paradox is that while major differences between people can provide a barrier to effective communication, differences can also be levers for positive change. Differences generally are seen as challenges and opportunities rather than problems or threats to be navigated.

TABLE 12.1 Cultural orientations framework

Categories	Dimensions	Description
Sense of power and responsibility	Control/harmony/humility	**Control:** people have a determinant power and responsibility to forge the life they want.
		Harmony: strive for balance and harmony with nature.
		Humility: accept inevitable natural limitations.
Time management approaches	Scarce/plentiful	**Scarce:** time is a scarce resource. Manage time carefully!
		Plentiful: time is abundant. Relax!
	Monochronic/polychronic	**Monochronic:** concentrate on one activity and/or relationship at a time.
		Polychrome: concentrate simultaneously on multiple tasks and/or people.
	Past/present/future	**Past:** learn from the past. The present is essentially a continuation or a repetition of past occurrences.
		Present: focus on the 'here and now' and short-term benefits.
		Future: have a bias towards long-term benefits. Promote a far-reaching vision.
Definitions of identity and purpose	Being/doing	**Being:** stress living itself and the development of talents and relationships.
		Doing: focus on accomplishments and visible achievements.
	Individualistic/collectivistic	**Individualistic:** emphasize individual attributes and projects.
		Collectivistic: emphasize affiliation with a group.

Organizational arrangements	Hierarchy/ equality	**Hierarchy**: society and organizations must be socially stratified to function properly. **Equality**: people are equals who often happen to play different roles.
	Universalist/ particularist	**Universalist**: all cases should be treated in the same universal manner. Adopt common processes for consistency and economies of scale. **Particularist**: emphasize particular circumstances. Favour decentralization and tailored solutions.
	Stability/change	**Stability**: value a static and orderly environment. Encourage efficiency through systematic and disciplined work. Minimize change and ambiguity, perceived as disruptive. **Change**: value a dynamic and flexible environment. Promote effectiveness through adaptability and innovation. Avoid routine, perceived as boring.
	Competitive/ collaborative	**Competitive**: promote success and progress through competitive stimulation. **Collaborative**: promote success and progress through mutual support, sharing of best practices and solidarity.
Notions of territory and boundaries	Protective/ sharing	**Protective**: protect oneself by keeping personal life and feelings private (mental boundaries), and by minimizing intrusions in one's physical space (physical boundaries). **Sharing**: build closer relationships by sharing one's psychological and physical domains.
Communication patterns	High-context/ low-context	**High-context**: rely on implicit communication. Appreciate the meaning of gestures, postures, voice and context. **Low-context**: rely on explicit communication. Favour clear and detailed instructions.
	Direct/indirect	**Direct**: in a conflict or with a tough message to deliver, get your point across clearly at the risk of offending or hurting. **Indirect**: in a conflict or with a tough message to deliver, favour maintaining a cordial relationship at the risk of misunderstanding.
	Affective/neutral	**Affective**: display emotions and warmth when communicating. Establishing and maintaining personal and social connections is key. **Neutral**: stress conciseness, precision and detachment when communicating.

As noted earlier, when working with the idea of cultural orientations and dimensions, there is a risk of stereotyping. The advantage of the COF is that it gives you and your coachee valuable information about the coachee's individual cultural orientations, which may be similar to or different from the coachee's national, community or organizational culture. Through the COF you may find, for example, that your coachee enjoys change and is an 'outlier' within his or her cultural environment, which favours stability. This situation offers opportunity for leveraging the differences. Your coachee may be an ideal candidate for leading change management processes in the company in the event of a merger or acquisition. It may also help your coachee to understand frustrations and tensions he or she has been experiencing at work.

The global coaching process

The three-stage global coaching process (Rosinski, 2003a) provides a structure for embracing diversity in coaching. From the first meeting to the completion of the formal sessions, the coach encourages coachees to consider their lives in the broader context of their relationships and their society – always with a view to unleashing the coachee's potential.

Stage 1. Assessment

The assessment phase includes a systematic consideration of the self, as well as family and friends, organization, community and the world. Through exploration there comes a gradual emergence of objectives that separate the coachees from what others expect and turn them towards a future that is consistent with their individual desires, preferences and unique contexts. The coach may encourage coachees to assess approximately where they might be in relation to the stages of cultural sensitivity (outlined above) and to discuss their associated levels of effectiveness in cross-cultural adjustment and functioning. The COF may be used to assist the coachee in understanding his or her current orientations and those of others. It requires that the coach adopt an inherent bias of believing in coachee potential.

Stage 2. Setting targets

In the second stage, the global scorecard (see Figure 12.1) invites the coachee to devise measures of internal and external success across a broad variety of

FIGURE 12.1   The global scorecard

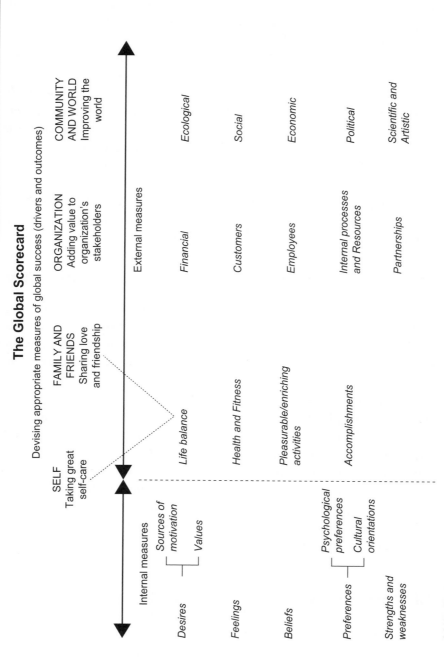

The Global Scorecard

Devising appropriate measures of global success (drivers and outcomes)

SOURCE: Rosinski (2003a)

stakeholders, including self, family and friends, organization, community and the world. This process emphasizes the centrality of human relationships in personal and professional growth and extends the coaching outside of individual experiences and perceptions.

The categories help to incorporate the various cultural perspectives that influence the coachee's reality. There are various other indicators that are effectively used in individual coaching and in organizational development. What has been missing is a comprehensive framework for conceptualizing and tying together previous and disparate scorecards and extending the scope. The global scorecard seeks to fill this gap. By including the stakeholder category of 'Community and the world', the global scorecard focuses attention on an area that individual coaching sometimes neglects. Coaching relationships can enter the challenging and critical areas of business ethics, sustainable development, corporate citizenship, human rights, poverty and human creativity.

Stage 3. Making progress towards the target objectives

This is the action stage where coach and coachee focus on monitoring and making progress towards the targets. The objectives – like culture – are not static. Targets are revised as new experiences and new learning are integrated. The approach is pragmatic in focusing on what works in the context of the coachee.

The global coaching process is the vehicle for opening up possibilities through the overlay of a cultural perspective. It is a multilevel approach that acknowledges the influence of culture in our lives, while remaining consistent with the general principles and practice of high-quality coaching. Our view of how intercultural coaching fits within the broader profession of coaching is shaped by the very practice of intercultural coaching. It is not an either/or choice. Culture is an 'and' in our profession. You lose nothing by including a cultural perspective. Instead you enhance the depth and the impact of whatever other approaches you favour.

Cross-cultural work in practice

As a coach, it helps to keep in mind some of the following questions, particularly when the coaching relationship does not seem to be flowing:

- What are the cultural orientations of your coachee?
- What are your own cultural orientations?

- How might the interaction between your and the coachee's orientations be impacting on the coaching process?
- How might you leverage the different cultural orientations?

Below are two examples where the coach (in this case Geoffrey Abbott) was able to work with coachees to leverage differences. The cases are real but some details have been changed to protect confidentiality.

Direct vs indirect communication style

Julio felt stuck in his position as an expert problem-solver in the middle levels of a South African multinational company operating in his country in Latin America. Through the global coaching process, Julio clarified and explored the ambitions for himself, his family, his company, his community and his country. He wanted to move out of specialized project work into management, to give his children an opportunity to live and study overseas, to add value to his company, and demonstrate that local managers could make an impact in a multinational company. He also wanted to have an impact in promoting inclusive and empowering management practices in the company and his country.

Julio was receiving negative feedback about his communication and presentation skills, even though he rated himself highly on these. He had been a line manager in two large Latin American companies. He had given many presentations and training courses and had invariably received positive feedback.

In the first coaching session I noticed that Julio was expansive and rather indirect in the way he described his situation and how he responded to my questions. His language was also very formal, laced with technical terms and jargon. Julio confirmed a preference for an indirect and formal communication style (see Table 12.1). We discussed the cultural aspect of this style. I was familiar with the local business culture and was aware that Julio's style was quite typical in his country (though in other ways Julio was very atypical). We then discussed the dominant cultural orientation in the multinational company. Julio had been to South Africa for training. I had worked with several of the South African managers. It was obvious to both of us that the South Africans preferred a direct approach and were not interested in formality. The discussion quickly moved Julio to a realization that he needed to alter his communication style if he wanted to make a bigger impact in the company.

Through parts of the subsequent sessions I became more of a trainer than a coach in assisting Julio to be more direct. My Australian business background meant that I was comfortable and familiar with a style very similar to the South African approach. We worked with role-plays and practice presentations. Sometimes as we moved across discussions of some of Julio's other objectives I stopped the coaching session and invited Julio to reflect on how he was communicating (particularly if Julio was indirect in response to a direct question).

Julio's strength – and the reason why he was of such value to the company – was his grasp of detail and complexity. Our task therefore was to leverage difference, ie for Julio to keep control of the detail in a complex environment, but for him to succinctly present the ideas in an appropriate style. I used the metaphor of a back office full of organized files that were available from the front desk if requested. Within six months, Julio had successfully made representation to senior management to establish a new department in the company – the department in charge of the interface between complex financial data and operational systems. Julio had made short, high-impact presentations backed by detailed documentation. Also, Julio persuaded them to make him the departmental head and was able to put into practice his management philosophy and to open up a new future for himself and his family.

Perhaps coincidentally, Julio changed his diet, joined a gym, went from 215 pounds to 155 pounds, and became more active in playing with his children. At the traditional extended family barbeque each Sunday, Julio took his own lean meat and drank a glass or two of wine in place of beer. After some initial incredulity and resistance, some of Julio's friends and family members quietly asked him for the phone number of his nutritionist and began their own change processes.

Affective vs neutral communication style

Tracy was an African American information technology manager who was having some difficulty with her supervisor. In my introductory meeting, Tracy suggested that she perceived some racial issues in the attitude that her manager demonstrated towards her. I was conscious that I was of a similar demographic to her manager – ie white, male, Anglo background, 40s. We didn't meet again for some months. When we met outside my hotel, Tracy hugged me warmly. We then went to her office and began our coaching session.

The conversation moved slowly and I felt a tension similar to the one I experienced in our first meeting. There was no problem, but an underlying sense of separation and difference. I mentioned to Tracy that I had been slightly uncomfortable in receiving her warm hug when we met earlier in the day. She responded that she had noticed my reticence. I explained my Anglo heritage and how in my family and in my culture there was not the same spontaneity in the expression of emotions. While we had strong love for each other and our family was very close, we were the typical Anglo family in favouring a more neutral communication style (see Table 12.1). The conversation extended into a broader conversation about family and community connections in Tracy's life – in contrast to my rather mobile and sometimes self-contained life with my partner (see the COF individualistic and collectivist dimensions under definitions of identity and purpose). We started to understand each other much better and the tone moved to a kind of relaxed playfulness that for me was an indication that the coaching session was becoming a learning environment. The playful interaction around our differences was my way of helping the two of us to leverage cultural difference.

Later, these conversations proved very helpful for both of us in understanding other situations in Tracy's life, including her relationship with her manager.

When and how to raise such issues with a coachee are matters of professional judgement. However, the aim in intercultural coaching is to bring culture to the surface, so when in doubt it is probably better to raise the issue. How you raise the issue for maximum impact is best determined to some extent by the cultural orientation.

Conclusions

We are ambitious for the role of intercultural coaching in an expanding global economy. Intercultural coaching can unleash the potential of leaders and produce tangible benefits including empowerment, vision and creativity, and more effective cross-cultural communication (Rosinski, 2003b).

Intercultural coaching encourages the coaches to look deeply at themselves. The coach's own desires, strengths, weaknesses, contexts, and cultural and psychological preferences are directly relevant to the success of the coaching in unleashing coachee potential. We need to open ourselves to the possibility that our own cultural values, assumptions or backgrounds may potentially inhibit our effectiveness with a coachee. By being aware of ourselves and sensitive to our coachees we can be ready to develop authentic strategies to leverage contrasts we encounter.

The principles and practices of intercultural coaching we have described above can be applied when working with cultural diversity in many forms. Diversity can come through cultural difference based on nationality, sex, faith, sexual preference, disability, etc. The essence of intercultural coaching is to assume that the experience and perspective a client has gained by being part of a group opens up potential and possibility. When one has, for example, experienced extreme hardship through some form of discrimination and managed not only to survive but also to prosper, the perspectives gained can be utilized to create solutions to new problems and issues. We do not suggest culture be treated in isolation in coaching. Intercultural coaching is multidisciplinary and draws on multiple sources of evidence (see Abbott and Rosinski, 2007). We advocate a global coaching approach that calls on multiple interconnected perspectives.

Culture is becoming an increasingly important focus of attention. Technology is bringing people together more easily and rapidly. There are demographic shifts driven by social, political, religious and environmental forces that are placing diverse cultures in proximity and often in tension. Coaching is a methodology for finding possibilities and opportunities in the VUCA world. Intercultural coaching is challenging and goes to the essence of who we are. Hall (1989: 240) writes about the difficult journey beyond culture, 'because the greatest separation feat of all is when one manages to gradually free oneself from the grip of unconscious culture'. Coachees may initially be resistant to the idea that they are carrying assumptions and perspectives that are holding them back. Coaching can unleash potential by giving coachees greater understanding and choice about the way they are, the way they want to be, and the direction their lives will take.

Acknowledgement

Table 12.1 is reproduced with kind permission of Nicholas Brealey Publishing from *Coaching Across Cultures*, Philippe Rosinski.

References

Abbott, G and Rosinski, P (2007) Global coaching and evidence based coaching, *International Journal of Evidence-based Coaching and Mentoring*, 5 (1), pp 58–77

Bennett, M J (1993) Towards ethno relativism: a developmental model of intercultural sensitivity, in *Education for the Intercultural Experience*, ed R M Paige, pp 21–71, Intercultural Press, Yarmouth

Bennett, M J (1998) Overcoming the golden rule: sympathy and empathy, in *Basic Concepts of Intercultural Communication: Selected readings*, ed M J and Bennett, pp 191–214, Intercultural Press, Yarmouth

Bernstein, L E (2014) *The Perceived Importance of VUCA-Driven Skills for 21st Century Leader Success and the Extent of Integration of those Skills into Leadership Development Programs*, unpublished dissertation, Drake University, Iowa

Hall, E T (1989) *Beyond Culture*, Anchor House, New York

Hofstede, G (1980) *Culture's Consequences*, Sage, Beverly Hills

Moral, M and Abbott, G (2009, 2011) (eds) *The Routledge Companion to International Business Coaching*, Routledge, London

Nisbett, R E (2003) *The Geography of Thought: How Asians and Westerners think differently and why*, The Free Press, New York

Passmore, J (2009) (ed) *Diversity in Coaching*, Kogan Page, London

Peterson, D P (2015) 'Coaching Leaders in Turbulent Times: Dealing with complexity, chaos and constant change', Presentation to the Coaching in Leadership and Healthcare Conference, 25–26 September, Harvard Medical School, Boston

Rosinski, P (2003a) *Coaching Across Cultures: New tools for leveraging national, corporate and professional differences*, Nicholas Brealey Publishing, London

Rosinski, P (2003b) The applications of coaching across cultures, *International Journal of Coaching in Organizations*, 1 (4), pp 4–16

Rosinski, P (2010) *Global Coaching*, Nicholas Brealey Publishing, London

Schwartz, S H (1999) A theory of cultural values and some implications for work, *Applied Psychology: An International Review*, 48 (1), pp 23–47

Trompenaars, F and Hampden-Turner, C (1998) *Riding the Waves of Culture: Understanding cultural diversity in global business*, 2nd edn, McGraw Hill, New York

Coaching and stress

13

**DR M ALICIA PEÑA BIZAMA and
PROFESSOR SIR CARY L COOPER**

Why focus on stress?

Today it is common to hear people talk about being stressed as a result of increasing workloads, and of having to adapt to a rapid pace of organizational change. In addition, the extraordinary developments in technology are revolutionizing communications, and organizations adopting digital technologies which require developing new ways of working (CIPD, 2008). Although technology brings benefits, the easy access to e-mails on our smartphones, for example, has made it very difficult to take breaks from work demands. These developments are making it harder to maintain a work–life balance. The gradual loss of energy and tiredness reduces physical health and well-being, which in turn has a negative effect on our ability to be productive at work.

The subject of stress has drawn the attention of professionals interested in promoting health and well-being at work. Stress has been identified as the second factor of work-related health problems after musculoskeletal complaints, particularly in the non-manual worker population (Cooper, Dewe and O'Driscoll, 2001). Professor Sir Cooper commented that in the early 1990s the National Institute of Occupational Safety and Health estimated that workplace stress (in relation to alcoholism) cost the United States $51 billion due to decreased productivity and $4 billion as a result of lost employment. Recent press releases on the American Psychological Association website (26 January 2006) reported that research had found that about 20 per cent of Americans are worried about the effects of stress on their health. It also mentioned that about 36 per cent of respondents commented that they coped by eating or drinking alcohol. Another article on the same website reported that a meta-analysis of 293 independent studies – between 1960 and 2001 – had found that long-term or chronic stress reduced the capacity of the immune system to protect the body from illness (Segerstrom and Miller, 2004).

From the research available it is evident that stress is a problem affecting individuals worldwide; Peterson (2005), *Occupational Health and Safety*, argued that stress and stress-induced illnesses are the largest and most debilitating epidemic of the 21st century. In the UK, The Health and Safety Executive (2004) survey indicated that at least half a million in the UK population were experiencing work-related stress, and about one in five workers reported extreme symptoms of work-related stress (CIPD, 2004). A European research of work-related stress (Cox, Griffiths and Rial-Gonzalez, 2000) found that 28 per cent of workers interviewed experienced stress. Also, the research found that in 1998 about 200 million days were lost due to sickness absence. Stress and mental health problems were cited as main causes of long-term absence (CIPD, 2004). This report also indicated that three-quarters of executives mentioned that stress had a negative impact on their health as well as on their performance. Main factors mentioned as causes of stress were workload, tight deadlines, lack of support and feeling threatened at work (HSE, 2004/5).

This data provides clear indication of the scale and severity of the impact of stress on individuals. The interest in finding ways to support people's health has increased, and an indication of the importance of this topic is that stress at work has become a prominent area of research in occupational psychology both in the United States and Europe (Cox *et al*, 2000).

The cost of work-related stress to the UK economy has been estimated to be between £10 and £12 billion annually (HSE, 2004). The Health and Safety Executive encourages organizations to take preventative measures to reduce the impact of stress in the workplace, and it has developed management standards to achieve this aim. The management standards focus on six key areas:

- demands (being able to manage the job);
- control (having enough discretion over work that needs to be done);
- support (good support from managers and peers);
- roles (clarity of responsibilities);
- relationships (good environment with no unacceptable behaviour);
- change (awareness of, and participation in, changes within the organization).

Given the incidence of stress, and its potential to lead to mental ill health and long-term sickness, it is critical to take preventative action. The damaging effects of stress can be prevented by providing support to individuals and organizations to promote health and well-being at work. Increasingly organizations are promoting well-being at work, and these practices are encouraged by governmental institutions who are developing guidelines focusing on working conditions to promote mental health and well-being (NICE, 2012). Coaching offers an effective intervention which can help individuals both manage work demands in the short term and also develop new coping mechanisms which help over the long term.

What is stress?

The topic of stress has been discussed extensively. There is considerable debate on how to define it, and depending on the definition there are implications for research as well as for the design of interventions to manage stress (Cooper *et al*, 2001). The Health and Safety Executive (2004) defined stress as individuals' reaction to excessive pressure or demands, and this develops as individuals worry about their ability to cope. In the 1950s, Selye first described stress as a non-specific response of the body to a demand, and defined it as a general adaptation syndrome (Selye, 1976). He identified a three-stage response: a) an alarm reaction (emergency) with an immediate psycho-physiological response to prepare the body to take action; b) an adaptation response (resistance) where energy is depleted over time; and c) exhaustion.

One way of viewing stress is to consider it from a relational perspective. This approach views stress as a result of transactions between the individual and the environment (Cox *et al*, 2000), and the intensity of the stress response would depend on the individual's perception of their ability to respond to the threat or challenge (Lazarus, 1991; Cooper *et al*, 2001). A work task could be perceived as demanding of resources that the individual might not have. Karasek and Theorell's (1990) demand-control model purports that the main sources of work-related stress are the psychological demands of the job, and job decision latitude. They expanded their model to include social processes as social relationships with co-workers influence productivity, and the level of support experienced influences behaviour as well as the perception of well-being.

How does it affect us?

When demands exceed our resources this challenges the natural tendency of the human body to maintain a stable internal state, and stress is the response to keep it balanced (Sapolsky, 1994). Stress puts strain on psychological and physical functioning, creating an imbalance that affects health (Cartwright and Cooper, 1997), and the effectiveness of the responses to stress will depend on the level of energy available to deal with it. A prolonged period of stress depletes energy, increasing the risk of developing anxiety or depression, in addition to the potential risk of physical injury (if working with machinery, for example). This can lead to ill health and to the need to be absent from work to restore health (Tehrani, 2004).

The depleted energy resources result in symptoms of stress. These are effectively raising the alarm that it is urgent to take action to prevent ill health. Symptoms of stress include those listed in Table 13.1.

If no action is taken, energy reserves are not restored and this can then result in exhaustion. If individuals do not have the opportunity to replenish their resources they may experience burnout – a state of mind accompanied by distress and low motivation that can derive from disillusionment (Maslach and Leiter, 1997; van Dierondonck, Garssen and Visser, 2005). Increased work demands and high expectations can lead to a negative attitude towards work as the individual gradually becomes exhausted (McMillan, O'Driscoll and Burke, 2003). Individuals who are strongly motivated to work, and have a high sense of responsibility, are more vulnerable to burnout. This is likely to happen because people do not pay attention to signs of stress and therefore extend their efforts beyond their capacity, exhausting their energy resources, which then may result in ill health. Pearsall (2002) refers to striving to achieve as toxic success – when despite achieving, somehow individuals experience a sense of lack of meaning, disconnection from others and a sense of disappointment.

How can coaching help to manage stress?

Most of us spend a significant amount of time working and interacting with others, and at times we can face stressful situations that reduce our sense of well-being. The number of self-help books giving guidance on how to improve our lives indicates that there is a growing interest in learning how to experience less dissatisfaction and more enjoyment. Events that are stressful can prevent us from achieving this aim.

TABLE 13.1 Symptoms of stress

Physical	Behavioural	Psychological	Work performance	Other behaviours
Sweating	Withdrawal	Easily upset	Reduced/inconsistent performance	Isolation
Tiredness	Lack of exercise	Lack of concentration	Loss of control	Sensitivity to feedback
Lethargy	Increased/decreased eating	Memory difficulties	Lack of motivation	Nervousness
Altered sleep	Impulsivity	Indecisiveness	Increased number of errors	Difficulty communicating
Restlessness	Out of character behaviour	Increased worry thoughts	Procrastination	Irritability
Tense	Increased alcohol/drugs/smoking	Fluctuating mood	Lack of planning	Aggression
Aches and pains	Unkempt appearance	Loss of meaning	Difficulty delegating	Bullying or harassment
Minor ailments		Feeling alone	Staying longer at work	Increased conflict
Weight gain/loss		Low mood	Absenteeism	
Headaches		Anxiety	Recklessness	
Burnout		Depression		
		Lack of confidence		

We have already seen in Chapter 1 that the aim of coaching is to promote a positive approach to the improvement of performance and well-being. To support this aim, coaching can benefit from Positive Psychology's study of positive emotions, optimal functioning and its focus on the understanding of human strengths (Linley and Harrington, 2005).

In the last fifteen years or so, coaching has become an accepted strategy to manage stress as well as to improve performance. Through coaching, individuals can identify stressors and work towards the development of strategies to manage them and reduce the effects of stress. There is some evidence that those who have engaged in coaching practice have reported a reduction of stress and burnout as a result of the process (Gyllensten and Palmer, 2005).

Research indicates that work is good for us. If we are prevented from working when we would prefer to be doing so, our self-perception and self-confidence can be affected. Understanding positive emotions can help us to develop these and increase our sense of well-being from engaging more authentically in our lives (Seligman, 2002). Having more optimal experiences can boost our sense of mastery and a feeling that we are more in control of our lives. This would lead then to experiencing flow – a state of mind of inner harmony that enhances motivation and a sense of contentment (Csikszentmihalyi, 1992). So, by learning to prevent the experience of stress – and manage symptoms when it occurs – we are likely to be able to remain at work, and also more likely to find meaning and satisfaction in what we do both at work and in our personal life.

Managing stress: a comprehensive approach

A comprehensive approach to the management of stress, both at an organizational and individual level, is essential to maximize the potential of reducing the effects of stressors and encourage a culture where people can work while maintaining their health (Cox *et al*, 2000; Cooper *et al*, 2001).

Employers can support the organization's health by demonstrating that reducing stress is a priority. Making sure that policies that support employees' well-being are in place, and monitoring that they are implemented, is an essential first step. Designing policies that provide clear guidelines on how to deal with stress, bullying and harassment, and return to work can facilitate the reduction of the incidence of sickness absence, turnover, costly litigation and compensation cases (Nice and Thornton, 2004; Tehrani, 2004).

How can coaching help individuals?

Coaching provides individuals with the opportunity to develop to maximize their potential to work effectively. The process allow identify their needs (eg career development), and what they wou achieve to enhance their performance while maintaining their sen: being. Identifying strengths, and using them regularly, can help this aim (Seligman, 2002).

A coaching process for well-being and performe

The effectiveness of coaching depends on designing a process s: individual and adopting a flexible approach to be able to resp(needs. It is recognized that it is essential to develop a trusting and c relationship. It is also critical to assess the motivation of the readiness to engage in the coaching process. Establishing limits tiality and having clearly defined aims for the process are also

The expertise of the coach matters, particularly when dealing with health issues. Some coaches have a psychology degree, although this is not a requirement for coaching. Having training in counselling skills and experience in dealing with health issues and supervision (or consultation with an experienced colleague) are strongly recommended. It is important that coaches are aware of when it is appropriate to refer to health professionals. Monitoring individual professional practice and reflecting on professional issues maintain and promote best practice.

Figure 13.1 describes some key components of a practical approach when coaching for well-being and performance.

1. Identifying areas to work on

The first aim is to identify the coachee's needs. Obtaining information about what is causing concern, and how the individual is feeling in general, allows the coach to identify the sources of stress. The coach needs to consider both work and personal factors, which are summarized in Table 13.2.

A discussion of these areas, and others considered relevant in agreement with coachees, helps to identify objectives and define what can realistically be achieved. This process is a useful intervention as it encourages coachees to reflect, away from external pressures, and allows them to clarify their thinking and feelings about what has been concerning them. Increasing understanding of the issues, and beginning to establish positive action, raises confidence in their ability to self-manage and direct their own learning process.

FIGURE 13.1 Flowchart of coaching for well-being and performance

Identify needs ↗ Establish rapport →	Identify symptoms of stress / Health status ↗	Refer: YES →	Contact HR Occupational Health for specialist treatment	
		Refer: NO →	Identify objectives → / Identify performance issues/ / Development areas / Manage stressors / Work-life balance	Identify approach / Define boundaries →
←				Raise awareness stress symptoms and impact on health, performance →
Prevention →	← Increasing self-efficacy and resilience →	← Communication skills →	← Coping strategies to manage stress symptoms, develop health and increase performance →	← Identify values / Priorities
* Become proactive * Monitor health * Monitor stressors * Regular meetings with line manager	* Identify strengths * Build confidence * Awareness of resources and support	* Managing conflict * Assertiveness * Problem solving * Decision making	* Challenging negative thoughts * Relaxation * Exercise * Nutrition	

TABLE 13.2   Stress factors

About work	About the individual
Job demands (tasks, relationships, skills)	Family/personal responsibilities
Level of job complexity	Interests, expectations (what is
Level of control/discretion	aiming for, would like)
Roles and responsibilities (role clarity,	Perception of self (abilities,
objectives)	experience, strengths)
Relationship with manager/peers/staff	Health (stamina)
Resources	Obstacles to achieving aims
	Communication style (conflict)
	Support
	Motivation
	Meaning of work
	Values and priorities

At this stage it is essential to identify whether it is appropriate to work with the individual in a coaching process or whether they require the support of health professionals.

When should the coach refer?

When the coach becomes aware that the individual's needs are beyond what can be dealt with in a coaching session, the best support they can provide is to make a timely referral for treatment with health professionals. This may be the person's GP and a health professional with clinical expertise. Some indicators of mental health problems are:

- high levels of distress;
- persisting low mood and negative thinking (negative outlook);
- high levels of anxiety;
- low self-esteem (high self-criticism);
- inability to find positive aspects;
- issues discussed are predominantly related to personal life;
- sense of hopelessness;
- sense of helplessness;
- poor physical health.

2. Identifying approach

Before starting to address issues it is essential to discuss with coachees how they prefer to work. In order to engage in the process some individuals prefer a very pragmatic and logical approach applied to the work environment only, whereas others prefer to engage in self-exploration and wish to discuss the wider picture, including aspects of their personal life. Understanding different preferred styles (such as those described by MBTI, learning styles), level of self-awareness and their motivation for learning can provide information to identify which approach to adopt. The choice made will also depend on the individual's interests and the expertise of the coach.

3. Raising awareness of stress symptoms

It is likely that the individual will have been working under considerable pressure before engaging in coaching. As a result he or she may have learnt to overlook signs of stress and might have developed a tolerance to them. Individuals who are very conscientious and take responsibility too seriously are likely to be most at risk. Some may increase the time they spend at work as a means to manage the increasing demands. The more senior the position (although not exclusively) the more likely that they might display this pattern, and feelings such as increased irritability can lead to conflict. The ability to manage conflict tends to be reduced owing to the lack of energy and increased tension, which affects their ability to use their interpersonal skills effectively. Senior managers in particular, who have a responsibility for others, require their strength to make critical decisions (McMillan *et al*, 2003). Therefore, helping them to identify the symptoms, and giving them information on how they can cope more effectively, is a positive intervention in itself.

Coaches can use a number of strategies to help their coachees develop awareness of the impact of stress. An initial interview where attention is directed to how the individual is functioning can trigger awareness and further exploration. Sometimes individuals express that stress is good for them; in this case it is important to explain the difference between pressure and stress. We all need an optimum level of pressure to summon our internal resources to keep us motivated and the stamina to function well. However, when we are effectively demanding that our bodies function without the resources to cope with the demand, we develop symptoms of stress. It is interesting to observe reactions when a similarity is drawn to the care we take of our car. When the flashing red light on the dashboard indicates that the car is running low on petrol, even if we are late for a very important and critical meeting, we are unlikely to say, 'I will continue to drive and I will fill up after the meeting.' We know we have to stop and go to a petrol station because the car will not go anywhere once it runs out of petrol. Symptoms of stress are like the red light warning us that we are running out of energy. We should do the same, stop and take time to restore energy so that we take good care of ourselves.

The Myers–Briggs Type Indicator (MBTI) is a very useful tool to help individuals identify the areas that may be more demanding of their energy. We can make the most of our resources when we can work in our preferred style; however, when working in our non-preferred style we can experience more strain. Coachees generally express relief when they identify that the symptoms of stress may be due to working in a different style rather than necessarily an indication of a lack of ability. The areas of work that they find most difficult and demanding tend to be those tasks that require they use the opposite dimension from their preferred style. Quenk (1993) paid attention to the dynamics of types and suggested that job burnout symptoms could be the result of overuse of a particular dimension. Identifying strengths and areas that could be developed would help coachees increase their ability to manage tasks.

An effective technique to raise awareness is to use the initial illustration of signing as we normally do, and then with the opposite hand. For example, those who normally write with their right hand after the exercise tend to apologize for not writing well with their left hand (the same vice versa). When asking them 'how long have you been writing with your right (left) hand?' they are likely to say 'many years, or all my life'. Then asking 'and how long have you been writing with your left (right) hand?', a common response is 'rarely, never' ... and a smile! This illustration helps to identify their expectations to perform well despite the lack of practice. They can be encouraged to keep the illustration in mind so that when they face a difficult task, or when they perceive they are not doing things as well as they would like, it is likely to be a task in which they are writing with their left (or right) hand! This tends to reduce the pressure they put themselves under, and encourages a positive attitude towards learning new ways to increase their competence in working with the opposite of their preferred style. For example, individuals who have a preference for intuition may find it difficult to present specific details; or a manager whose preferred style is introversion may find managing meetings very draining. Both can benefit from information about how they can develop strategies to manage work that demands more of other dimensions.

Coaches can draw attention to the need to complement the preferred style with developing the opposite dimensions. Some useful strategies are to take time and pace energy, and time to reflect on experiences, so that coachees can practise skills and develop confidence in their abilities. Adapting expectations and applying strategies can reduce the pressure individuals experience when performing tasks that are more demanding. By building a sense of self-efficacy – increasing our belief in our ability to perform tasks – we can enhance our self-confidence (Bandura, 1997).

4. Identifying priorities

When stressed, there is a tendency to pay more attention to symptoms and to what is going wrong, and as a result we can easily lose perspective. It is difficult to manage time when we are not clear about what is important and meaningful. In order to prioritize we first need to identify what is of value to us. Helping coachees to identify their priorities can allow them to channel their energy and direct their efforts to achieve their aims.

5. Communication style: managing conflict

We spend a significant amount of our time communicating with others, and even with the best of intentions at times we end up having difficult conversations. According to Tannen (1998), different interpretations of words and the different styles can lead to friction. Interpersonal relationships can produce great satisfaction and a sense of belonging. However, when arguments occur and differences cannot be reconciled, tensions prevail. Developing strategies to establish cooperation to achieve resolution can reduce tensions and increase self-confidence.

Difficulties in relationships at work can emerge for a variety of reasons – disagreement on how to approach a task, a perception of not being liked or not being treated with respect. These difficulties can be managed by exploring communication style and attitude towards conflict. Dealing with difficult situations, such as a negative relationship with the line manager, for example, can be very stressful and can seriously affect individuals' ability to cope at work. The Thomas and Kilmann (2002) conflict questionnaire can be a useful tool to explore attitudes and approach to conflict. Again, the MBTI is a useful tool that can facilitate raising awareness of how we can manage conflict more constructively (Killen and Murphy, 2003).

Effective communications involve self-expression and listening. Communication skills can be strengthened by following a few steps: reflecting on the message to be communicated, expressing thoughts and feelings clearly, being direct and honest, addressing the issue not the individual,

asking questions to check understanding of what the other said, and adopting an open attitude with the aim of creating understanding.

6. Developing coping strategies

The literature on counselling and clinical psychology provides information on various coping strategies that are effective in helping individuals restore their mental health. Using a solution-focused approach, where emphasis is on paying attention to the present, focusing on developing strengths and enhancing the positive can provide tools to help individuals maximize their resources (O'Hanlon and Weiner-Davis, 1989). In order to help coachees develop resilience to be able to cope with stressors it is useful to draw attention to the mind–body connection. Integrating physical, mental and emotional dimensions can increase the potential to restore a sense of wellness. It has been suggested that it is also important to address the spiritual dimension as identifying what is of meaning to individuals will have an impact on their lives (van Dierendonck *et al*, 2005).

Challenging negative thinking

It is not the event that distresses us but how we perceive the situation. A negative perception can be distorted or magnified out of proportion, resulting in considerable distress. A cognitive behavioural approach focuses on tackling the negative thinking that prevents us from being able to use our creativity to find solutions (Beck, 1979). These negative thoughts erode self-confidence and the belief in the capacity to manage complex and stressful situations. Meichenbaum (1977) developed a stress inoculation programme and used cognitive restructuring to help people manage stress. The aim is to help individuals modify their internal self-dialogue to build up positive thoughts. This process guides individuals to pay attention to the thoughts that run through their mind when dealing with stressful situations. Then, they are encouraged to challenge these thoughts and replace them with more realistic and constructive ones.

The approach used to deal with the situation will depend on how the situation is perceived, and what meaning it is given (threat or challenge). A problem-focused approach is where individuals make attempts to deal with the event, and an emotion-focused approach is when individuals try to deal with the emotional distress experienced as a result of the difficulties being faced (Lazarus, 1991). When using a problem-focused approach the first step is to examine the situation to understand what is happening exactly. Here the aim is to clarify whether the event presents a threat or a challenge, and questions such as 'What is the difficulty?', 'What information do I need?', 'Do I need to respond now?', 'What would I like as an outcome?', 'Who else is affected?', 'Who could provide support?' can help to explore and understand the situation better.

In order to find creative solutions it is essential to allow the imagination to freely explore ideas. Maintaining the mind alert and being curious, looking for what is new or unusual, can help free the mind from assumptions or negative thoughts. Asking oneself questions such as 'What would be different if this was not a problem?', 'What would be the ideal situation?', 'What would happen if I did the opposite of what I normally do?' can help to identify options. Other techniques such as mind mapping (Buzan, 1994) and lateral thinking (de Bono, 1994) can help to develop our capacity for generating creative solutions. Next, identify the options available, choose the best one, take action and then observe what happens, and learn from what works and what does not. This process of evaluation provides information to modify actions so that the outcome can be improved.

Developing resilience

Why do people react differently to stressors? The study of resiliency – the ability to bounce back from setbacks – suggests that those who cope with stress without developing ill health are flexible and have a positive attitude. Siebert (2005) says that people who are resilient accept life's setbacks, allowing themselves to experience loss, grief and distress because they see it as a temporary situation. They do not develop a victim response. Individuals who have a high level of internal control can cope more effectively, whereas those who blame others or feel victimized tend to score high in external control and are likely to believe that they cannot make a difference to their situation. Those who are resilient expect to be able to recover after a setback and consciously decide to survive; by believing in their capacity to deal with the situation they reinforce their self-motivation and this allows them to thrive.

Resiliency can be increased by developing self-awareness. Individuals who are resilient ask themselves 'What can I learn from this?', 'What would I do different next time?' Imagining an effective outcome helps to prepare for the next time. They do not undermine themselves with self-criticism and defeating thoughts that only reduce self-confidence and create a self-fulfilling prophecy. Maintaining a curious and playful spirit increases resiliency because of the ongoing questions we may create, and these allow us to keep learning from our experiences.

Healthy eating and exercise

A prolonged period of stress will deplete our energy and will reduce the effectiveness of our immune system to protect us, increasing the risk of developing an illness (Sapolsky, 1994). Not only are we more likely to become ill, but we are also less likely to be effective in what we do. In order to function properly our nervous system and muscles get energy from glucose as well as oxygen in our blood. We increase the use of energy when we engage in mental activity, so if our energy is low our body is less efficient and our ability to function as well as we would like is reduced (Dienstbier, 1989). Health professionals will encourage healthy eating to restore energy and maintain good health. Eating well and taking exercise stimulate the brain and promote a positive attitude, increasing our potential to live and age well (Weil, 2005).

Studies on the effects of exercise show it promotes psychological well-being (Hayes, 1986). Exercise has a number of positive effects, such as helping to channel energy to release negative energy (aggression), and also it can cultivate self-esteem and self-efficacy. For example, when engaging in exercise we can derive a sense of satisfaction because we know that we are doing something that is good for us. Another benefit is that exercise helps to reduce muscle tension and lifts our mood. As the body releases tension, in addition to deriving a good feeling, it can also help to restore sleep as the mind and body are not overloaded as a result of stress (Dienstbier, 1989).

Exercise should be enjoyable so that we can maintain our efforts and make it a regular activity. By engaging in exercise – although not in excess – we can increase our sense of well-being and our resilience.

Relaxation

Coachees are encouraged to engage in activities that reduce tension. Currently, there is greater awareness of the importance of calming our bodies through breathing exercises, as when using mindfulness techniques (Kabat-Zinn, 2005). Using these techniques on a regular basis helps to regulate breathing and promote muscle relaxation to dissipate tension, restoring a sense of calm.

How can stress be prevented?

Organizations can be proactive and increase their efforts to provide their employees with a healthy work environment. Healthy employees have a better chance to develop their skills and abilities to increase their effectiveness at work. Acknowledging and actively working to manage stress can help to begin to dispel the stigma attached to mental health and turn it into an issue that is dealt with constructively. Raising awareness of stress and how to cope with it proactively is the first step. Through stress management, training information about the symptoms of stress and coping strategies can be shared with all employees. This approach can enhance the potential to change the organizational culture to one where maintaining health is perceived as a priority. Increased information and coping strategies can encourage individuals to be proactive and seek solutions before their health is compromised.

Individuals who have experienced stress for a long time are likely to experience health problems and may need time off work to rehabilitate. It is important then to recommend that they seek professional support. The first port of call is their GP who could then refer them for psychological treatment, although waiting lists may be long. Alternatively, they could benefit from a private referral for psychological treatment. Some employers do offer medical advice through Occupational Health and psychological support through their Employee Assistance Programmes, or have access to independent psychological treatment. The use of a case management approach, where cooperation is established between various professionals, can be an effective way to support individuals to restore their health.

When there is concern about an individual's health due to stress then the case manager can liaise with Occupational Health, HR and the line manager to coordinate the support to help the individual. Early intervention can prevent the development of chronic illness and the likely loss of confidence in the ability to return to work. If individuals are off work due to mental health issues they can be supported by providing a facilitated return to work process (Tehrani, 2004; Peña Bizama, 2010).

References

American Psychological Association website, http://www.apa.org/, retrieved on 26 January 2006

Bandura, A (1997) *Self-Efficacy: The exercise of control*, Freeman and Company, New York

Beck, A T (1979) *Cognitive Therapy of Depression*, Guilford Press, New York

Buzan, T (1994) *The Mind Map Book: How to use radiant thinking to utilize your brain's untapped potential*, EP Dutton, New York

Cartwright, S and Cooper, C (1997) *Managing Workplace Stress*, Sage, London

Chartered Institute of Personnel and Development (CIPD) (2004) *Employee Absence 2004: A survey of management policy and practice*, CIPD, London

CIPD (2008) *Smart Working: The impact of work organisation and job design*, CIPD, London

Cooper, C L, Dewe, P J and O'Driscoll, M P (2001) *Organizational Stress: A review and critique of theory, research and applications*, Sage, London

Cox, T, Griffiths, A and Rial-Gonzalez, E (2000) *Research on Work-related Stress*, European Agency for Safety and Health at Work

Csikszentmihalyi, M (1992) *Flow: The psychology of happiness*, Rider Books, London

de Bono, E (1994) *Parallel Thinking, from Socratic to de Bono Thinking*, Penguin, Harmondsworth

Dienstbier, R A (1989) Arousal and physiological toughness: implications for mental and physical health, *Psychological Review*, **96** (1), pp 84–100

Gyllensten, K and Palmer, S (2005) Can coaching reduce workplace stress? *The Coaching Psychologist*, **1**, pp 15–17

Hayes, D (1986) Body and mind: the effect of exercise, overweight, and physical health on psychological well-being, *Journal of Health and Social Behaviour*, **27** (4), pp 387–400

Health and Safety Executive (2004) Management standards for work-related stress, HSE, London, www.hse.gov.uk/stres/standards/index.htm

Health and Safety Executive (2004/5) *Stress-related and Psychological Disorders*, www.hse.gov.uk/statistics/causdis/stress.htm

Kabat-Zinn, J (2005) *Coming To Our Senses: Healing ourselves and the world through mindfulness*, Hyperion, New York

Karasek, R A and Theorell, T (1990) *Healthy Work: Stress, productivity, and the reconstruction of working life*, Basic Books, New York

Killen, D and Murphy, D (2003) *Introduction to Type and Conflict*, CPP, Inc, Palo Alto, CA

Lazarus, R S (1991) Psychological stress in the workplace, *Journal of Social Behaviour and Personality*, **6**, pp 1–13

Linley, A and Harrington, S (2005) Positive psychology and coaching psychology: perspectives on integration, *The Coaching Psychologist*, **1**, pp 13–14

Maslach, C and Leiter, M (1997) *The Truth about Burnout: How organisations cause personal stress and what to do about it*, Jossey-Bass, San Francisco

McMillan, L H W, O'Driscoll, M P and Burke, R J (2003) Workaholism: a review of theory, research, and future directions, in *International Review of Industrial and Organizational Psychology*, vol 18, ed Cary L Cooper and Ivan T Robertson, pp 167–89, Wiley, Chichester

Meichenbaum, D H (1977) *Cognitive-Behaviour Modification*, Plenum Press, New York

National Institute for Health and Care Excellence guidelines (2012) *Workplace health*, NICE local government briefings http://publications.nice.org.uk/lgb2

Nice, K and Thornton, P (2004) *Job Retention and Rehabilitation Pilot: Employers' management of long-term sickness absence*, Research Report N.227, Department for Work and Pensions, London

O'Hanlon, B and Weiner-Davis, M (1989) *In Search of Solutions: A new direction in psychotherapy*, W.W. Norton & Company, New York

Pearsall, P (2002) *Toxic Success: How to stop striving and start thriving*, Inner Ocean, Maui (printed in Canada)

Peña Bizama, M A (2010) *An Exploratory Study of the Factors Influencing Individuals' Recovery and Ability to Return to Work After Experiencing Stress, Burnout, Anxiety or Depression*, professional doctoral dissertation

Peterson, C (2005) The epidemic of stress, in *Occupational Health and Safety: International influences and the 'new' epidemics*, ed C Peterson and C Mayhew, Baywood Publishing Co, Amityville, NY (Monash University, Faculty of Medicine, Nursing & Health Sciences, Australia)

Quenk, N L (1993) *Beside Ourselves: Our hidden personality in everyday life*, Davies-Black, Palo Alto, CA

Sapolsky, R M (1994) *Why Zebras Don't Get Ulcers: An updated guide to stress, stress-related diseases, and coping*, WH Freeman and Company, New York

Segerstrom, S C and Miller, G E (2004) Psychological stress and the human immune system: a meta-analytic study of 30 years of inquiry, *Psychological Bulletin*, **104**, pp 601–30

Segerstrom, S and Miller, G (2006) *Stress Affects Immunity in Ways Related to Stress Type and Duration, as Shown by Nearly 300 Studies*, American Psychological Association, press releases, www.apa.org/releases/stress_immune.html

Seligman, M E P (2002) *Authentic Happiness: Using the new positive psychology to realize your potential for lasting fulfillment*, Nicholas Brealey Publishing, London

Selye, H (1976) *Stress in Health and Disease*, Butterworths, London

Siebert, A (2005) *The Resilience Advantage: Master change, thrive under pressure, and bounce back from setbacks*, Berrett-Koehler, San Francisco, CA

Tannen, D (1998) *The Argument Culture: Changing the way we argue and debate*, Virago Press, London

Tehrani, N (2004) *Recovery, Rehabilitation and Retention: Maintaining a productive workforce: a guide*, Chartered Institute of Personnel and Development, London, www.cipd.co.uk/subjects/health/mentalhlth/recrehabretent.htm

Thomas, K W and Kilmann, R H (2002) *Thomas–Kilmann Conflict Mode Instrument*, Xicom, Inc (CPP, Inc, Palo Alto, CA)

van Dierendonck, D, Garssen, B and Visser, A (2005) Burnout prevention through personal growth, *Journal of Stress Management*, **12** (1), pp 62–77

Weil, A (2005) *Healthy Aging: A lifelong guide to your physical and spiritual well-being*, Alfred A. Knopf, New York

Wilson, P (2006) *Stress and Emotions Can Negatively Affect Heart Health*, American Psychological Association, Press Releases (January), www.apahelpcenter.mediaroom.com

Coaching ethics: integrity in the moment of choice

14

ALLARD DE JONG

Why are ethics important in coaching?

As I sit down to write this chapter on ethics, I'm utterly convinced that what we have here is one of the most important and stimulating topics in coaching today. I am not making this statement from the dark recesses of an inflated ego or as a deluded attempt to affirm my self-importance, but rather from the conviction that a) sound ethics are the essence and underpinning of good coaching, and that b) people acting as professional coaches must adhere to the highest standards of responsibility and account-ability to protect the interests of the coachee.

The importance of getting training as a coach before practising the art of coaching should not be underestimated. One can understand that there are those who strongly favour different certification procedures in order to ensure a consistent quality of the coaching profession. But we must place ethics – in the Aristotelian sense of customs and character – above both training and professional accreditation. Why? Because it doesn't matter how well trained you are or how many stripes you have on your shirt, if you're not ethical you can potentially do harm to your coachee. If on the other hand, you act ethically and in accordance with the qualities of your spirit, you will make up for the training and/or certification that are not yet yours.

In contributing this chapter to this book, it is not my intention to convert you to accept my personal points of view on ethics or coaching. Nevertheless, I hope that you will share my passion for ethics and my wish for ethics to become a more conscious part of your coaching practice. There remains considerable debate about meanings and thus over the next few pages we will review several definitions and descriptions, simply to provide us with a common platform for reflection. As coaches I would invite you to question and challenge the ideas you come across in this chapter. As always, we all have something to learn and something to teach – but never is this truer than in the field of ethics.

So then, what is my intention? It is hoped that upon completing this chapter you'll approach the task of ethical decision making as a coach and a person with a deeper understanding of – and respect for – the difficulty and the complexity of the act of determining right from wrong and acting accordingly.

My goal in this chapter is to share my passion by investigating the links that exist between coaching, ethics and modern society at large, as represented by Figure 14.1.

More specifically, this chapter will attempt to provide answers to some of the questions that arise from the diagram:

- What is meant by 'ethics'?
- What is the place of ethics in today's society?
- What is the role of coaching in society and how can coaches (or coaching) be a role model for moving towards a more ethical society?
- What are the main ethical considerations for our profession?

Before we get to these questions, allow me to rapidly clarify some of the terms that we'll use throughout this chapter in order to start this investigation from a common platform of understanding.

FIGURE 14.1   The links between coaching, ethics and modern society

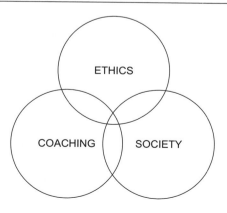

What is meant by ethics?

Let's look, first of all, at the word 'ethics' itself. It's hard to believe the number of ways in which writers in the field have answered this seemingly easy question, 'What is ethics?' Often, ethics is concisely and simply described as the science of morality. Morality here is understood as a collection of relative judgements people make about what is right or wrong, good or bad, in the relations between people or groups of people. Others will define ethics as an intellectual practice that develops our perspectives of right and wrong. Merriam-Webster defines 'ethics' as: 1) the discipline dealing with what is good and bad and with moral duty and obligation and, 2) a set of moral principles or values, a theory or system of moral values, the principles of conduct governing an individual or a group and a guiding philosophy. One thing is for sure: as these definitions indicate, ethics is inseparably connected to the issue of morals or morality. The necessary relationship between ethics and morals is best summarized by reminding ourselves that ethics calls for moral practice. Indeed, the notion of ethics takes on its fullest sense when we translate theories into moral principles that can be used as drivers towards ideal ends.

It should also be noted that principles or values play an important part in all ethical decision making. Values are based upon our belief systems about what is desirable, rather than what is right and wrong. This means that ethics based on value systems is very relative, yet our values invariably come into play as we make ethical decisions. Principles make up our individual code of conduct and allow us to act with integrity. Principles are, therefore, based at least in part upon our values, and they may differ widely from one individual to another.

Last, but not least, this review of definitions would not be complete without taking into account the notion of professionalism. Professionalism is yet another term that is directly related to ethics and to ethical behaviour, given that high personal standards tend to bring about the emergence of both ethical and professional behaviour. Do note, however, that not all unprofessional behaviour is necessarily unethical. For example, while showing up late for a meeting with a coachee could be considered unprofessional, it is not deemed to be unethical.

As far as the rest of this chapter is concerned, ethics will be viewed as the way in which we determine what's right and wrong and being moral in doing the right thing. To be ethical means one is able to differentiate between acts that are good and those that are bad. What one does after that differentiation is made, is what determines whether or not we are moral persons. After all, distinguishing right from wrong is one thing – but to actually do what we believe to be right, and to refrain from doing what we believe to be wrong is quite another.

The foundations of ethical thinking

The meaning of 'ethics' and the definition of moral standards have changed throughout history. In early Greece, *ethos* meant character or customs. In early Latin, *mos* – from which we got our word morals – also referred to customs. The discussion of ethics in Aristotelian Athens referred not just to 'good versus bad', but also to such character traits as courage, justice or temperance. During the Middle Ages, much of ethics was replaced by religious or church-issued dogma and rules. Moral matters were no longer 'customs' or character qualifications but became matters of 'right' and 'wrong'.

Later still, ethics emerged as an intellectual pursuit, a discipline of philosophy. It is useful to quickly review the conclusions of theorists dealing with leading ethical theories as they attempt to define and defend a series of principles that we can use to reflect upon specific ethical actions and choose what we ought to do or what kind of persons we ought to become:

Results-based ethics

Sometimes called 'consequentialism', this theory states that moral goodness or badness is determined by the results or consequences of an act or rule. According to this theory, lying about our coaching experience is morally wrong because of the damage this lie will cause to the coach, the coachee and to an entire profession that depends on honest relationships. One model derived from this theory is called 'utilitarianism'. It was originated by Jeremy Bentham (*An Introduction to the Principles of Morals and Legislation*, 1789) who argued that the morally correct rule was the one that provided the greatest good to the greatest number of people.

Standards-based ethics

Also called the 'deontological' theory, standards-based ethics says we determine if an act or rule is morally right or wrong by investigating whether or not it meets a moral standard. One famous contributor to this theory was the German philosopher Immanuel Kant. He developed a 'universal test' to see if a rule could be a universal standard (*Groundwork of a Metaphysics of*

Morals, 1785). For example, violating client confidentiality is morally wrong because you cannot make it a universal law that everyone can knowingly violate client confidentiality.

Ethical intuitionism

Ethical intuitionism was the dominant moral theory in Britain for much of the 18th, 19th and early 20th centuries, yet it is part of an older family of theories that ascribe to humanity a common moral faculty. Origins include the moral sentiment theories of David Hume (*Of the Original Contract*, 1758). Under this view an act or rule is determined to be right or wrong by appeal to the common intuition of a person. This intuition is sometimes referred to as your 'conscience'. Any coach with a normal conscience will know that it is wrong to promise a client or a coachee something you know you can't deliver.

Virtue ethics

According to this ethical theory, ethics should develop character traits or virtues in a person so he or she will do what is morally right because he or she is a virtuous person. Aristotle was a famous exponent of this view and felt that virtue ethics was the way to attain true happiness.

Ethical principles that guide coaching practice

All codes of ethics and all ethical decision making should be guided by a set of underlying values or principles. In this section we'll quickly review the principles that have guided the fields of medicine, counselling and psychotherapy and how these have influenced ethics in coaching.

Biomedical ethics

The guiding principles of biomedical ethics, as outlined by Beauchamp and Childress (1979), represent a foundational piece in the field of medical ethics. The authors defend the four principles of respect for autonomy, non-malfeasance, beneficence and justice. Not only did these principles become very popular in writings about medical ethics, they also influenced ethics in the coaching field. In coaching decisions, our respect for the autonomy of the coachee would mean that the coachee has the capacity to act intentionally and that the coach's role is to foster that capacity and sense of responsible independence. Non-malfeasance requires that we do not intentionally create a needless harm or injury to the coachee. Beneficence refers to the coach's duty to be of benefit to the coachee, and justice in coaching can be defined as a form of fairness. As we'll see next, the same principles also found their way into the fields of counselling and psychotherapy.

Ethics in counselling and psychotherapy

In the book, *Guide to Ethical Practice in Psychotherapy*, Thompson (1990) proposes a set of underlying tenets or virtues upon which all ethical decision making should be based. Kitchner (1988) describes similar foundational principles. The concepts that these authors put forward are offered to guide us towards a more ethical practice, and an understanding of these authors' work may help us demarcate the role of ethics in our practice of coaching:

- Beneficence is the virtue of helping others and providing services that are in the other individual's best interest; the virtue of doing good; a commitment to promoting the client's well-being.

- Non-malfeasance is the virtue of, and commitment to, not doing harm to the client; ensuring that our actions do not result in harm to anyone.

- Fidelity is the virtue of faithfulness; being true to our commitments and obligations to others. It's about honouring the trust placed in the practitioner, about being trustworthy. An important component of fidelity, veracity, implies we will be truthful and honest in all our endeavours.

- Promoting the autonomy of those one provides services to, is one of psychotherapy's overarching goals. This includes respect for the client's right and ability to be self-governing.

- Justice is the virtue of providing fair and impartial treatment to all clients and the provision of adequate services.

- The virtue of self-interest stresses the importance of adequate and appropriate attention to our own self-care so our competence and judgement do not become impaired. Self-interest, or self-respect, means fostering the practitioner's self-knowledge and that the practitioner appropriately applies all of the above principles to his or her own professional efforts, ie they walk their talk.

As an example, the British Association for Counselling and Psychotherapy's list of ethical principles, which is shared by the large majority – if not all – of practitioners, is clearly based on the principles presented above, namely fidelity, autonomy, beneficence, non-malfeasance, justice and self-respect.

What the principles outlined above teach us is that in general, ethical decisions – in medicine, counselling and psychotherapy – that are strongly supported by one or more of these principles may be regarded as reasonably well founded. As such, they have been used as a platform for the establishment of ethical guidelines in the field of coaching that will be discussed later on in this chapter.

Modern society and 'new ethics'

To what extent are the ethical principles outlined so far actually visible in today's society? What role do ethics play in today's world? It has been said – somewhat provokingly – on more than one occasion that we won't survive the 21st century with 20th-century ethics. There is strong evidence to support this affirmation. Indeed, a quick look at our planet today reveals a global situation that is characterized by the widening of at least three important gaps:

- between the 'haves' and the 'have nots';
- between rhetoric and reality;
- between those that heed the well-being of others and those that ignore it.

These gaps are indicators of eroding ethics. In spite of the loftiest ethical intentions, we can't seem to translate our ideals into action and collectively work towards bridging these gaps in an organized and sustainable manner. The Dalai Lama convincingly argues (2001) that much of today's troubles are due to a fundamental neglect of our inner dimension and that, until we address this underlying neglect, we will not solve our problems. Others such as Blanchard writing from a Christian perspective have echoed this call in his writing on leadership (Blanchard *et al*, 2003). He calls for a reawakening of certain qualities of the human spirit and concludes this idea by pointing out that the common denominator among these qualities is a concern for others' well-being and an ethical restraint through which we 'curb our own harmful impulses and desires'. In essence, and if one agrees with this point of view, what is required is a form of inner bonding, if you wish, with our spirit.

At the same time, modern society is characterized by high levels of uncertainty regarding questions of right and wrong and people are unsure as to who or what to turn to for answers and direction. Zohar and Marshall (1999) have argued that 'unlike IQ, which orients itself with respect to rules, and EQ, which is guided by the situation in which it finds itself SQ [spiritual intelligence] lights our way to what mystics have called the "eye of the heart".' As such, they too recommend reconnecting with our source, our ground of being, our spirit, in order to recapture a feeling of certainty, guidance and ultimately ethics.

One way to respond to this erosion of ethics in modern society may well be to turn to within ourselves, rather than established or emerging external sources. For practical purposes, we could refer to this emerging alternative as 'new ethics'.

What exactly is meant by 'new ethics'? New ethics takes on the view that our ethical viewpoints, decisions and actions are determined to be right or wrong by using our spiritual intelligence to access and bond with our human 'beingness', a shared inner source of knowing. New ethics holds that all forms of externally imposed ethics are, in the long run, unsustainable due to lack of ownership and subjective morality – and ultimately a degrading form of alienation and estrangement of people from themselves. New ethics trusts people to know for themselves how to act with integrity and treat other people well. As such, new ethics suggest that people are able to develop their own 'vows' in a manner that is harmonious with others and in due course positive for mankind as a whole. Though most probably not an exact definition quite yet, I will refer to this description throughout the remainder of this chapter.

There exists a huge role for coaching in bringing about ethical practice in society. Why? Because a new ethics-based society cannot be implemented by an outside authority. People will need to be encouraged to develop their spiritual qualities from within, to reconnect with their source of inner wisdom. This is a central way in which ethics can become a conscious, attractive and creative part of our daily lives as coaches and as citizens. While sharing the opinion of those that claim that coaching is a powerful force for making the world 'a better place', one might underline that the responsibility lies with 'coaching' and not 'coaches'. What is meant by this is that as coaches, we are change agents, stimulating and supporting change at the individual level. One of the motives that attracts many of us to this work is the possibility of doing good and making the world a better and more ethical place. This thrusts upon us the responsibility of placing integrity at the centre of our work. The word integrity comes from the Latin *integritas*, meaning integer or entire, and has connotations of incorruptibility, soundness, completeness, honesty, sincerity, fairness and straightforwardness of conduct.

How can we, as coaches and role models for tomorrow's society, continue to develop our ethics? What is required of us to advance in our quest to resolve the specific ethical questions that arise in our work as coaching professionals? We know from observing the world around us that it does not always follow that a person who distinguishes between right and wrong automatically does the right thing, and refrains from doing wrong; there is work to be done. Furthering the cause of ethics in ourselves, our work and our world will only be achieved through the informed and conscientious practice of new ethics and by observing specific codes to guide our decisions.

So in answer to the question, 'Can we actually be ethical?', one reply could be that we indeed have the necessary capacity, knowledge and tools to be so and that the power of choosing right and wrong, good and evil, is within the reach of all. But the question begs another: 'Can we be moral?' This is a lot more difficult to answer than the previous one. In spite of all the books, codes and guidelines we have been handed over the years, the answer remains elusive to say the least. By definition, and in truth, the only way to be moral is by putting the qualities of our spirit, of our heart, into action.

What better way to tap into ourselves and into the self of others than coaching? New ethics and coaching are intrinsically linked. Action taken from our deepest sense of self, the core of what makes us human beings, can be stimulated by stirring our own and our clients' connection with what Moore (2001) called our 'original self'.

New ethics, in coaching and in life, must come from that place of personal and intrinsic power – and again, isn't that what coaching is all about? At the end of the day, only you can ensure your integrity in your moments of choice.

Ethical standards for coaching

To help us walk a path of ethical practice, organizations such as the Association for Coaching in the UK offers, in one way or another, a code of ethics and good practice. The code sets out the essential elements of sound ethical practice and are called into life to ensure that members operate in accordance with ethical, competent and effective guidelines. The code of conduct can indeed be very useful, as coaches can expect to run into a series of ethical questions arising from such issues as maintaining confidentiality and objectivity, managing conflicts of interest, being clear about what they can or cannot deliver, or correctly representing the coaching process to existing and potential clients. Yet any code of conduct should be seen as a collective position and a transitory phase as we move towards the development of new ethics.

What about situations that are not specified in the current standards? No ethical code can provide coaches with guidance on how to act in all situations or how best to respond to all possible ethical dilemmas. Merely following these guidelines, therefore, will not be sufficient for responding to the myriad of ethical dilemmas by which coaches are regularly confronted. So it bears repeating that what is needed is a deeper connection to one's own sense of new ethics.

Ethical themes and scenarios from coaching

So far we have made the case for ethics to be used by coaches to bring about ethical change. However, what about the responsibility that coaches have in their relationships with their coachees? Maybe this issue is best explored by imagining a series of not so improbable scenarios and seeing how some of the main guidelines set forth by the Association for Coaching's code of ethics and good practice apply.

Scenario 1

Suppose that a romantic attraction develops between your coachee and yourself. Having reviewed the Association for Coaching's code, you know that coaches must act in a manner that does not bring the profession of coaching into disrepute and that coaches are required to respect the coachee's right to terminate coaching at any point during the coaching process. Coaches need to be aware of this danger, one that results in the largest number of complaints to the BACP (British Association for Counselling and Psychotherapy). Therefore, as soon as you become aware of the budding reciprocal passion, you could suggest to your coachee that the two of you come to a mutual agreement to terminate the formal coaching relationship and that you set a period aside, maybe four to eight weeks, as a cooling-off period. This allows space and time between the old professional coaching relationship and a new personal relationship. It also recognizes that attraction may be generated from transference within the intimate space of the coaching relationship, and that this interest may wane when the coaching relationship is terminated.

Scenario 2

As a seasoned executive coach, you are approached by a former coachee who wants to find a romantic partner and wants to hire you with that objective in mind. You explain that, as someone specializing in business issues, you are not an expert in that area. After exploring the coachee's objectives in some more depth, you suggest that he might want to consider a dating service. He informs you that he has been down that road but to no avail and that he just knows that working with you is the right thing for him to do at this time. Coaches are required to recognize both personal and professional limitations. As per the code of ethics, you would indeed want to assess whether or not your experience is appropriate to meet the coachee's requirements. Should this not be the case, the coachee should be referred to other appropriate services, such as more experienced coaches, counsellors, psychotherapists or other specialist services.

Scenario 3

Imagine a coachee who complains of constant tiredness, wants to stay in bed, is irritable, cannot sleep and expresses feelings of hopelessness about his condition, thinking he will never get better. The coachee denies being depressed and instead simply expresses frustration at a host of circumstantial factors. As a coach, you are required to be sensitive to the possibility that some coachees will require more psychological support than most coaches are trained to offer. In these cases, referral should be made to an appropriate source of care. This might be the person's GP, a counsellor or coaching psychologist.

Scenario 4

A professional acquaintance has just referred a close friend to you. She is very enthusiastic about beginning the coaching straight away, based on your acquaintance's flattering introduction. Even though she does not have a clear idea of what coaching really is, she tells you money is not an issue and that it won't be necessary to prepare a coaching contract. Coaches are responsible for ensuring that coachees are fully informed of the coaching contract, terms and conditions, prior to or at the initial session. These matters include confidentiality and the cost and frequency of sessions. It is your responsibility to generate a frank discussion around what this potential coachee may or may not expect and respond to her requests for information about the methods, techniques and ways in which the coaching process will be conducted. This should be done both prior to contract agreement and during the full term of the contract.

Scenario 5

Suppose that during a coaching session a coachee discloses a desire to do himself harm. He has just lost his job, feels ashamed about the situation and can see no way forward. All information obtained in the course of coaching relationship is confidential, but on occasions there can be a compelling reason for this rule to be broken. The coach should include this as part of the contracting discussion. Such occasions would be where there is genuine concern that coachees would do harm to themselves or others, or where a serious criminal offence has been committed, and a failure to disclose would itself be a criminal offence.

Scenario 6

You are working with a coachee and it's just not going well; both she and you are frustrated with the pace and the lack of results. Rather than simply terminating the coaching by telling the coachee she is not coachable, you might want to look into the value of the coaching you provide and the dynamic of the relationship between you. Coaches are required to monitor the quality of their work and to seek feedback, for example at the end of each session. If things are not working in a relationship, this may be due to the coach and his or her ability to adapt, but may also be a product of the relationship. Talk frankly about this and identify a suitable alternative, such as a referral for the coachee.

References

Beauchamp and Childress (1979) *Principles of Biomedical Ethics*, Oxford University Press, Oxford

Blanchard, K, Hodges, P, Ross, L and Willis, A (2003) *Lead like Jesus: Beginning the journey*, Thomas Nelson Books, Nashville, TN

Dalai Lama, His Holiness (2001) *Ancient Wisdom, Modern World: Ethics for the new millennium*, Abacus, London

Kitchner, J (1988) Dual role relationships: what makes them so problematic?, *Journal of Counselling and Development*, **67**, pp 222–26

Moore, T (2001) *Original Self: Living with paradox and originality*, Harper Perennial, London

Thompson, A (1990) *Guide to Ethical Practice in Psychotherapy*, Wiley, New York

Zohar, D and Marshall, I (1999) *Spiritual Intelligence: The ultimate intelligence*, Bloomsbury, London

Coaching supervision

15

PETER HAWKINS

> *Learning to see anything truly cannot occur without a significant deepening of self-knowledge.* **CHRISTIE 2013: 146**

What is coaching supervision?

In the exponential growth and development of coaching in the last 35 years (Hawkins, 2014c) we often forget that coaching is not done by a coach. Coaching is always a collaborative, co-creative and triangulated endeavour that involves at a minimum a coachee, a coach and a challenge or challenges from life. Each part of the triangle has its role to play and each is necessarily part of the systemic process. As part of the relational system of coaching, the coach inevitably will be unable to see clearly the system he or she is part of. Coaching supervision provides a parallel reflecting system where the coach is enabled by the coach supervisor to reflect on the coaching relational system. Coaching supervision is not done by the supervisor. It too is always a collaborative, co-creative and triangulated process involving a coach, their coaching work and the challenges it inevitably presents and the supervisor. This new relational system of coaching supervision therefore is always part of a series of nested systems: the world of the client; the coaching relational system; the supervisory system; and the wider environmental context in which the work takes place. The last of these involves the organizations and communities in which the client, the coach and the supervisor work; the stakeholders of these organizations and communities, the wider social, political, economic and cultural contexts and the environmental ecology on which all human beings are entirely dependent.

Supervision, like coaching, flows around the Kolb learning cycle (Hawkins and Smith, 2013). It starts with reflection on the work and the challenges that this is presenting. From the reflection it develops new awareness, understanding and thinking. These are then applied to creating new ways of being and fast-forward rehearsals of new strategies of action. This then leads to new action post the coaching or supervision meeting, which can be reflected on at the next meeting. Thus the learning continues to cycle.

This systemic understanding has led me to define coach supervision as:

> the process by which a coach with the help of a supervisor, can attend to understanding better both the client system and themselves as part of the client-coach system, and by so doing transform their work and develop their craft. Supervision should also be a source of organisational Learning. (Hawkins and Smith, 2006, 2013)

Coaching supervision has three elements:

1 Coaching the coach on his or her coaching.

2 Mentoring the coach on his or her development in the profession.

3 Providing an external perspective to ensure quality of practice.

This three-function model parallels the three functions that Kadushin (1992) put forward for social work supervision and Proctor (1997) espoused for counselling supervision. Kadushin talked of the 'managerial, educative and supportive' aspects of supervision and Proctor of supervision being 'normative, formative and restorative'.

Having worked with these two models for many years we have found both to be rather confined to their own field, Kadushin in social work and Proctor in counselling, and so have developed our own model that defines the three main functions as developmental, resourcing and qualitative (see Table 15.1). Kadushin focuses on the role of the supervisor, Proctor on the supervisee benefit, and our new distinctions on the process that both supervisor and supervisee are engaged in.

In Hawkins and Shohet (1989, 2000, 2006, 2012) we outlined a number of the primary foci of supervision and we have now linked these to the new categories (see Figure 15.1).

I believe there is a fourth key function for coaching supervision and that is providing a source of organizational learning. Ways of harvesting the organizational learning from multiple coaching engagements within an organization while preserving appropriate personal confidentiality are described in Hawkins, 2012.

TABLE 15.1   Three main functions of supervision

Hawkins and Smith, 2006, 2013	Proctor, 1997	Kadushin, 1997
Developmental	Formative	Educational
Resourcing	Restorative	Supportive
Qualitative	Normative	Managerial

FIGURE 15.1   Primary foci of supervision

Main categories of focus	Function Category
To provide a regular space for the supervisees to reflect upon the *content and process* of their work	Developmental
To develop understanding and skills within the work	Developmental
To receive information and another perspective concerning one's work	Developmental/resourcing
To receive both content and process feedback	Developmental/resourcing supportive
To be validated and supported both as a person and as a worker	Resourcing
To ensure that as a person and as a worker one is not left to carry, unnecessarily, difficulties, problems and projections alone	Resourcing
To have space to explore and express personal distress, restimulation, transference or counter-transference that may be brought up by the work	Qualitative/resourcing
To plan and utilize their *personal and professional* resources better	Qualitative/resourcing
To be proactive rather than reactive	Qualitative/resourcing
To ensure quality of work	Qualitative

Role and purpose of supervision

Supervision is a key element in both the training process for coaches and lifetime continuing professional development (CPD). In training it is the process of rigorous supervision that helps the trainee link the theory and skills they learn on courses to the real-time experience of working live with coachees. In workshops you can learn models and develop competencies, but these do not by themselves produce an excellent coach. Supervision provides the reflective container for the trainee to turn his or her competencies into capabilities and to develop his or her personal and coaching capacities.

Why is coaching supervision so widely promoted and yet so little practised?

At the core of CPD is continual *personal* development, where our own development is woven through every aspect of our practice, where every coachee is a teacher, every piece of feedback an opportunity for new learning, and we have practices that support the balanced cycle of action, reflection, new understanding and new practice. In Hawkins and Smith (2006, 2013) we have shown why we believe that having supervision is a fundamental aspect of continuing personal and professional development for coaches, mentors and consultants, providing a protected and disciplined space in which coaches can reflect on particular coachee situations and relationships, the reactivity and patterns they invoke for them and by transforming these live in supervision, can profoundly benefit the coachee.

O'Neill (2000) does not use the term 'supervision', but talks of the importance of coaching for the coach. She writes:

> Everyone needs help to stay on track in the powerful interactional fields of organizations ... One of the best ways that coaches can stay effective in their role is to receive coaching themselves ... I used to think that my need for a coach would diminish once I had worked with numerous clients and had many years under my belt. Twenty years and over a hundred clients later, my effectiveness has dramatically increased, but my desire to use a coach myself has remained high. I no longer see using a coach as a sign of incompetence but as a smart investment.

For too long the themes of continuing development and supervision of coaches and mentors has been neglected. Flaherty (1999), writing in the United States about the area of coaches' continuing development, says:

> I haven't found this aspect of coaching in any other text on the topic, but self-development seems to be a self-evident component of coaching ... Psychiatrists, physicians, teachers and lawyers all confer with peers and mentors in difficult cases. Coaches are, it seems to me, no exception to this practice.

Downey (2003), writing in the UK, says: 'Very few coaches have any supervision, but it is a vital ingredient in effective coaching.'

So what is the lack of practice due to? In carrying out research into supervision for CIPD in the UK, we explored the reasons for the lack of development of coaching supervision (Hawkins and Schwenk, 2006). In interviews and focus groups with experienced coaches we were given a number of different explanations:

- lack of clarity about what supervision involves;

- lack of well-trained supervisors;

- lack of commitment to personal development as it makes us *3.4* vulnerable;

- lack of discipline among coaches;

- addiction to being in the role of the person enabling others, rather than receiving enablement.

Since 2006 there has been a rapid growth in coaching supervision, particularly in the UK and Europe where it has been endorsed by most of the major professional coaching bodies and where there has been a number of new significant publications (Bachkirova, Jackson, and Clutterbuck, 2011; Passmore, 2011; de Hahn, 2012; Hawkins and Smith, 2013).

In 2014 Eve Turner and I (Turner and Hawkins, 2015) carried out some new research, primarily on multi-stakeholder contracting in coaching; however, we used the opportunity to update the 2006 research on coach supervision. The research had responses from 717 coaches from many different parts of the world; 76 organizations that employed coaches and 61 clients. Out of 428 coaches who responded to the questions on supervision, 72 said they never have supervision. Broken down by geographic region it suggests that the highest numbers without supervision are in the United States and Canada and Asia and the lowest numbers are in the UK, Africa and Latin America (though on a small response rate in the case of the latter two):

- UK 18/234 (18 out of 234 coaches who replied to this question, 7.69%)

- Europe 18/93 (19.35%)

- Africa 1/10 (10%)

- Asia 6/17 (35.29%)

- Australia/New Zealand 6/22 (27.27%)

- Latin America 1/9 (11.11%)

- United States and Canada 22/42 (52.38%).

The key reasons coaches stated for not having supervision were that they did their own reflective practice, or are part of peer networks. Cost was not a key factor, cited by 9 coaches (9.1 per cent) out of 99 who said they didn't have supervision.

Where coaches did have supervision the top two reasons given were positive ones:

It is part of my personal commitment to good practice	92.6%
It contributes to my CPD	51.6%
It is a requirement of a professional body of which I am a member	33.9%
It is a requirement for accreditation by a professional body	26.5%
It is a requirement of organizations using me as an external coach	19.2%
It is a requirement of organizations using me as an internal coach	14.7%

The research showed that increasingly coach supervision is being adopted as a key aspect of best practice in coaching, particularly in the UK and Europe, but less so in North America.

Similarities and differences to counselling and psychotherapy supervision

Whether we call the process supervision, or coaching on one's coaching, the need to have another attend to one's practice is increasingly being recognized as essential. There is much each of the helping professions can learn from each other, but it is also important to recognize the difference between the fundamental work of each professional group, and hence the dangers of over-applying the theories and models of one group to the work of another. One of the dangers of a coach going for supervision to a counsellor or counselling psychologist is that the supervisor's professional focus will tend towards understanding the psychology of the coachee. Depending on their orientation the supervisor might also focus on the relationship of coach and coachee and may have a tendency to focus more on pathology than on health! The biggest danger is when a fundamental orientation that is more interested in individuals than organizations tips over into an unrecognized tendency to see individuals as victims of 'bad' or 'unfeeling' organizations. At worst this can create a classic drama triangle of 'organization as persecutor; coachee as victim and coach as rescuer'.

The stages in a supervision session

The earliest model I developed for supervision in the 1980s was to apply my five-stage coaching model CLEAR (Contract, Listen, Explore, Action, Review) to the stages of supervision.

In this model the supervisor starts by *contracting* with the supervisee on both the boundaries and focus of the work. Then the supervisor *listens* to the issues that the coach wishes to bring, listening not only to the content, but also to the feelings and the ways of framing the story that the coach is using. Before moving on, it is important that the supervisor lets the coach know that he or she has not only heard the story, but has got what it feels like to be in the coach's situation. Only then is it useful to move on to the next stage to *explore* with the coach what is happening in the dynamics of both the coaching relationship and the live supervisory relationship, before facilitating the coach to explore new *action*. Finally, *review* the process and what has been agreed about next steps. In this short chapter I will just write about the contracting phase, which is the foundation for all that follows.

Contracting for supervision

All forms of supervision relationship need to begin with a clear contract, which is created and formed by both parties, and also reflects the expectations of the organizations and professions involved.

In Hawkins and Smith (2013) we propose that in contracting there are five key areas that should be covered:

1 practicalities;

2 boundaries;

3 working alliance;

4 the session format;

5 the organizational and professional context.

1. Practicalities

In forming the contract it is necessary to be clear about the practical arrangements such as the times, frequency, place, what might be allowed to interrupt or postpone the session, and any payment that is involved.

2. Boundaries

A boundary that often worries both coachees and new coaches is the one between coaching and counselling or therapy.

The basic boundary in this area is that coaching should always start from exploring issues from work and should end with looking at where the coachee goes next with the work that has been explored. Personal material should only come into the session if it is directly affecting, or being affected by, the work discussed, or if it is affecting the coaching or supervision relationships. If such an exploration uncovered more material than could be appropriately dealt with in the supervision, the supervisor may suggest that the worker might want to get counselling or other forms of support in exploring these personal issues.

A supervision contract should also include clear boundaries concerning confidentiality. Confidentiality is an old chestnut that is of concern to many new coaches and new supervisors. So many supervisors fall into the trap of saying or implying to the supervisee that everything that is shared in the supervision is confidential, only to find that some unexpected situation arises where it is necessary to share material from the supervision beyond the boundaries of the session.

Thus, in contracting the appropriate confidentiality boundary for any form of supervision, it is inappropriate either to say everything is confidential that is shared here, or to say nothing here is confidential. The supervisor should instead be clear what sort of information either would need to take over the boundary of the relationship, in what circumstances, how he or she would do this, and to whom he or she would take the information. Clearly every possible situation cannot be anticipated, but such a general exploration can diminish the possibility of what may be experienced as sudden betrayal.

We also give our supervisees the undertaking that we will treat everything they share with us in a professional manner and not gossip about their situation.

3. Working alliance

Forming the working alliance starts from sharing mutual expectations: what style of coaching the supervisee most wants, and on which of the possible foci do they wish the supervision to concentrate. The supervisor also needs to state clearly what his or her preferred mode of supervision is, and any expectations he or she has of the supervisee. We find it useful at the contracting phase to not only share conscious expectations but also hopes and fears. It can be useful to complete sentences such as: 'My image of successful supervision is ...'; 'What I fear happening in supervision is ...'.

A good working alliance is not built on a list of agreements or rules, but on growing trust, respect and goodwill between both parties. The contract provides a holding frame in which the relationship can develop, and any lapses in fulfilling the contract need to be seen as opportunities for reflection, learning and relationship building, not judgement and defence.

4. The session format

As well as sharing hopes, fears and expectations, it is useful to ground the discussions in an exploration of what a typical session format might be like. Will all the time be spent on one situation? Does the supervisor expect the supervisee to bring written-up notes or actual recordings of sessions?

5. The organizational and professional context

In most supervision situations there are other critical stakeholders in the supervision contract besides the direct parties. There is the expectation of the organization or organizations in which the work is being carried out. The organization may have its own explicit supervision policy where the expectations of supervision are clarified. Where a clear policy does not exist, it is still essential that the implicit expectations of the organizations are discussed. This could include what responsibility the organization might expect the supervisor to take in ensuring quality work and what report it requires on the supervision. Likewise, it is important to clarify the professional and ethical codes of conduct that both may be party to.

Most professional associations have codes of conduct and statements of ethics that stipulate the boundaries of appropriate behaviour between a coach and a coachee, and also provide the right of appeal for the coachee against any possible inappropriate behaviour by the coach. A number of professional coaching bodies are becoming clearer about their code of practice for supervision. We do not want to prescribe what we think are appropriate ethical standards for supervision, because this must invariably vary from one setting to another. However, we do consider it imperative that all new supervisors check whether there are ethics statements covering supervision within their profession and/or organization. If no such statement exists, we suggest that you review the ethical standards for work with coachees, and become clear yourself which of them you feel apply to the supervision context. It is important that all supervisors are clear about the ethical boundaries of their supervision practice and are able to articulate these to their supervisees.

The seven-eyed coaching supervision model

In 1985 I developed a more in-depth model of supervision (Hawkins, 1985; Hawkins and Shohet, 1989), which later became known as the 'seven-eyed supervision model', and has been used across many different people professions in many countries. In the 1990s and early years of this millennium, as coaching supervision first began to get under way, I developed a version of this particularly for supervision of coaches, mentors and consultants (Hawkins and Smith, 2006). Its purpose is the exploration of the various different influences on supervisory activity in the room. It is based on the systemic understanding of both coaching and supervision articulated at the beginning of this chapter. The four nested systems (the world of the client, the coaching relational system, the supervisory system and the wider contexts) provide seven different modes of focus. I will set out in more detail these seven areas of potential focus available to both supervisor and supervisee in reviewing their practice.

1. The coachee's system

Here the focus is on the content of what happened with the coachee's system, the problem the coachee system wants help with and how the coachee is presenting the issues.

Mode 1 skill

The supervisor's skill in this mode is to help coaches accurately return to what actually happened with the coachee; what they saw, what they heard and what they felt, and to try to separate this actual data from their preconceptions, assumptions and interpretations. It is also useful for coaches to be helped to attend to what happened at the boundaries of their time with the coachee, their arrival and exit, for it is often at the boundaries that the richest unconscious material is most active.

2. The coach's interventions

This looks at what interventions the coach made and alternative choices that might have been used. It might also focus on a situation that the coach is about to intervene in and explore the possible options and the likely impact of each.

Mode 2 skill

Often coaches will ask for help with an impasse they have arrived at in facilitating the change process. They will often present this impasse in the form of an 'either/or' such as: 'Should I collude with this situation or confront the issue?' The skill of the supervisor is to avoid the trap of debating the either/or options, and instead to enable coaches to realize how they are limiting their choice to two polarized possibilities and facilitate a shared brainstorming that frees up the energy and creates new options. Then the benefits and difficulties of these options can be explored and some possible interventions can be tried out in role-play.

3. The relationship between the coach and the coachee

Here the focus is neither solely on the coachee and his or her system nor the coach, but the relationship that they are creating together.

Mode 3 skill

The supervisor has to facilitate the coach to stand outside of the relationship that he or she is part of and see it afresh, from a new angle. The Chinese have a proverb, that the last one to know about the sea is the fish, because they are constantly immersed in it. In this mode the supervisor is helping the coach to be a flying fish, so he or she can see the water in which he or she is normally swimming.

4. The coach

The focus is on coaches beginning to look at themselves, both what is being re-stimulated in them by the coachee's material, and also themselves as an instrument for registering what is happening beneath the surface of the coaching system.

Mode 4 skill

In this mode the supervisor helps coaches to work through any re-stimulation of their own feelings that has been triggered by the work with this client. Having done this, the coaches can also be helped to explore how their own feelings may be very useful data for understanding what the coachee and their system is experiencing but unable to articulate directly. The coaches also explore how their own blocks may be preventing them from facilitating the coachee and their system to change.

FIGURE 15.2   The seven-eyed model of coaching supervision

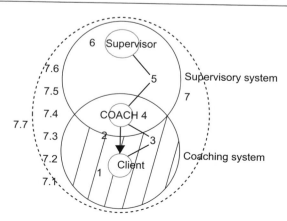

5. The parallel process

Here the focus is on what the coach has absorbed unconsciously from the coachee system and how it may be being played out in the relationship to the supervisor. The coach can, unaware, treat the supervisor the way his or her coachee treated them.

Mode 5 skill

Here the supervisor needs to be able to attend not only to what he or she is being told about the coaching system, but also what is happening in the relationship in the room. Having acquired this skill, the supervisor can then at times offer tentative reflections on the impact of the presented material on the coaching relationship to illuminate the coaching dynamic. When done skilfully this process can help the coaches bridge the gap between their conscious understanding of the coaching relationship and the emotional impact it has had upon them.

6. The supervisor self-reflection

The focus for mode 6 is the supervisor's 'here and now' experience while with the coach and what can be learnt about the coach/coachee relationship from the supervisor's response to the coach and the material he or she presents.

Mode 6 skill

In this mode the supervisor has to attend not only to presented material and its impact on the 'here and now' relationship, but also his or her own internal process. The supervisor can also discover the presence of un-conscious material related to the coaching relationship by attending to his or her own feelings, thoughts and fantasies while listening to the presenta-tion of the coaching situation. These can tentatively be commented on and made available as possible indicators of what lies buried in the relationship with the coachee. The additional skill is to have a means of sharing this with the coach in a non-judgemental and speculative way.

7. The wider context

The focus of mode 7 is on the organizational, social, cultural, ethical and contractual context in which the coaching is taking place. This includes being aware of the wider group of stakeholders in the process that is being focused on; these may be the client organization and its stakeholders, the coach's organization and its stakeholders, and the organization or profes-sional network of the supervisor.

Mode 7 skill

The supervisor has to be able to bring a whole-systems perspective to understand how the systemic context of what is being presented is affecting not only the behaviour, mindsets, emotional ground and motivations of the coach and coachee, but also themselves. The skill is to appropriately attend to the needs of the critical stakeholders in the wider systems, and also to understand how the culture of the systemic context might be creating illusions, delusions and collusions in the coach and oneself. To attend to mode 7 also requires a high level of transcultural competence (see Hawkins and Smith, 2013, Chapter 14).

Using all seven modes

In talking with both supervisors and coaches who have gone to others in search of help in exploring coaching situations, we have discovered that often different supervisors are stuck in the groove of predominantly using one of the seven modes of working. Some focus entirely on the situation out there with the coachee and adopt a pose of pseudo-objectivity (mode 1). Others see their job as coming up with better interventions than the coach managed to produce (mode 2). This can often leave the coach feeling inadequate or determined to show that these suggested interventions are as useless as the ones he or she had previously tried. Other coaches have reported taking a problem with a coachee and having left supervision feeling that the problem was entirely their pathology (mode 4).

'Single-eyed vision', which focuses only on one aspect of the process, will always lead to partial and limited perspectives. This model suggests a way of engaging in an exploration that looks at the same situation from many different perspectives and can thus create a critical subjectivity, where subjective awareness from one perspective is tested against other subjective data.

Each mode of supervision can be done in a skilful and elegant manner, or ineffectively, but no matter how skilful one is in one mode, it will prove inadequate without the skill to move from mode to mode. We have devised a training method for helping the supervisor use each of the modes with skill and precision and to explore the timing and appropriateness for moving from one mode to another.

The most common order for moving through the modes is to start with mode 1, talking about specific coaching situations, then to move into modes 3 and 4 to explore what is happening both in the coaching relationship and for the coach/supervisee. This may well explore the here and now relationship in the room between the coach and the supervisor (modes 5 and 6), and/or bringing into awareness the wider context (mode 7). Finally, having gained new insight and created a shift in the supervisory matrix, the attention may turn back to mode 2, to explore what different interventions the coach might use in the next session to create the needed shift in the coaching matrix. The coach might even try out some of these interventions in what we term a 'fast-forward rehearsal'. From our experience we have learnt that if the change starts to happen live in the supervision, it is far more likely to happen back in the coaching.

The model has also been used as a way of empowering the coach, who is receiving the supervision, to be able to give feedback on the help he or she is being given and request a change in focus. It can be used as a framework for a joint review of the supervision process by the coach and supervisor.

Supervising team coaching

In the last five years there has been a very rapid development of team coaching (Hawkins, 2011, 2014a, 2014b). Good team coaching is by its very nature systemic and it is essential that the team coach has a place to reflect on their work. Without this it is very easy for the team coach to become flooded and ensnared by the complex team and organizational dynamics. Supervising systemic team coaching requires additional skills and methodology. These are described in Hawkins, 2014, Chapter 13, which includes a 10-eyed model of supervision of team coaching.

Training as a coaching supervisor

In 2002 the debate about the need for supervision in coaching began to change. The professional coaching bodies, such as the Association for Coaching and the European Mentoring and Coaching Council, started to argue that all coaches should receive supervision from trained and qualified supervisors. In response, the Bath Consultancy Group led the way in the development of a certified training programme in the supervision of coaches and mentors (**www.bathconsultancygroup.com/coachingsupervision/**). Our starting belief was that these professions had much in common with other helping professions when it came to supervision, but were also significantly different. The difference was particularly in the fact that as a counsellor, psychotherapist, psychologist, nurse, etc the work was focused primarily on the individual client, whereas coaches, mentors and organizational consultants always have a minimum of three clients:

1 the coachee or mentee;

2 the organization he or she works in and for;

3 the relationship between him or her and the organization.

This led us to design a training programme that had a foundation module and final advanced supervision module just for people who were experienced executive coaches, mentors and consultants, but required the participants to choose two further modules that they would undertake alongside other helping professionals.

Our second assumption is that learning to be a supervisor is best undertaken through cycles of action learning, not by sitting in a classroom. Thus the training involves a great deal of supervision practice in threes, comprising a supervisor, supervisee and shadow supervisor, who gives feedback to the supervisor, sometimes at the end of the practice session, and sometimes in the middle, in structured 'timeouts'. The trainee supervisors, as well as undertaking the modules, receive 10 hours of supervision on their supervision, from an experienced supervisor, as well as two tutorials to help them maximize their individual learning programme.

We constantly learn more from each cohort of new trainees about the fascinating craft of supervising coaches and the lifelong journey to develop this craft. Increasingly we are reminded that at the heart of being a good coach or a good coaching supervisor is not academic knowledge, a collection of theories and models, or an armoury of tools and techniques, but a constant dedication to developing one's human capacity to be fully present for another, acting with what we term 'ruthless compassion'. For it is the ruthless compassion we can bring, not only for our coachee but also the work they do in the world and for our craft, that ultimately allows the fear and anxiety that pervades so many work situations to be overcome, and for our coachees to find new strength to act courageously.

References

Berglas, B (2002) The very real dangers of executive coaching, *Harvard Business Review*, June, pp 86–92

Christie, D E (2013) *The Blue Sapphire of the Mind: Notes for a contemplative ecology*, OUP, Oxford

Downey, M (2003) *Effective Coaching: Lessons from the coaches' couch*, Texere/Thomson, New York

Flaherty, J (1999) *Coaching: Evoking excellence in others*, Butterworth-Heinemann, Woburn, MA

Hawkins, P (2011, 2nd edn 2014a) *Leadership Team Coaching: Developing collective transformational leadership* (translated into Spanish and Japanese), Kogan Page, London

Hawkins, P (2012) *Creating a Coaching Culture* (translated into Dutch), Open University Press/McGraw Hill, Maidenhead

Hawkins, P (ed) (2014b) *Leadership Team Coaching in Practice*, Kogan Page, London

Hawkins, P (2014c) The Challenge for Coaching in the 21st Century in *e-Organisations and People*, **21** (4), Winter 2014, www.amed.org.uk

Hawkins, P and Shohet, R (1989, 2000, 2006, 2012) *Supervision in the Helping Profession*, Open University Press, Milton Keynes

Hawkins, P and Smith, N (2006, 2013) *Coaching, Mentoring and Organizational Consultancy: Supervision and development*, Open University Press, Milton Keynes

Kadushin, A (1992) *Supervision in Social Work*, 3rd edn, Columbia University Press, New York

O'Neill, M B (2000) *Coaching with Backbone and Heart: A systems approach to engagingleaders with their challenges*, Jossey-Bass, San Francisco, CA

Proctor, B (1997) Contracting in supervision, in *Contracts in Counselling*, ed C Sills, Sage, London

Scharmer, O and Kaufman, K (2013) Leading from the Emergent Future: from ego-system to eco-system economies, Berrett-Koehler, San Francisco

Turner, E and Hawkins P (2015) *Multi-stakeholder contracting in coaching*, Research Report for the AC, EMCC and ICF

Evaluating coaching programmes

16

ALISON CARTER and DAVID B PETERSON

Most of the literature on evaluating coaching outcomes has been written by three groups. First, academics and scientist-practitioners have produced the majority of the 'serious' research as well as detailed reviews of this work (eg De Meuse, Dai and Lee, 2009; Feldman and Lankau, 2005; Joo, 2005; Levenson, 2009; Passmore and Gibbes, 2007; Peterson, in press; Schlosser *et al*, 2006), most of which has actually been conducted by graduate students. Second, organizations which hire coaches have evaluated their own coaching programmes, often based solely on self-report from coaching participants or the programme sponsors themselves (eg many of the case studies in Carter, 2006; Clutterbuck and Megginson, 2005; Hunt and Weintraub, 2007; and Jarvis, Lane and Fillery-Travis, 2006; as well as the surveys of organizations using coaching reported in CIPD, 2004; Corporate Leadership Council, 2004; McDermott, Levenson and Newton, 2007; and Thompson *et al*, 2008). Finally, many coaching organizations have evaluated the coaching services they provide, typically seeking information for marketing and promotion purposes as well as for improving the quality of the work they do (eg Corbett and Colemon, 2006; McGovern *et al*, 2001; Rock and Donde, 2008). Each group has its own biases (eg rigour for the academics, relevance and value for the organizations, and substantiating return on investment (ROI) for the practitioners), with associated strengths and weaknesses in their research methodologies. Nevertheless, the aggregate research by these three groups provides a compelling case for the value of coaching (Peterson, in press).

This chapter, based on our own experiences as coaches and researchers, provides coaches with a practical, easy-to-use process for evaluating, improving and demonstrating the value of their work. We aim to give you guidance, illustrated by actual case studies, on measuring three different levels of evaluation – effectiveness (Did the coaching work?), impact on individuals (What did the person do as a result of being coached?), and organizational and business results (What was the value of the coaching to the organization?).

Why evaluate?

In researching this chapter we have been surprised to discover that evaluation is largely ignored by coaches (Coutu and Kauffman, 2009; Peterson, 2009). A minority of coaches seem to actively avoid it, perhaps fearful of what they or their clients might find out. Others see the additional time and cost making it an optional extra rather than routine. Coaches' lack of expertise in evaluation and research methods may be another factor. So why are we urging coaches to embrace evaluation?

For one thing, evaluating your coaching can provide evidence to back up your marketing claims about the difference your coaching has made, and therefore why your coaching is worth the money you charge. As the coaching industry continues to grow and enters the market maturity phase of its life cycle, the pressure on suppliers to prove that coaching works and adds additional value is likely to intensify (Maher and Pomerantz, 2003). Evaluating coaching can also give you feedback to improve your practice as well as identify sources of greatest client satisfaction and dissatisfaction. Russ-Eft and Preskill (2001) believe that it is imperative for professionals to view evaluation as an essential part of our craft, to continue to challenge our thinking, build our confidence and pursue personal growth and development. Carter, Kerrin and Wolfe (2005) suggest that coaches need to be braver about having upfront conversations about evaluation with prospective corporate purchasers and be willing to use different evaluation tools for different client organizations.

But are clients interested enough in evaluation to pay for it? Gil Schwenk, an executive coach and consultant with the Bath Consultancy Group who also serves as a board member of the European Mentoring and Coaching Council (EMCC), thinks they are. He told us:

> We are noticing a change in the way big companies negotiate organizational requirements. There's a much greater willingness to spend money on evaluation-related activity as part of the coaching assignment. For instance, one client we are in start-up phase with is extremely interested in agreeing outcomes expected, how they will know the value that is returned from the coaching and who is

best placed to give feedback. Indeed it is one of their key requirements that evaluation underpins the whole approach. We are agreeing clear behavioural outcomes: different for each individual to be coached ... The double benefit for us as coaches is that it engages the clients in meaningful dialogue about behaviour change, plus it gives us something to evaluate.

We have encountered the occasional coach who evaluates all his or her coaching engagements even where the client organization has no initial interest and does not pay for the additional time involved. For example, Carol Wilson, managing director of Performance Coach Training and head of accreditation at the Association for Coaching, who says: 'Producing an evaluation report of the coaching outcomes is a key marketing tool which invariably leads to additional work. Measuring progress continuously also allows coaches to give periodic feedback to the client organization to demonstrate the value of the coaching programme.'

Professional bodies like EMCC, the International Coach Federation (ICF) and Academy of Executive Coaching (AoEC) offer little guidance about how practitioners can evaluate the impact of their own work. The emphasis is more often on the need for coaches to have supervision and seek regular client feedback to monitor their quality and effectiveness.

How to evaluate

It is beyond the scope of this chapter to give you a tutorial on the techniques of research project design or statistical analysis techniques. Instead we present a practical step-by-step approach to evaluation and point out some common pitfalls.

Evaluation steps

Adapting Peterson and Kraiger's (2004) evaluation process for examining organizational coaching programmes, we recommend five steps for you to consider (see Figure 16.1).

Step 1: Preparation

Evaluation begins with a consideration of your goals and what you wish to evaluate. Do you want to measure business results – perhaps efficiency (was the coaching worth the cost?) or return on investment from the coaching? Or are you interested in changes in performance or behaviour in those you will be coaching? Alternatively, are you interested in the effectiveness of the

FIGURE 16.1 Evaluation process steps

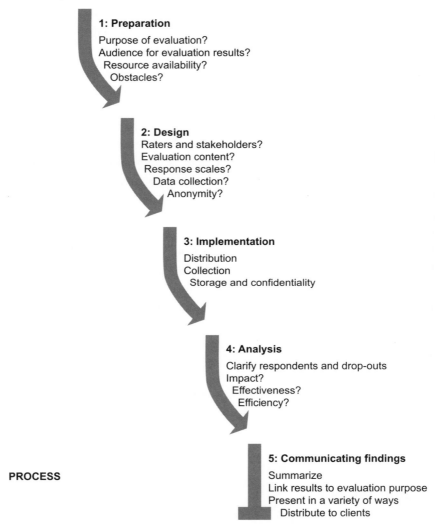

1: Preparation

Purpose of evaluation?
Audience for evaluation results?
Resource availability?
Obstacles?

2: Design
Raters and stakeholders?
Evaluation content?
Response scales?
Data collection?
Anonymity?

3: Implementation

Distribution
Collection
Storage and confidentiality

4: Analysis

Clarify respondents and drop-outs
Impact?
Effectiveness?
Efficiency?

PROCESS

5: Communicating findings

Summarize
Link results to evaluation purpose
Present in a variety of ways
Distribute to clients

SOURCE: Adapted from Peterson and Kraiger (2004)

coaching process itself, the quality of the relationship, or your own coaching skills? Do you want to find out which of the organization's systems helped or hindered achieving the benefits expected? Thinking through the various goals you might have will help you choose the right ruler before you start measuring.

Think through not just your purposes in embarking on evaluation but also the resources available and the challenges you are likely to face. Ensure you are clear about your evaluation budget, whether that is limited by time or money. Check constraints and scope before you start. For example, ROI may take significant time, expertise and money to do well (Anderson and Anderson, 2004; Peterson, in press; Phillips, 2007a, 2007b).

Step 2: Design

Here you decide who will provide the information you need, generate the specific questions you will ask them to respond to, choose the appropriate rating scales to be applied, and then decide how to collect your data (eg face-to-face interviews, online or paper-based surveys, or personal/group reflection).

Decide what counts as evidence. In general, numbers serve to convince stakeholders who are sponsoring coaching, while individual success stories can easily be remembered and used by way of illustration (Carter and Chapman, 2009). The most convincing evidence is that gathered over time. You might want to consider using pre- and post-coaching measures if they are sensitive enough to detect meaningful change. It is also feasible to ask people for degree-of-change ratings on their coaching objectives after the coaching is done (Peterson, 1993a, 1993b), but it is essential to clearly specify the goals of coaching ahead of time to ensure objectivity. Following up six months to a year later is useful to see how well changes or benefits have been sustained. To demonstrate that coaching was the true reason for the change, it's best to have some sort of control group, either a separate group of individuals who have development objectives but are not participating in coaching, or even have coaching participants rate how much they changed on a set of 'control items' that are not part of the coaching process itself (Peterson and Kraiger, 2004). Consistently showing that people change in the areas in which they receive coaching more than they change in other skill areas helps build credible support.

Do a stakeholder analysis. Although coaching is a one-to-one process, it takes place in a context with a multitude of stakeholders with different priorities, needs and expectations. You will need to decide whom to include and find out what data to collect in order to satisfy these needs. Be clear about who the stakeholders are and establish what influence they have and their expectations from the coaching, and make sure that your evaluation plan finds out whether their expectations have been met. Identify who else might have an interest, eg the coached and their bosses, as well as their direct reports and customers. What do they hope for? Stakeholders might also be in a position to help you identify changes. Consider using them all as data sources.

Be pragmatic. Stick within your planned budget and select a data collection method(s) that meets the objectives of stakeholders and the purpose of evaluation.

For a simple all-purpose instrument for use with clients, Peterson and Kraiger recommend using a pre- and post-coaching rating of 8–10 specific learning objectives for each participant. For the pre-coaching survey, they recommend using either a current effectiveness or current vs desired performance scale. For the post-coaching survey, they recommend same scale again plus a level of improvement scale.

Step 3: Implementation

Here you implement the design decisions you made in step 2.

Keep survey questionnaires short to get a better response rate – lack of time is one of the primary reasons people don't respond. Response rates will increase further with reminders and follow-up. They can be improved again if you distribute and collect evaluation forms during sessions, or by asking managers to reserve time for them to be completed. Bear in mind that clients may not give such honest answers in the presence of their coach or manager.

It is important to offer confidentiality to maximize the quality of the data you get. Building trust and explaining honestly the purpose(s) for the evaluation and the use of their ratings is also good practice. This also means you should store data securely and ensure that you do not use it for anything other than the intended purpose without explicit consent.

Step 4: Analysis

Here is when you analyse the data you have collected to answer the questions raised by the purpose(s) of your evaluation. The most basic approach is simply to read each survey and study it carefully for concerns and new insights. More helpful is to set up a spreadsheet where you can enter the data and keep a running average of all the quantitative feedback data. Keeping all the qualitative answers in one place is useful if you periodically, perhaps quarterly or annually, review all the written feedback at once and search for trends. It's also important to consider your response rate; how many responses are you getting and are there consistent variations in who responds and who doesn't? If you find that you are not getting completed forms from participants who drop out early or who don't seem fully satisfied with the coaching, you will need to find ways to get that feedback.

Step 5: Communicating results

It is likely that some of the feedback will be solely for your benefit. Other information may be appropriate for marketing purposes, such as client satisfaction with you and the type of significant outcomes achieved. If you are doing a lot of work with a particular organization, you may want to provide them with regular updates, at least annually, on the feedback you are receiving. As you think about what information you are using and what else would be helpful, you may want to go back to Step 1, re-evaluate your purpose and modify your process. Using the same questions over and over again allows you to measure your own progress, while adapting and incorporating new questions helps make sure that you are seeking the most useful information.

Pitfalls to avoid

Common pitfalls in evaluating coaching include (Carter, 2006; Peterson and Kraiger, 2004):

- Leaving it until too late. Not planning how to evaluate the coaching before the programme starts.

- Making evaluation too clever. Keep it simple. A focus on a small handful of key indicators can be sufficient, even if you are looking at business results, eg sales figures that are already being collected for those coaching participants who are working in sales.

- Relying on a single measure from a single source at one time, eg merely asking for satisfaction data from those you are coaching. Different types of measures at different times and from different stakeholders ensure a more complete picture.

- Not telling everyone upfront that you will evaluating the coaching, how it will be done and what they will need to contribute.

- Seeking only marketing data or information that may appear self-serving. As the coach, you may be perceived as having a financial interest in the coaching outcome, so make sure you gather information that will be credible to others you may present it to.

- Failing to anticipate relevant cultural, diversity and language issues. Seek advice on how those with different cultural values may perceive the evaluation process. Consider how you will gather data from those who speak different languages.

- Not challenging some buyers who assume that ROI is the only way to demonstrate the utility and worth of coaching.

- Not knowing what to do with the data, once collected, or failing to follow through on your plans to communicate it to key audiences.

Cases in point

In this section we will give two examples from our own experience of evaluating coaching processes and outcomes in a work context. The first example describes an external independent evaluation commissioned on behalf of a consortium of organizations jointly operating a coaching scheme. The coaches in this context were all employees of the organizations specially trained and supervised by external coach training providers, all of whom were expected to cooperate with the evaluators. By contrast, the second example is situated in one large organization and involves the organization in hiring consultancy advice on how to develop and then evaluate their own coaching scheme utilizing hired coaches. Despite the differences of context, both cases involved thinking through what the evaluation was for, its design, analysis and communication of findings. Both also necessitated the coaches' cooperation and participation in the evaluation.

Keep in mind that evaluation is essentially about asking questions, being curious, making decisions and putting a value on things. It pays to keep things simple.

CASE STUDY ONE

In 2008 Alison, the first-named chapter author, was commissioned through a competitive tendering process to undertake a comprehensive external early evaluation of all the coaching activities of a pool of coaches (Carter *et al*, 2009). The coaching pool is a partnership of 13 organizations within the same region. It operates by training and deploying selected employees as coaches throughout the region to coach colleagues from other organizations within the partnership. The coaches operate under supervision from external coach training providers. The timing of the evaluation was shortly after the coaching pool completed its development and start-up phases and commenced full operations.

Objectives

Objectives of the evaluation were threefold:

1 Explore the impact on individuals. The idea was that any early successes could support marketing and promotion of the pool within the partnership organizations.

2   Develop tools to explore impact on partnership organizations. Although too early to expect business results to be seen, data that can be used and compared with future evaluations could be collected.

3   Identify strengths or weaknesses in coaching pool operational processes. Identifying any problems in the way the coaching pool is designed or managed at an early stage, and suggesting improvement action to be taken, can allow necessary changes to be made prior to full launch and implementation.

Methods

A combination of qualitative and quantitative elements based on self-reported data was suggested. The views of sponsors/line managers were considered of particular importance when it comes to a 'third party' confirmation of claims made by clients for the organization-level impact of coaching. The methods used were: in-depth telephone interviews with a sample of 'matched trios' of client, coach and line manager/sponsor; and web-based impact surveys of all accredited coaches, all clients and selected line managers/sponsors.

The same measure of individual behaviour and organizational performance re-measured over time was unfeasible given the timescale available for the evaluation and the fact that so few clients had actually completed their coaching. Instead, all individuals were surveyed, whatever the stage they had reached in the coaching process by the single time point at which the evaluation was undertaken.

All three interview guides asked if there was anything they would like to see changed in the way in which the coaching pool operates. All three stakeholder groups were also asked (variously phrased) to 'describe any behaviour changes or impact on your colleague that you have noticed following their coaching' and 'please describe any impact on business results your colleague has made in the last six months'.

Additional interview questions to line managers/sponsors included: 'Why did you choose or support coaching for your colleague?' and 'Can you tell me about your involvement in setting objectives for your colleague's coaching?'

Additional interview questions to coaches included: 'What do you think of the training (in coaching) that you received?' and 'Has supervision helped with your coaching practice? How has it done that?'

Additional interview questions to clients included: 'What criteria did you use in choosing your coach from among those offered to you?' and 'What support did you get from your manager?' Where any impact on business results was identified, follow-up questions were 'How did you have an impact?', 'Can you quantify the extent of your impact?', 'What percentage was due to the coaching?' and 'How did your approach differ from what you might have done before coaching?'

Data on impact on individuals were obtained from three online surveys by asking individuals in all three stakeholder groups about their perceptions of any changes occurring since starting coaching. A series of statements was suggested against a six-point rating scale, from 'Very strongly disagree' to 'Very strongly agree'. Items included: 'Is more aware of own strengths and weaknesses', 'Manages his/her own team better', 'Is more effective in managing stakeholders' expectations' and 'Puts more effort into developing and sharing a vision'. In addition, the surveys asked about all the coaching pool's operational processes, including coach selection and deployment, marketing to potential clients, matching, quality of coaching, administrative support and line manager/organization support.

Results

All clients said that they found the coaching worthwhile and would recommend it, and there was a clear perception that the coaching is a high-quality product. This was very helpful to the coaching pool in terms of marketing to potential clients. Coaches, clients and managers/sponsors listed the most noticeable improvements in individuals as greater confidence, greater emotional intelligence and self-awareness, and improvements in interpersonal and management skills. In particular, they have identified significant improvements in the client's confidence to lead change (a mean client self-report rating of 5 out of 6) and make a greater effort to find innovative approaches to solving problems (also rated 5 out of 6). This was helpful in promoting the coaching pool to chief executives and potential sponsors as a scheme worth putting someone forward for.

Not all managers had been involved with the contracting process for objective setting, and there was a distinct lack of business objectives being built into coaching objectives. This information enabled the implementation of more quantifiable links with organizations' needs to increase business impact moving forward. Changes made since the launch of the programme include: prioritizing clients working in circumstances where they and their organization are likely to gain most benefit; more targeted and performance-orientated publicity; and guidance for coaches to ensure that at least one of each client's objectives is explicitly linked to a business priority.

Coaches were relatively under-utilized at this early stage, meaning there was scope to secure a faster return for the upfront monies invested in coach training. The partnership is undertaking ongoing evaluation itself moving forward, using the evaluation tools developed selectively. Some will be used regularly and others on an annual basis.

CASE STUDY TWO

David, the second author of this chapter, consulted several years ago with an organization to help them design their coaching programme (Peterson, 2002; Peterson and Little, 2008), including their evaluation process. They were interested in four specific objectives:

1 Gather data to market and promote coaching inside their organization. To address this goal, they incorporated items such as 'This is a high-quality programme', 'My time was well worth it' and 'I would recommend this programme to others'. On a five-point scale, from Strongly Disagree to Strongly Agree, they found that 97–99% of participants responded 4 or 5 to all of these questions. Thus they could claim that virtually all participants found their coaching to be valuable.

2 Evaluate the quality and effectiveness of the coaches, the aim being to maintain high standards and use each coach where they were most effective. Here, they used items such as 'My coach was credible, professional, and helpful' and 'I would recommend my coach to others' as well as soliciting input through open-ended questions about the types of people and situations where people thought their coach would be most effective. Coaches who received high ratings were moved up the priority list of coaches they would use again. If a coach received a rating of less than 4, the sponsors interviewed the participant to get more information. In some cases, they removed the coach from their approved list and in others they proceeded on a case-by-case basis to get more data and evaluate fit with specific needs.

3 Justifying the programme to senior executives and corporate sponsors to ensure continued support. Primarily, they focused on using coaching to address specific business needs and then demonstrating business impact through items such as 'My leadership skills improved significantly as a result of my coaching', 'I learnt skills that increase my value to the organization for current and future roles' and open-ended questions such as 'What specifically did you learn through coaching and what was the demonstrable business impact?' They also asked participants' managers for feedback on the value they perceived and learned that over 90% saw a tangible improvement in the person's job performance and more than 80% reported improvement in the skills required for advancement. Early in the process, the HR director in charge of the corporate coaching programme interviewed each

participant in person to obtain specific examples and vivid stories of the impact which she could use to promote coaching and to share with senior executives.

4   Assessing participant satisfaction to find where they could improve the process. They sought ratings of the coach and all aspects of the process, including scheduling, communication, feedback tools, homework assignments, in-person vs telephone coaching conversations, organizational resources, and support from their manager and HR partner. In the early stages, satisfaction with the coach, feedback tools and the coaching process was high, but low with the communication and administrative aspects, and very low with boss and organizational support. The organization was able to incorporate the feedback to improve communication, scheduling, and administrative support. Although the numbers have increased somewhat, they have been less successful in enhancing perceptions of boss and organizational support.

This organization has modified its evaluation process over time to make it shorter and more focused on the key goals. They have eliminated items where there is little variability and no new information (eg homework assignments) and where they already have what they need (eg sufficient information for marketing purposes), and they have modified items to zero in more specifically on elements they can use to improve the process. Because they see this information as key to their ongoing success, they continue to summarize their information quarterly and communicate it to the relevant stakeholders.

Final thoughts

In this chapter we have suggested that more coaches should embrace evaluation. We have also provided references to some of the relevant literature and hope that you will be interested enough to read a few and take your thinking and practice on evaluation further. We hope we have demonstrated that actually conducting your own evaluation research can be a relatively straightforward, manageable process. Clearly, the potential benefits can be significant in terms of personal learning and commercial value. In an increasingly crowded marketplace, good coaches need to make sure they stand out. Demonstrating your willingness and ability to contribute to a company's thinking about the quality of its coaching is a compelling way to enhance your professional credibility and impact.

References

Anderson, D L and Anderson, M C (2004) *Coaching that Counts: Harnessing the power of leadership coaching to deliver strategic value*, Elsevier, Burlington, MA

Carter, A (2006) *Practical Methods for Evaluating Coaching*, IES Research Report, No 430, Brighton, UK

Carter, A and Chapman, M (2009) How to . . . evaluate coaching programmes, *Coaching at Work*, **4** (2), pp 54–55

Carter, A, Fairhurst, P, Markwick, C and Miller, L (2009) *Evaluation of West Midlands Regional Coaching Pool: Summary of findings*, IES Research Report, Brighton, UK

Carter, A, Kerrin, M and Wolfe, H (2005) Employers and coaching evaluation, *International Journal of Coaching in Organizations*, **3** (4), pp 63–72

CIPD (2004) *Training and Development 2004*, survey report, Chartered Institute for Personnel and Development, London

Corbett, B and Colemon, J (2006) *The Sherpa Guide: Process-driven executive coaching*, Texere, Mason, OH

Corporate Leadership Council (2004) *ROI of Executive Coaching*, Corporate Executive Board, Washington, DC

Coutu, D and Kauffman, C (2009) What can coaches do for you?, *Harvard Business Review*, **87** (1), pp 91–97

De Meuse, K P, Dai, G and Lee, R J (2009) Evaluating the effectiveness of executive coaching: beyond ROI?, *Coaching: An International Journal of Theory, Research, and Practice*, **2**, pp 117–34

Feldman, D C and Lankau, M J (2005) Executive coaching: a review and agenda for future research, *Journal of Management*, **31**, pp 829–848

Joo, B K (2005) Executive coaching: a conceptual framework from an integrative review of practice and research, *Human Resource Development Review*, **4**, pp 462–88

Levenson, A (2009) Measuring and maximizing the business impact of executive coaching, *Consulting Psychology Journal*, **61**, pp 103–21

Maher, S and Pomerantz, S (2003) The future of executive coaching: analysis from a life cycle approach, *International Journal of Coaching in Organizations*, **1** (2), pp 3–11

McDermott, M, Levenson, A and Newton, S (2007) What coaching can and cannot do for your organization, *Human Resource Planning*, **30** (2), pp 30–37

McGovern, J, Lindemann, M, Vergara, M, Murphy, S, Barker, L and Warrenfeltz, R (2001) Maximizing the impact of executive coaching: behavioral change, organizational outcomes, and return on investment, *The Manchester Review*, **6** (1), pp 1–9

Passmore, J and Gibbes, C (2007) The state of executive coaching research: what does the current literature tell us and what's next for coaching research?, *International Coaching Psychology Review*, **2**, pp 116–128

Peterson, D B (1993a) *Skill Learning and Behavior Change in an Individually Tailored Management Coaching Program*, unpublished doctoral dissertation, University of Minnesota, Minneapolis

Peterson, D B (1993b, March) *Measuring Change: A psychometric approach to evaluating individual coaching outcomes*, Presented at the annual conference of the Society for Industrial and Organizational Psychology, San Francisco

Peterson, D B (2002) Management development: Coaching and mentoring programs, in *Creating, Implementing, and Managing Effective Training and Development: State-of-the-art lessons for practice*, ed K Kraiger, pp 160–91, Jossey-Bass, San Francisco

Peterson, D B (2009) Does your coach give you value for your money?, *Harvard Business Review*, **87** (1), p 94

Peterson, D B (in press) Executive coaching: a critical review and recommendations for advancing the practice, in *APA Handbook of Industrial and Organizational Psychology*, ed S Zedeck, American Psychological Association, Washington, DC

Peterson, D B and Kraiger, K (2004) A practical guide to evaluating coaching: translating state-of-the-art techniques to the real world, in *The Human Resources Programme-Evaluation Handbook*, ed J E Edwards, J H Scott N S Raju, pp 262–82, Sage, Thousand Oaks, CA

Peterson, D B and Little, B (2008) Growth market: the rise of systemic coaching, *Coaching at Work*, **3** (1), pp 44–47

Phillips, J J (2007a) Measuring the ROI of a coaching intervention, part 2, *Performance Improvement*, **46** (10), pp 10–23

Phillips, J J and Phillips, P P (2007b) Show me the money: the use of ROI in performance improvement, part 1, *Performance Improvement*, **46** (9), pp 8–22

Rock, D and Donde, R (2008) Driving organizational change with internal coaching programmes: part two, *Industrial and Commercial Training*, **40** (2), pp 75–80

Russ-Eft, D F and Preskill, H (2001) *Evaluation in Organizations: A systematic approach to enhancing learning, performance and change*, Perseus, Cambridge, MA

Schlosser, B, Steinbrenner, D, Kumata, E and Hunt, J (2006) The coaching impact study: measuring the value of executive coaching, *International Journal of Coaching in Organizations*, **4** (3), pp 8–26

Thompson, H B, Bear, D J, Dennis, D J, Vickers, M, London, J and Morrison, C L (2008) *Coaching: A global study of successful practices: Current trends and future possibilities 2008–2018*, American Management Association, New York

Coach accreditation

17

DIANE BRENNAN and ALISON WHYBROW

Introduction

Coaching's success over the past 20 years has prompted many to join this growing industry. According to the 2012 ICF Global Coaching Study conducted by PricewaterhouseCoopers (PwC), coaching represents a nearly US$2 billion annual industry worldwide (PwC, 2012). The positivity and potential associated with coaching also attracted many to offer programmes to those wanting to become a coach. At the time of first writing, in 2010, there were fewer restrictions than currently and whilst it is more of a challenge to enter more mature coaching markets, it is still the case that anyone can call themselves a coach or create a programme to train and certify coaches. This context presents opportunities and challenges for the coach as well as coachees, coaching buyers and the coaching profession. There is further complexity across the globe as the coaching industry emerges, blossoms and matures at different times in different countries.

In 2015, those looking to develop their coaching practice through a recognized accreditation or qualification can clearly assess the credibility of different providers as the level of insight, understanding and consolidation around coaching as a profession continues. The number of accredited coaches for the International Coach Federation (ICF) alone has increased since 2010 from 5,000 to 16,000. According to the European Mentoring and Coaching Council (EMCC), more organizations are looking to have their internal coaches accredited and more coaching buyers are seeking accredited coaches. The forecast for the coaching industry remains bright. The coaching industry has survived and thrived in the face of significant challenges to individual and corporate budgets. Further, coaching skills and coaching interventions, as many coachees, clients and coaches will testify, can enable and have enabled individuals, teams and organizations to thrive in a world that is volatile, uncertain, complex and ambiguous (VUCA).

The demand for coaching is not reducing. Clients' insight into what good coaching looks like is increasing. The requirement for robust accreditation systems in order for the industry to sustain, develop and grow remains. Through this, the coaching industry is enabled to ensure effective delivery of coaching services to an increasingly sophisticated client base and expanding set of client needs.

Our intention in this chapter is to inform individual practitioners, coaching buyers and wider stakeholders in the coaching industry as to the value of accreditation; to raise some useful questions for the coaching profession; and to provide some insight into the current state of play in relation to coach accreditation and qualification. Questions such as:

- How can accreditation systems enable the distinction of good practice?
- What trends around accreditation are occurring within the coaching industry?

We present the results of an updated survey of many of the main coaching professional bodies in the English-speaking world exploring their views on the value of accreditation and reviewing what is on offer.

The case for accreditation

What is the purpose of coach accreditation? What is it for? Whom does it serve? Accreditation processes have a number of purposes and functions, ranging from a values-based perspective to an economic one.

Primarily, accreditation is presented as a means of protecting and informing the client, assuring coach quality and client safety. This is achieved through the intention to clarify and enhance standards of coaching practice. Accreditation systems ideally support the client to find responses to questions such as:

- What do I need to do to find a coach?
- What is the process of selecting a coach?
- How do I know whether the coach I have is any good?
- How do I know whether my coach is safe?
- How do I know that I am investing my money wisely by employing this coach?

Accreditation systems can be designed to outline recognizable standards of practice within a professional body that can be expected from an individual (or organization) who is deemed as meeting that standard.

Accreditation also supports the development of the coaching profession. There is the view that for any discipline to be considered a profession (rather than an industry), there 'is the recognition of legitimacy and quality of the work performed by those practicing the trade' (Bennett, 2008). One of the 11 criteria for determining a profession includes:

> Evaluation of merit (credentialing) and self-regulating, encouraging diversity of thought, evaluation, and practice – for example, accepted requirements for coaches: systems for accessing competence; systems for monitoring and regulating service delivery by coaches; means of encouraging a wide array of thought and discussion about the practice of the profession. (Bennett, 2006)

In line with this, professional bodies might also support the appropriate education of coaching buyers by answering meta questions such as:

- Is coaching the right intervention?
- What are the opportunities and limitations of coaching as an intervention in relation to other methods?

Being able to clarify what good looks like and to evidence the likely impact builds trust and credibility. As Amstat simply puts it, accreditation strengthens the profession by setting the standards that relate to the quality of work a buyer can expect (Amstat, 2007).

Coaching accreditation, as well as setting a standard, provides a level of aspiration to those developing their coaching skills, clarifying what excellence consists of.

It seems a robust accreditation system that aligns to Bennett's criteria can have a positive impact on the quality of the coaching practice that emerges through:

- **Mastery of a body of knowledge.** As part of professional development such mastery can support creativity, accelerating and spurring innovation (Khurana and Nohria, 2008).

- **Increased self-awareness and understanding.** A robust coaching programme is likely to request some form of reflection regarding what principles and beliefs the individual coach holds or other underpinnings of his or her coaching practice.

- **Critical reflection on the ethics of coaching practice that is required as part of an accreditation process and adherence to an ethical code of practice.** Coaching remains a predominantly one-to-one activity, often conducted in a private, confidential space. An understanding of the boundaries that need to be held in such an environment, the value of such boundaries and some form of recognition of good practice in relation to those boundaries to ensure coach and client psychological and physical safety would seem essential.

- **Supporting coaches to articulate their coaching practice more explicitly.** As coaching is such a diverse and eclectic mix, a more explicit articulation may enable a more effective matching process between coaches and their clients and greater understanding among potential buyers and recipients.

There is a strong case for the value of robust accreditation systems for the individual coach, the buyer and the profession. Coach accreditation, however, is not straightforward. There are different levels of accreditation currently on offer, different terms used to mean accreditation, and an abundance of certificates available, and potential confusion.

Coach accreditation does not happen through professional bodies alone. Van Oudtshoorn (2002) noted that accreditation in coaching happens at three levels – personal, professional and academic:

- Personal accreditation is the simplest form, where a personal recommendation is made by an individual client who has benefited from coaching with the individual. This form of recommendation was perhaps one of the only ways of a coach being accredited up until the latter part of the 1990s. This approach is still highly used alongside (rather than instead of) other forms of accreditation.

- Professional accreditation, where a professional coaching body establishes a benchmark for standards and ethics in coaching practice and coach education, conducts research and educates key stakeholders. Krigbaum (2006) states that certification by an independent professional body gives the coach, as well as the public, a more transparent measure of skill that ensures both that the schools are training well and that the student is learning well.

- Academic accreditation, where academic institutions review the academic standards and quality of coach education against national qualifications frameworks. This is considered one of the most independent forms of accreditation as accreditation is independent of the profession itself.

The word 'accreditation' itself is derived from 'accredit', that is, 'to give official authorization to' (**www.oxforddictionaries.com**). Official authorization (professional or academic accreditation) provides formal recognition by a government body or some type of overarching organization that has the authority to award or authorize that an individual or training organization has achieved a certain standard.

Coaching is a largely unregulated industry; qualifications are still voluntary. This means that despite the level of maturity in any particular coaching market, any body (commercial or otherwise), may award 'accreditation' to coaches and coach training programmes without fear of censure. It's not surprising that certificates and qualifications for coaches abound; for example, Anne Scoular found over 50 organizations in the UK alone issuing certificates to coaches (Cotu and Kauffman, 2009: 96). Rather than enabling distinction for the coach and the consumer, this proliferation of certificates and qualifications does the opposite, overwhelming, confusing and further blurring the market. This was found to be the case in the 2009 ICF Global Coaching Client Study (PwC, 2009), which indicated that there are a number of misconceptions about coaching, the types of coaching and the process of coaching in the marketplace.

To add to the confusion, accreditation, certification, credential and registry are at times used interchangeably in reference to coaching qualifications. A registry (as opposed to accreditation) often refers to an agency or government body that keeps a record of certain items. Accreditation can refer to a training programme *or* to an individual coach. Within the domain of coaching, no government-sanctioned registers of coaches exist; however, organizations (including commercial organizations as well as professional bodies) might keep a register of coaches to promote registered members who have demonstrated a particular level of coaching competence that is relevant to that organization's coaching strategy.

As a coachee or buyer of coaching services, it is clear that there are many choices on offer. For this chapter we have chosen to focus on the development of accreditation systems which, as far as possible, are neutral, independent of particular business interests and individual agendas. The term we will use is *Individual Accreditation*, to encompass accreditation and credential as we discuss the formal qualifications of a coach. We define Individual Accreditation as: '*certification of an individual by a professional coaching body*'.

Research into best practice and professional standards in coaching indicates that there are opportunities to be explored and value to be gained through coach accreditation systems. Hawkins, drawing on the work of Jessica Jarvis and colleagues (CIPD, 2004), highlights three areas that the buyers of coaching services saw as important for coaching in the future:

- greater clarity in defining coaching and its main component;
- better quality control of the coaching provided to organizations;

- less fragmentation in the profession, with the major bodies working together to define standards and accredit coaches and training.

This was supported by the findings of the 2009 ICF Global Coaching Client Study (PwC, 2009).

Given the diversity of coaching on offer and the confusion around accreditation, it is not surprising that respondents in the ICF study (2009) viewed personal referral/word of mouth as their primary source of information when selecting their coaching (46 per cent of respondents rated this as their preferred option). Additionally, the importance of a coaching credential or certificate was rated as 'Very Important' by 41 per cent of respondents, and not as important as other interpersonal attributes (such as a coach's confidence, personal rapport, personal compatibility and the effectiveness of their coaching process).

There are some indications that, at least in more mature markets, the trends are shifting in the direction indicated by Hawkins (CIPD 2004). A level of consolidation is in process across some of the major professional coaching bodies in the English speaking world. Additionally, the importance of formal accreditation appears to be growing.

The importance of a coaching qualification appears to be growing. In the 2014 ICF Global Consumer Awareness Study of those consumers who have been in a coaching relationship, 83 per cent rated a coaching credential or certification as 'Important' or 'Very Important'. Accreditation from a trusted source is likely to play a more prominent role in the selection decision. More and more, individuals are not considered for organizational coaching registers unless they can provide evidence of coaching accreditation.

In summary, a coach's formal credentials or individual accreditation can:

- assure a level of service and play an important part in the decision to hire a coach (particularly when an existing personal recommendation or relationship is not present);
- protect those receiving *and* those providing the service;
- lead to enhanced standards of practice across the industry;
- promote learning and development;
- support the establishment and growth of a coaching profession across different areas of the globe.

The historical confusion and potential misinformation in the coaching arena provides a cautionary note. Without regulation of the industry through voluntary processes, such as valid and useful accreditation systems, formal regulation at the level of national governments may be forthcoming, following trends in other areas of professional practice.

Coach accreditation: recent history and developing trends

The coaching industry itself has a long history. Prior to the 1990s the industry was relatively small, consisting of specialist areas of practice such as coaching in relation to sporting achievements, or coaching in relation to performance. In contrast, the coaching industry today is very broad and includes professional coaching in business and organizations, executive coaching and life coaching. The industry has never been regulated; however, trends towards greater self-regulation have been noted by Palmer (2008) as coaching develops and matures from an industry into a profession.

In becoming a profession, standards of practice that are clarified through representative professional bodies are a key factor (Whybrow, 2008). Indeed, Khurana and Nohria (2008) note that 'true professions have codes of conduct, and the meaning and consequences of those codes are taught as part of the formal education of their members. A governing body composed of respected members of the profession, oversees members' compliance' (p 70). Indeed, Palmer comments on another sign of increasing professionalization, the fact that the coaching field 'is represented by one or more established professional bodies, eg the Association for Coaching, British Psychological Society Special Group in Coaching Psychology, European Mentoring and Coaching Council, International Association of Coaching and the International Coach Federation who have developed codes of ethics and practice for their members and accreditation and/or credentialing processes so members can work towards recognition as qualified coaches by their peers and others' (Drake, Brennan and Gørtz, 2008: xvii–xviii). In some of the more specialist areas of coaching practice, notably sports coaching, the accreditation for coaches is possibly at its most established, with nationally recognized schemes in some countries (for example, a National Coach Accreditation Scheme across Australia).

The emergence of a mature coaching profession is of interest to professional bodies that are stakeholders in the coaching industry. Dialogue of a collaborative nature (as called for by Brennan and Prior, 2005) has progressed conversations about standards of practice. When we originally reviewed coach accreditation for the second edition of *Excellence in Coaching*, we wrote that each professional body remained distinct and there was no clamour for the unification of standards (Brennan and Whybrow, 2010). Currently, the Association for Coaching, the European Mentoring and Coaching Council, and the International Coach Federation are working toward aligning competencies and identifying common standards of ethics within the construct of the Global Coaching and Mentoring Alliance (ICF, 2015). While we would hope to see involvement across more of the professional bodies, this is a beginning. A different approach to more consolidated standards is modelled in the area of Coaching Psychology, where the International Society for Coaching Psychology (ISCP) offers accreditation in its own right, as well as supporting emerging coaching psychology bodies around the globe to develop systems of accreditation locally.

Hawkins and other scholars (Bennett, 2006; Drake, 2008; Hawkins, 2008) acknowledge the work towards professionalization in the coaching industry and, at the same time, warn of the need to proceed with caution. There appears to be value in the existing diversity within the coaching industry. The eclectic nature of the coaching community, with various levels of education, experience and expertise, presents challenges and opportunities that are important to understand, to learn from and to grow, both as individual practitioners and as a community of professionals. Adopting a single set of standards across the industry may limit the potential and diversity of this emerging field (eg Hawkins, 2008) and reduce the coaching industry to the 'middle layers of competence'.

Understanding existing and emerging professional accreditation systems in the coaching space

Individual accreditation systems continue to emerge and develop as new and established professional bodies continue to shape their thinking and accreditation activities. For this chapter, we have explored the development of individual professional accreditation across the coaching industry, drawing on results from a survey of many of the main coaching bodies across the English-speaking world.

In 2010, we approached professional bodies that were viewed as the most central stakeholders in the development of the emerging coaching profession. In addition, we contacted the well-known leadership and management bodies in the UK and North America. In 2015, we approached the same group of professional bodies, using an online 10-item questionnaire. The professional bodies spanned the United States, Europe and Australia (see the appendix at the end of the chapter).

Individual Accreditation Survey: findings

In reviewing the 2010 findings, first we looked at what had been developed in broad terms, and how long different accreditation systems had been in place. We then looked at some of the detail of the structure of individual accreditation systems and what assessment methods were involved in assessing capability. Second, we looked at the underpinning purpose of accreditation as declared by the different professional bodies, how the systems have been validated, and the underpinning values, incidents and ideas that shaped the different accreditation systems. Finally, we explored the impact of coach accreditation systems on members, clients and the professional body itself. While we referred to coaching throughout, more than a third of the professional bodies approached were specifically focused on coaching psychology as an area of professional practice and provided insight into the accreditation systems that were emerging in that space. We drew out some of the elements that relate specifically to this group of practitioners. In 2015 we repeated many aspects of this enquiry. The results are outlined below.

What individual accreditation systems have been developed for coaches?

In 2010, the majority of the professional bodies who responded to the survey (9 of the 13) had individual accreditation systems in place, including one accreditation system specifically for coaching psychologists (that of the International Society for Coaching Psychology). For organizations that didn't have their own individual accreditation system, only one professional grouping (Asia Pacific Alliance of Coaches (APAC)) recommended the system within another body (that of the International Coach Federation (ICF)). The remaining three organizations that did not have an individual accreditation system for people working specifically as coaches were those who were part of a broader psychological professional body.

All professional bodies were in the process of developing, or at least considering the development of, a route to individual accreditation. Additionally, where systems were established in coaching professional bodies, these are not static; as one participating body noted, they are 'currently working on significant upgrades to the existing system'.

In 2015, all the coaching and most of the coaching psychology bodies surveyed had an individual accreditation process in place. The sophistication and range of coaching accreditation offered is more diverse within many of the professional bodies than it was in 2010. This diversity goes beyond levels of coach accreditation to include specific accreditation of wider aspects of a potential coaching practice, such as individual accreditation for coaching supervision, and accreditation for team coaching.

How long have individual accreditation systems been around?

Individual coach accreditation systems have been in place since 1998, with the International Coach Federation being the first to develop an accreditation system for coaches. The next wave of accreditation systems were developed between 2003 and 2005 (Association for Professional Executive Coaching and Supervision (APECS); European Coaching and Mentoring Council (EMCC); International Association of Coaching (IAC); Association for Coaching (AC)). The latest wave of individual coach accreditation systems has been since 2006/7, with the Worldwide Association of Business Coaches (WABC) and the European Mentoring and Coaching Council UK (EMCC UK) developing a system in 2008. The first coaching *psychology*-specific individual accreditation system was developed in 2008, by the Society for Coaching Psychology (SCP).

The trend has been for more individual coach accreditation systems to develop, and, more recently, for coaching psychology professional bodies to develop specific routes to accreditation for psychologists specializing in coaching practice. The Special Group in Coaching Psychology (SGCP), the Society of Evidence-based Coaching of the Danish Psychological Association (SEBC) and the Interest Group in Coaching Psychology (IGCP) are all prioritizing accreditation for their members.

With rapid developments in the field of coaching in terms of the thinking that is taking place around standards (see Figure 17.1), the research being conducted and the development of coaching communities and coaching practice, there is challenge for professional coaching bodies to stay up to date. Periodically, established accreditation systems are being reviewed and updated.

What different levels of individual accreditation are offered?

As well as the offering of an individual accreditation/certification system, we were interested in what levels of individual accreditation were offered by the professional bodies (see Table 17.1 for an overview). Some immediate observations include:

FIGURE 17.1 The rate of development of individual accreditation systems

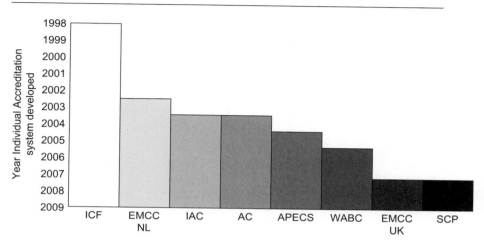

- There is a good range of accreditation options to choose from as an individual practitioner – from foundation through to mastery.

- Titles of the different awards differ significantly from one body to another; this renders the level denoted by the title alone relatively meaningless in comparison to other individual accreditation systems in the profession.

- Some professional bodies offer different levels of individual accreditation (AC, EMCC, ICF, ISCP, WABC), while some bodies offer one level of individual accreditation (APECS, IAC, SGCP). Of those bodies that offer only one level of individual accreditation, in the case of APECS, IAC and the SGCP, this denotes a level of mastery of individual coaching practice (rather than an entry level accreditation).

- The level of theoretical underpinning, hours of practice, and demonstrable evidence required to be eligible for a particular type of accreditation vary widely.

In 2010, several of the bodies indicated that they were in the process of reviewing and updating. The table reflects the 2015 responses and updates from the professional bodies.

TABLE 17.1 The different levels of accreditation provided by different professional bodies

Professional body	Individual accreditation options offered by different professional bodies	
	Entry level	**More advanced options offered**
European Mentoring and Coaching Council (EMCC)	**Foundation level**	**Intermediate level** **Practitioner level** **Master level**
International Coach Federation (ICF)	**Level 1 – Associate Certified Coach (ACC)**	**Level 2 – Professional Certified Coach (PCC)** **Level 3 – Master Certified Coach (MCC)**
International Society for Coaching Psychology	**Level 1:** Portfolio Approach for Associate Members	**Level 2:** Accreditation process for Qualified Psychologists
Worldwide Association of Business Coaches	**Level 1 – WABC Accredited (Practitioner Level)**	**Level 2 – WABC Accredited (Master Level)** **Level 3 – WABC Accredited (Chartered Level)**
APECS	**Level 1 – Associate Practitioner**	**Level 2 – Accredited Executive Coach**
International Association of Coaches	**Level 1 – IAC-Certified Coach** This is a master-level accreditation based on an assessment of coaching demonstration	
Association for Coaching	**Associate Coach**	**Level 2 – Professional Coach;** **Level 3 – Master Coach**
	Associate Executive Coach	**Level 2 – Professional Executive Coach;** **Level 3 – Master Executive Coach**
Special Group in Coaching Psychology (SGCP, BPS)	**Level 1: Register of Coaching Psychologists**	

What do the individual accreditation systems require by way of evidence?

In 2010, there were many different ways of evidencing capability or competence to be eligible to become accredited. The different methodologies that individual accreditation systems require are shown in Figure 17.2.

Evidence of study of a body of knowledge is asked for in all cases. As stated earlier, the principle of mastering a body of knowledge can lead to creativity, accelerating and spurring innovation (Khurana and Nohria, 2008). What was not explored in this survey is the nature of that knowledge base. What are the similarities and differences across the coaching and coaching psychology bodies in terms of the detail of what is considered relevant 'knowledge'?

As would be expected in an area that is about practice excellence rather than theoretical expertise alone, evidence of practice is required in all cases. One coaching body that did not require evidence of practice in the

FIGURE 17.2   Different forms of evidence used to demonstrate standards

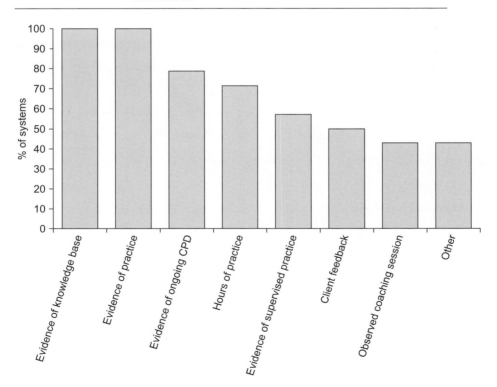

application form requested observation of a coaching session as part of the accreditation process. Most accreditation systems required evidence on ongoing continuous professional development (CPD) (79 per cent), evidence of hours of coaching practice (71 per cent) and evidence of supervision (57 per cent). Half of the professional bodies asked for client feedback (50 per cent), while less than half required observation of coaching practice (43 per cent).

It seems that a range of evidence of practice was required by professional bodies in order for individuals to demonstrate their capability. It would be interesting to explore the validity of these different methodologies in determining the capability of individuals to practise in line with the professional bodies' explicit standards and purpose for accreditation.

In addition to the aspects detailed in the table below, there are other criteria that are considered in accreditation systems. For example, length of experience, number of clients, evidence of performance against competences, reflection on practice, contribution to the profession and evidence of appropriate professional insurance.

TABLE 17.2   Different forms of evidence used by selected professional bodies

Professional body	EMCC	ICF	ISCP	SGCP, BPS	WABC	APECS	AC	IAC
Evidence of knowledge base	✓	✓	✓	✓	✓	✓	✓	✓
Evidence of coaching practice	✓	✓	✗	✓	✓	✓	✓	✓
Evidence of ongoing CPD	✓	✓	✓	✓	✓	✓	✓	✓
Minimum number of hours of coaching practice	✓	✓	✓	✓	✓	✓	✓	✓
Evidence of supervised practice	✓	✗	✓	✓	✓	†	✓	†
Client feedback	✓	✗	✗	✗	✓	✓	✓	✓
Observed coaching session	✗	✓	✗	✗	✓	✗	✗	✗
Recorded coaching session	✗	✓	✗	✗	✓	✗	✗	✓
Evidence of ethical practice	✓	✓	✓	✓	✓	✓	✓	✓

Coaching and coaching psychology

Here we looked at the commonalities across the coaching professional bodies and coaching psychology professional bodies before exploring the specific points for coaching psychology professional bodies that have emerged.

The purpose of coach accreditation – survey responses

Responses to the individual accreditation survey indicated that coaching professional bodies saw their accreditation system as having a range of purposes. Some appeared to be based around values and principles:

- to contribute to standardization of the profession and upholding standards in this unregulated industry, to advance the profession;
- to provide a yardstick to coaches and provide a benchmark that gives confidence to coaches;
- to set international standards for business coaches;
- to promote high-calibre leadership in business coaching services for the benefit of clients;
- to provide a personal development guide for coaching psychologists;
- to contribute to the definition, development and self-regulation of the emergent [business] coaching profession;
- to assist the public and the purchasers of coaching services to identify effective coaches and provide an assurance of quality, to provide protection to the public;
- to allow the market and stakeholders of coaching to differentiate between more or less qualified practitioners;
- to enable the users of coaching to distinguish the amateurs from the professionals.

Other articulated purposes appear more utilitarian:

- to give professional status to members, to provide marketplace credibility;
- to provide designations to members;
- to promote membership of the body.

These articulated purposes are thought provoking and a number of questions emerge. For example, what is to be standardized and what is it important not to standardize in the accreditation process? What are the principles on which the accreditation is based? How are we certain that these standards lead to assured quality? To what extent are 'public' interests being served and the 'public' being protected? Can we say that a coach with a particular accreditation is better, more effective, safer, than one without?

The utilitarian purposes are easier to evaluate. It is easy to ascertain whether an individual coach appears more professional as a result of a designated accredited title; we can see immediately that members of professional bodies are provided with designated titles that do carry some authority; and we can also see how the availability of an individual accreditation system promotes membership growth of that particular body.

Whether the appearance of professionalism through a given designation does indeed deliver a more professional service depends on the evidence of impact of those who have a particular accreditation and those who don't. This is a fertile area for research.

What underpinning values, incidents, ideas and experience have shaped accreditation systems?

We were interested here to understand what drivers helped shape the accreditation system. Was this about avoiding poor standards? Was it about moving towards a particular philosophical perspective? The responses from participants in the survey are varied, and include:

- a commitment to maintaining good practice, driven from an ethical and experiential perspective;
- a belief in having the highest standards of mastery, to distinguish professionals;
- a modelling of mainstream professional chartered standards;
- a range of values such as inclusiveness, quality, fairness, objectivity, reliability, legal defensibility;
- competition with other coaching organizations;
- the desire for successful outcomes of coaching with clients rather than mere training hours.

How have the accreditation systems been validated?

We explored the extent to which the accreditation processes have been validated and there was a broad range of responses. Responses to this question included comments on how the process of accreditation was validated:

- multiple certifiers scoring recordings and comparing findings between recordings;
- a system created by experts in the field;
- a validating committee provided the suggestions;
- extensive evidence-based research.

Another way of looking at the validity of the accreditation system is to look at the outcomes of the systems. There were some responses to the question on validity that made explicit reference to a validation measure: increased demand and market acceptance; whether a significant group of practitioners would apply.

We recognize that the responses to this question very much depend on individual respondents' construct of validation; even then, the survey responses were very limited in their detail. What can be drawn from this is that the construction of the systems of accreditation is diverse across the field and assumptions cannot be made about what accreditation systems are based on or how they have been constructed without further investigation.

What is the impact of accreditation?

In this survey, we looked at impact at a very superficial level across a number of potential areas: members' clients, members themselves, and the professional body. One impact that completes the circle is that the very existence of individual coach accreditation systems supports the establishment of the profession itself (eg Bennett, 2006).

The impact on members' clients

The expected benefits for members' clients include:

- quality assurance – a key benefit cited by a number of professional bodies, whereby the accreditation system can act as a substitute for due diligence;
- safe, secure and effective coaching services;
- enables clients to identify highly experienced and qualified coaches;
- transparency.

The impact on members

From the purposes outlined above, it might be expected that the accreditation systems provide credibility to those that meet the requirements, that practitioners' 'marketability' is increased, that their confidence in their capability is assured. The impact of accreditation systems on members, as described by the coaching professional bodies, is purely seen as a beneficial development and includes providing:

- a recognized, high-quality certification that builds up coaches' professional reputation;
- assurance, credibility, increased branding, appropriate exposure and market representation;
- confidence as a professional and recognition of the knowledge and skill required as a coach;
- a road to professional development;
- a forum for skilled, highly qualified coaches to meet, network and exchange ideas and experiences.

The impact on the professional body itself

Accreditation is viewed as having a significant impact across the activities of the professional body. It is seen to increase the profile of the professional body and its opportunity to affect both members and the profession. The impact more specifically is seen as:

- realization of one of the main reasons for existing as a professional body;
- establishing standards and going on to further strengthen ethics and raise standards;
- development of professional expertise and self-regulation;
- enhancing the image and brand of the professional body;
- a primary service and a major incentive for members to join.

Coaching psychology

In 2010, 5 of the 13 respondents to our survey were coaching psychology bodies. The responses indicate that coaching psychology bodies are focused on the development of coaching psychology as part of the coaching profession *and* as an area within the profession of psychology. This duality means that coaching psychology professional bodies may at times experience uncomfortable tensions in both of the professions that they represent. Here we have drawn out responses that pertain to this specific group of professional bodies that are stakeholders in this area.

The purpose of coaching psychology accreditation systems (developed or in development), while sharing many of those of other coaching professional bodies, is specifically: to support quality of development and service provided by psychologists who focus on coaching as an area of practice, and the development of coaching psychology as a specific area of psychological practice; to draw coaching psychology together at an international level; and to support the credibility of psychologists within the coaching marketplace.

Looking at what underpinning values, incidents, ideas and experience have shaped the accreditation systems of coaching psychologist, of particular note is:

- a desire to have a particular representation for psychologists who coach;
- to articulate coaching psychology as a non-medical model of psychological practice, and the application of a positive psychological frame;
- a psychological cornerstone;
- a concern for the well-being of client populations.

The impact of coaching psychology accreditation systems (in addition to what has been articulated above in relation to coaching) is that, through the establishment of such systems, potential coachees and clients may have greater clarity about whom it might be appropriate to seek as a coach and with what psychological background. The contexts within which psychologists practise are diverse and it is not simply a case of a psychologist being able to work across multiple contexts without some reconstruction of his or her practice in each context. So, while some elements are transferable between contexts, other aspects may need to be relearned in the context of coaching. To those outside the profession, these differences are not often apparent.

For members of coaching psychology bodies, specific accreditation for coaching psychologists will support them to define their practice more clearly and provide them with a specific professional qualification route that differentiates coaching psychology from other areas of psychological practice.

For coaching psychology bodies, accreditation systems specifically for their membership could be seen to strengthen the coaching psychology body with a view to enhancing the role and the perceived value of psychology and psychological approaches in the coaching industry. Further, accreditation systems will support the credibility of coaching psychology within the broader domain of the psychological profession.

Where to from here?

There is on the one hand similarity across the accreditation systems being offered, but there is also great diversity in the tone, in the presentation and in the purpose of different systems. While there are many differences among the professional bodies, commitment to high standards, ethical practice and competence are foundational to why most have entered into this process.

For all professional bodies, their accreditation systems appear to serve multiple purposes: on the one hand, serving a more altruistic purpose 'to add value', whatever that articulated value might be; and on other, serving a basic function of supporting the survival of the industry itself. Without professionalization and a focus on sound practice, coaching might well, even now, have been a passing infatuation. As the profession of coaching continues to develop, the stakeholders in this area continue to navigate the challenge of exploring areas of similarity and points of leadership for the benefit of the broader profession, while at the same time clarifying their differences in order to maintain their own coherent community of practitioners.

This diversity and difference offer an important resource to the development of the professions of coaching and coaching psychology. The higher purpose of ensuring competent professionals to serve the public is important to keep at the forefront and may serve as the common goal for further dialogue. In moving forward, it would be particularly interesting to see how differences can be appreciated, and how each professional body can articulate and develop their strengths. For, after all, isn't this what coaching is about? Appreciating the diversity and resourcefulness of others and optimizing strengths in the pursuit of achieving fulfilment and potential? The alternatives one might imagine could include a scenario where professional bodies might further their individual purpose at the expense of the profession as a whole; the emergence of a 'merged' super coaching professional body seems less constructive to the development of this professional area of practice at this point in time.

For those seeking to become a coach there is work to be done. While individual accreditation is not, by default, going to lead to the professionalization of coaching, a coach has a responsibility to ensure that he or she is professionally qualified. As a client interviews a coach when seeking to find the right match, so should a coach explore the professional bodies to find their best fit. It is also important to note that there may be more than one route to accreditation that suits your purpose as a professional. Some questions for the coach to consider:

- What is the organization's purpose around individual accreditation?
- How does this fit with your purpose, your vision and your values?
- How were the individual accreditation standards and measures established?
- Does the process assess knowledge as well as skill?
- Are there any other requirements?
- What do members say about the process?
- What is the value of the accreditation in the marketplace that you want to work in – locally, nationally, globally?

Individual accreditation as a coach can offer much more than just a piece of paper. In choosing to become accredited, you may be embarking on a learning journey that has a positive impact beyond just your practice as a coach, and may include you becoming part of a professional community of practice that acts as a resource and guide far beyond the length of time it takes to become accredited.

In writing this chapter, some thoughtful questions have arisen from the diversity and difference we have observed. Curiously, while individual accreditation systems have been developed and appear to be robust and all-encompassing, there has been less peer-reviewed research than there might be as to the impact of that accreditation on the achievement of the purposes outlined by the professional bodies. It could be seen that the basis for accreditation is economically grounded, where coaching buyers are buying the idea of the value of accreditation and its link to professionalism, and members of professional bodies are joining and becoming accredited to enable them to show their value to buyers of coaching services and their professionalism.

But, what is the real value for the users of coaching services? What evidence is there to support the idea that the purposes of individual coach accreditation systems are achieved? Are we in danger of making the assumption that because accreditation is valuable to us as professionals, the accreditation systems that are in place are delivering a broader value? What is the link between accreditation, practice and outcomes? Has the link between accreditation and practice been robustly explored? The case study by Mortlock and Horner (2009), reports the initial review of a very thorough coach selection process to provide a register of coaches for a public sector body in the UK, the observation of coaching practice was critical in providing insight into how people actually coach.

This leads to a further area of exploration: what aspects of the individual accreditation systems provide what value? For example, there are significant differences between professional bodies in relation to the evidence required for the individual accreditation system. Of particular note is the requirement by some of the professional bodies for accredited members to demonstrate that they receive regular supervision for their practice, and the requirement for members to demonstrate ongoing professional development. What value is attached to these requirements and what impact does fulfilling these requirements have?

Yet still there is the question of how the professional bodies might collaborate to support those who are buying coaching services (individuals and organizations) in easily understanding the value of the accreditation systems in relation to practice. Currently the coaching and coaching psychology professional bodies have a significant opportunity to lay the groundwork for such a system and potentially developing such a system before a system is imposed by an external regulatory body as has happened with other professions.

In considering the opportunity for dialogue and discussion that has been generated, and the potential challenges in taking that forward, it is useful to reflect that whether coaching evolves to be truly recognized as a profession or continues to be perceived as an industry, the professional bodies play a key role for the future.

Conclusion

The awareness and impact of coaching continue to grow and expand, and accreditation, while not formally required yet, is an increasingly important consideration. Our survey gave us a glimpse of the professional bodies and their accreditation systems. They include a variety of requirements and measures, many of which support ongoing learning and professional development for the coach as well as those involved with the standards and assessment processes.

We acknowledge the work of the professional bodies for their foresight in introducing accreditation systems, beginning with ICF in 1998. The focus on standards, ethics and competencies that form the basis for the accreditation systems lays a significant foundation for professionalization of coaching.

References

Amstat.org (2007) Accreditation, http://www.amstat.org/committees/accreditation/individualaccreditationprograms.pdf, accessed 6/29/09

Bennett, J (2006) An agenda for coaching-related research: a challenge for researchers, *Consulting Psychology Journal: Practice and Research*, 58 (4), pp 240–49

Bennett, J (2008) *Is Executive Coaching an Academic Discipline?*, Conference paper Queens University, Charlotte, NC, retrieved from http://repository.upenn.edu/od_conf_2008/1/ on 4 February 2010

Brennan, D and Prior, D M (2005) *The Future of Coaching as a Profession: The next five years 2005–1010*, International Coach Federation, Lexington, KY

Chartered Institute of Personnel and Development (CIPD) (2004) *Coaching and Buying Coaching Services*, CIPD, London, http://www.cipd.co.uk/hr-resources/

Cotu, D and Kauffman, C (2009) What can coaches do for you? *Harvard Business Review*, Research Report, January

Drake, D B (2008) Finding our way home: coaching's search for identity in a new era, *Coaching: An international journal of theory, research and practice*, 1 (1), pp 15–26

Drake, D, Brennan, D and Gørtz, K (2008) *The Philosophy and Practice of Coaching: Insights and issues for a new era*, Wiley, Chichester

Hawkins, P (2008) The coaching profession: some of the key challenges, *Coaching: An international journal of theory, research and practice*, 1 (1), pp 28–37

ICF (2015) Global Coaching Mentoring Alliance, retrieved from www.coachfederation.org/about/ on 15 April 2015

Krigbaum, M (2006) Competence: getting, growing, and measuring coaching ability, in *Law and Ethics in Coaching: How to solve and avoid difficult problems in your practice*, ed P Williams and S Anderson, John Wiley & Sons, Hoboken, NJ

Khurana, R and Nohria, N (2008) It's time to make management a true profession, *Harvard Business Review*, October, pp 70–79

Mortlock, S and Horner, C (2009) *The Search for Excellence: How the NHS Institute selects coaches who are fit-for-purpose*, Paper presented at the CIPD Coaching at Work Conference, September, London

Palmer, S (2008) Foreword, in *The Philosophy and Practice of Coaching: Insights and issues for a new era*, ed D B Drake, D Brennan and K Gørtz, Jossey-Bass, San Francisco

PricewaterhouseCoopers (2014) *2014 International Coach Federation Global Coaching Study*. International Coach Federation, Lexington, KY. Retrieved from www.coachfederation.org/icfresearch/ on 15 April 2015

PricewaterhouseCoopers (2009) 2009 *ICF Global Coaching Client Study*, Lexington, JY: International Coach Federation. retrieved from www.coachfederation.org/icfresearch/ on 15 April 2015

PricewaterhouseCoopers (2009) *ICF Coaching Client Study*, International Coach Federation, Lexington, KY, retrieved from www.coachfederation.org/icfresearch/ on 15 April 2015

Van Oudtshoorn, M (2002) *Coaching: The catalyst for organization change?*, Professorial Lecture, 16 October, Middlesex University, London

Whybrow, A (2008) Coaching psychology: coming of age, *International Coaching Psychology Review*, 3 (3), pp 227–40

APPENDIX
Professional bodies who participated in the survey

We would like to express our heartfelt thanks to all the professional bodies that participated in our work exploring accreditation and as such have supported the writing of this chapter.

In the table below we have listed each of the participating bodies in alphabetical order and provided their web address.

Title	Acronym	Website address
Association for Coaching	AC	http://www.associationforcoaching.com
Association for Professional Executive Coaching and Supervision	APECS	http://www.apecs.org
European Mentoring and Coaching Council	EMCC – UK	http://www.emccouncil.org/index.php?id=5&L=1
International Association of Coaching	IAC	http://www.certifiedcoach.org
International Coach Federation	ICF	http://www.coachfederation.org
International Society for Coaching Psychology	SCP	http://www.isfcp.net
Society of Evidence-based Coaching of the Danish Psychological Association	SEBC	http://www.sebc.dk

Title	Acronym	Website address
Swedish Psychological Association	SPA	**http://www.psykologforbundet.se**
Worldwide Association of Business Coaches	WABC	**http://www.wabccoaches.com**
Special Group in Coaching Psychology, The British Psychological Society	SGCP	**http://www.sgcp.org.uk**
Interest Group in Coaching Psychology, Australian Psychological Society	IGCP	**http://www.groups.psychology.org.au/igcp**

Team coaching

18

KATE LANZ

Team coaching as a discipline is somewhat behind its individual coaching counterpart. This may be so but, that said, team coaching is catching up fast.

This is due in part to business recognizing that in an increasingly VUCA (volatile, uncertain, complex and ambiguous) world, effective teams are a key point of leverage within an organization, with the agility to exploit any perceived strategic advantage in fast-moving markets.

Since the 2008–09 financial crisis many teams in a wide variety of business sectors are being expected to both keep business as usual running, whilst at the same time building the platforms for growth and the change necessary to keep organizations relevant and fleet of foot. This can represent a considerable demand on the players who make up the team.

Additionally, post-crisis, there is a growing acceleration in the move away from the notion of the heroic leader, where the individual leader is expected to be the fount of all wisdom. There is now an increasing movement towards the idea of an 'ecosystem' where leadership is distributed across the organization – popularized under the title of leadership–exchange theory. This still requires leaders who are able to truly empower teams (not always as common as one might hope), and team members who are able to lead from any chair. Given the complex dynamics that can exist in teamwork, team coaching has a very important role to play in supporting effective distributed leadership, through enabling highly effective team performance.

The three key levels within team coaching

Team coaching needs to work at three levels to be effective. These are the individual level, the collective team level and the team's wider organizational relationship level.

In essence, teams are all about relationship. Relationship is one of the key units of measure, if you like, by which tasks do or don't happen. To reduce relationship to the notion of a unit of measure is of course entirely wrong, but it does help to make the point that, in essence, this is what organizations are. They are the sum total of the relationships that exist within them and it is the overall tone and quality of those relationships that make up the culture of the organization.

This does not at all mean that everyone has to be friends and get on all the time! Conflict is human and can result in organizational benefits. The ability to manage productive conflict is a key component in effective robust relationships. As humans, we function in relationship and the more relationship-insightful and competent we are, the more effective the organization will be. What goes on in teams and the way those teams interact with the whole in terms of relational insight and competence drives a significant element of task success or failure.

Good team coaching supports insight into and skill in building relationship at all these three levels. Firstly, at the individual level enabling team members to gain personal understanding of their own emotional and psychological patterns and how these show up at work – the self. Secondly, team coaching works to enable the relationships and dynamics at the collective level to be well understood, healthy and integrated, developing the behavioural habits that will keep them that way. Thirdly, team coaching works to support the team to have highly effective relationships with key parts of their organizational system and beyond.

These relationships are the means by which the team is able to deliver on its task in the most efficient, enjoyable and sustainable way possible. People who feel good about themselves do their best work.

Thus, my own definition of team coaching reflects this three-part approach.

> ### Team coaching defined
> 'Working with a whole team to support the development of healthy integrated relationships within the individual, between team members and key organizational stakeholders to support the delivery of the team task in the most efficient, enjoyable and sustainable way possible. The quality of relationships enables the team to get to true clarity of purpose, develop effective use of resources and focus on delivering the task.'

Again I must stress this is not about seeking harmony. Too much harmony can be bad for teams. Irving Janis's (1982) work on groupthink also highlights the dangers of teams becoming overreliant on agreeing with each other. The flawed decision of President Kennedy and his advisers to authorize the Bay of Pigs invasion of Cuba demonstrates the phenomenon of groupthink. Groupthink is characterized by excessive efforts to get to agreement, and a strong need for consensus that can override the team's ability to make the most appropriate decision. Symptoms of groupthink include group members' tendency to: believe the team to be more invulnerable than it is; to rationalize the team's decisions and believe stereotypes about its enemies/others; and also to feel increasing pressure to agree with others in the group.

It is about promoting overall relational health and competence. A large part of this is the ability to hold conflict and tension in a productive way. Good team coaching includes supporting team members to appropriately create and handle the conflict at the three levels.

Three core lenses for looking at team coaching effectiveness

There are three lenses that need to be applied to each of the three levels (individual/collective/systemic) as one both designs and carries out the work. These are:

- relationship;
- dynamics (arising from the relationships);
- business imperatives.

What do I mean by this? When you are designing your intervention, look for methods and techniques that are likely to enhance the quality of the relationship in question, that enable greater insight and appreciation of the relational dynamics in play and that link directly to the business imperative of that situation. This keeps the team coaching work relevant, drives real learning related to task and work context and moves the action forward in terms of results within the actual business.

An example in practice would be to get team members giving each other feedback in pairs on behaviours that are working/not working in relation to a real team task with which they are each involved and requesting a change of behaviour to drive a different business outcome. A very simple way of doing this is to get each team member to share:

> 'One thing I really appreciate about you is ... and the way it showed up in relation to task X was ...'

and

> 'One thing I would like you to change is ... and how this would help in task X ...'

This is a simple exercise which tackles all three lenses and two of the layers. You can get team members to do the same with all members of the team, thus building feedback capacity at the individual level and the collective team level. The exercise can be debriefed at the collective level and with that team you can start to develop a vocabulary for their behavioural dynamics and develop effective feedback habits that build (rather than disrupt) relationship.

At this point the exercise still remains only inwardly-focused on the internal team dynamic so needs framing up a level and repeating to get the team members applying the thinking and action to the wider system.

This overly inward focus is a very common pitfall in team coaching. Team coaches often lose sight of the fact that the team can only be truly successful in relation to the systemic whole. This perspective is supported by the ideas of Henrik Bresman (Bresman and Ancona, 2007), who has argued that the most successful teams reach out to stakeholders, develop extensive ties, work across tiers of their organization, and operate using flexible membership.

The six principles of team coaching – the 'how' of team coaching

There are six key principles that are helpful guiding principles when designing and delivering team coaching. Over the years these are the ones that I have found consistently support the best results in team coaching.

These are:

1 Create and hold the space; make the team do the work.

2 Create a strong sense of emotional and psychological safety. People can only change when they feel safe enough emotionally. This does not mean 'play it safe'.

3 Reveal the non-conscious dynamics that are playing out and help the team create their own vocabulary to describe them.

4 Uncover and understand the power dynamics within the team and in the system. Do this in a way that does not leave people feeling too exposed (remember principle two). This also supports the team in maintaining enough of an outwardly-focused view. Add this to the team's new vocabulary.

5 Always embed behavioural habits that support effective relationship insight and competence. People don't change easily; repetition and habit and a felt-sense of the shifts are vitally important to success.

6 Have fun – people remember more and change more when they are enjoying themselves, although this does not mean that there are no tense moments!

Let's look at these principles in more detail.

1. The coach creates and holds the space and the team does the work

Usually a team will come into coaching when something is not working already. Some smart teams will come into team coaching as a matter of course before anything has derailed. This is not common – yet. So normally there is a level of anxiety in the air already when the coach gets to meet the team for the first time. There are two primary ways this anxiety can manifest. The first is the 'Fix us, coach' projection, where team members become slightly helpless and passive and are waiting for the coach to work their magic on them and solve the problem. The second is a defiant stance which is more along the lines of 'show us what you've got, coach, and we'll see if we are willing to play' – a more aggressive approach. Whatever the coach gets coming their way, the important thing is to recognize the form the anxiety is taking and carefully position in the contracting phase the responsibility for what happens in the work so that it lies with the team not with the coach. This has to be done clearly, gently and firmly so as not to make the anxiety worse. At the first actual team coaching occasion this message needs to be followed quickly with some benign and encouraging exercises early in the process to make people feel relaxed and confident.

Example from practice: Contract with the whole team about what they want to get from the work and be very clear that they are the ones responsible for the outputs. You will hold the space; they will do the work. You can build on the diagnostic interviews that you may have already done pre-meeting the team. This personal contact before the team coaching starts is a really good idea. Then get team members thinking about their most positive experience in a team setting (at or outside work); get them bringing this personal team best to life through sharing the story with their team colleagues. This will get them in touch with their own competence, enjoyment and get them focused on what works right up front.

2. Create a strong sense of emotional and psychological safety

This is critical if the team coaching is to be successful and comes down in large part to the skill and confidence of the coach. It is in essence the trust that each of the team members feels individually with the coach and the trust that the team collectively feels with the coach and amongst each other. The sense of emotional safety will (hopefully) build steadily over the process of the coaching, and the coach needs to hold this in mind as a guiding principle at each point of the design.

It is very important to say that this is not the same as playing it safe with the coaching work – risks must be taken with the team in order to move the action forward. And if the risks are taken based upon a sufficient level of emotional safety at each stage they are more likely to be successful in outcome.

It is important to start this process during the initial contracting phase, before actually starting work with the whole team and inquiring at each of the three levels: individual, team/collective and systemic.

This inquiry also gets a view of the team by the team and from the wider system. This is best done through personal interviews and meetings so that the felt-sense of emotional safety with the coach can begin to be built up.

Example from practice: If you have made a good connection on the phone or in person beforehand this will already help a lot to establish the sense of emotional safety. Contract carefully that what comes up in the team coaching will remain confidential unless the team agree that it is information they want to share more widely. Personal information that gets revealed is the property of the person and is NOT for any other member of the team to share outside the room. Get everyone's voice in the room in agreement with this ground rule.

3. Reveal the team's non-conscious dynamics

Much of what inhibits a team's performance sits in the area of the non-conscious emotional dynamics or the conscious but unspoken emotional dynamics. The team coach needs to create the opportunity for the team to begin to see, understand and describe these dynamics in a way that feels sufficiently safe and that develops a vocabulary that the team can own themselves to describe them along with ways of dealing with the dynamics productively.

Revealing these dynamics is best done working with here and now examples of the behaviours that play out amongst team members. This can be done through calling short timeouts while a team is performing an exercise or team task and reflecting back what you are experiencing and observing as the coach and getting the team's response to that. It can also be done by asking the team an incisive question about something that just happened and finding out what team members noticed about it (or not). It is good to develop the vocabulary using the team's own language so that they feel a sense of ownership and that language that might smack to them of psychological jargon is avoided.

This is a central part of the work. It is especially useful to get the team working on their real business issues to do the here and now work. It works well to pick hot topics where there will be some tension between team members.

Example from practice: Carry out live coaching of one team member on a particular challenge they were facing and ask the rest of the team to observe and playback what they are noticing and picking up about the person, their situation, their verbal and non-verbal signals. Then asking them how they could help the individual. Develop some concrete and specific actions from the coaching session that involve team members helping each other. Use this data to facilitate the team talking about the non-conscious or not-spoken-about dynamics within the team. Use the exercise to flush out other non-conscious dynamics, name them and build a vocabulary. In one particular instance, for example, it emerged that the individual was very isolated. Even he had not realized this. This prompted some team members to think about how they could support him and it also flagged up others who felt isolated and struggled to reach out and ask for help for fear of looking weak. This led to a conversation about the things that represented weakness in the wider system and within this team. It was a very rich exchange and exposed in a productive way many of the things that were blocking team performance.

4. Uncover and understand the power dynamics within the team and the organizational system

I once worked with a team who described themselves (in our metaphor exercise) as the 'janitors – cleaning up everyone else's mess' – no wonder they felt pretty powerless within the wider system. This powerlessness was reflected in the way they were pretty passive with each other and low on stakeholder engagement. We worked on reframing their view of themselves and their role so that they could engage in an entirely different way.

It is vital to uncover, understand and discuss the power dynamics within the team and the wider system with which this team interacts. Without this understanding the team cannot be highly effective. The areas to explore with team members are to what extent the internal power dynamics support the team's task delivery and to what extent they block it. This is where it can get hot and uncomfortable. If some team members inappropriately wield too much power this will have to change and the team, with the coach's help, will have to work this out between them. This can be tough. Where some team members are revealed as lacking power or are weak, this can be embarrassing and result in a potential loss of face. These are the moments where some of the work might need to take place offline in one-to-one work or helping the team leader to support a particular individual. These are judgement calls to be made in the moment depending upon what one is uncovering. However, it is not OK to leave these dynamics unspoken or unattended to if they are genuinely in the way of the team stepping up to high performance.

Example from practice: A team where one team member considered himself smarter and more politically powerful than other team members. This was actually a reflection of the power structure at a company/systemic level. We invited the CEO into a portion of the event to set out how he saw the market changing and what this meant for the way the company needed to change. The CEO's view of the market shifts was a challenge to the old power structures. This clearly seeded the message that the game was changing. This was not a power shift that was going to change in one conversation and the team member's boss was one of the big holders of power on the operating board. This particular shift was going to take some time. It was felt from a team coaching perspective that bringing in higher authority early in the team coaching process to seed the changes in team members' minds would work well on a number of levels. Firstly, the changes were strategic and linked strongly to the business imperative; secondly, it gave other team members confidence in their own positions vis-à-vis the powerful member of the team; thirdly, it legitimized some of the mindset shifts the team would have to make in order to keep themselves relevant.

5. Always embed behavioural habits that support effective relational insight and competence

People find it hard to change. There are solid scientific reasons as to why, which are beyond the scope of this short chapter! What this means for the team coach is that you need to keep layering in (as soon after the moments of insight as possible) practice of the positive behaviours and replacements for the negative behaviours. More on layering as a team coaching technique later.

Give the team members lots of opportunities to practise in different groupings the types of behavioural habits that will support them. This work needs doing in duos, trios and within the whole team. It also needs doing with key stakeholders on whom the team depends for its success – likewise in different groupings. There may be some skills input that is required and the work may move momentarily into teach mode and then back into coaching. In my experience there are two key behavioural areas which are vital if a team is to make a sustainable step up to high performance where the behavioural habits have to be highly embedded before the coaching work stops. These are giving and receiving feedback between team members and holding other team members – laterally – accountable. The exercise mentioned earlier in the chapter is a good start. And these two behaviours need practising, practising and practising throughout the work.

This will give team members a felt-sense of what this is like and start to build the habit. If this is done enough times within the safe environment of the team coaching then it will be easier to do in the more scary environment of life back in the day-to-day.

Example from practice: Make sure that whatever the behavioural changes are that you identify together with the team, you practise them in different and engaging ways every time you work with the team. Focus on giving and receiving feedback. Use many different groupings (one-on-one, trios, the whole team) to model feedback giving. Talk about the experience of giving and receiving feedback at a whole team level so that this becomes a normal experience for team members. Use the team leader in particular to role-model feedback behaviours, especially at the beginning. This helps to build confidence quickly in the rest of the team.

6. Have fun!

Positive psychology has plenty to say and evidence to support the fact that people do good thinking when they are enjoying themselves (Fredrickson, 2001). This does not mean that the work has to feel frivolous or lightweight – on the contrary. Oscar Wilde said 'life is too important to be taken seriously' the same could be said of high performance team coaching. Fun connects and builds relationship and will happen if there is enough of a basic sense of emotional safety in the mix.

If one can create the fun whilst working on an actual team task the positive impact on the team dynamic is even greater.

Example from practice: We ran one team event at a football stadium and had a talk on teamwork from one of the marketing directors at the stadium followed by a tour. Working in an unusual location and where there is a connection with the topic and taking a close-up view of a different model of teamwork can stimulate new thinking. Mark de Rond (2012) shares a lot of lessons that can be learned from sport that translate to teamwork in business. Changing it up and translating and having some fun doing that can shake people's brains out of the normal ways of thinking and provide some enjoyable moments of insight. Even the folk who hate football were fascinated by some of the learnings from football for their own team performance.

Six core practices for team coaching

The overarching aim of team coaching is to support the team's ability to learn and keep learning. This is the whole point of the work. There are six key practices that I have found useful over time and, within each practice, tools, techniques and exercises from which a coach can choose to build up the design of their team coaching work. I have included one type of tool or technique here. There are of course many tools to choose from and too many to include in a single chapter!

These practices are:

1. Clear contracting – At each phase of the work. What do you agree with the team that they want to achieve and how will they know when they have achieved it?

Tools and techniques: Personal interviews prior to beginning the team coaching are an excellent way to build the relationship with you as coach as well as to gain important information about what the team needs. You can use one-to-one meetings or calls to gain insight at an individual level and of the team as a collective as well as interviewing other stakeholders to get the systemic view. Using the output from these interviews will support you to contract with the team as to what the objectives for the team coaching are. You can begin the work playing back what you have heard and using this information to help you contract clearly with the team.

2. Mirroring – What do the team see in the mirror about the way they are? What do they see when the mirror is held up to them by others? Bring fresh data to the team coaching that reflects back how the team is doing from a variety of perspectives.

Tools and techniques: There are a variety of processes to help coaches achieve this. One way is to use a 360° questionnaire: examples include a team 360 by Patrick Lencioni (see **www.tablegroup.com**), or the TLQ, Transform and BGC. Encouraging the team and their wider network to reflect on their own and other behaviours can be a useful starting point for a coaching conversation.

3. Layering – Continuously building up the team's connections within the system. Start with the team looking at themselves and their internal dynamics. Learn and improve here. Then create activities that extend the team's reach into the organizational system a layer at a time. The further you can help the team extend, the higher the positive impact of the work.

Tools and techniques: It can be very powerful to work with the team leader to identify real team tasks that the team has to achieve and to coach the team live. This can also include bringing in other stakeholders who are connected with the team. This provides really clear data about how the team connect outside themselves and builds real relationship across the organizational system.

4. Heat mapping – In order to facilitate learning the team coach has to be able to dial the heat up and down depending upon what you think the team can cope with. The temperature gauge is your sense of the degree of emotional and psychological safety you think the team individually and collectively are feeling. If you keep the team work too safe, the heat too low, the team won't learn.

Tools and techniques: A personal favourite is the hot seat exercise, where a team member has to sit and take feedback from the team on one thing they do especially well that contributes to team effectiveness and one thing that the team member giving feedback wants the hot seat person to change to help the team be more effective (Lencioni, 2007). You can do this with the whole team listening and taking part or you can take the heat out by doing it in pairs or trios. It is good to get the Team Leader to really take the hot seat early on.

5. Practising – It takes new habits for us to create a change of behaviour. Practise, practise, practise the new behaviours as the team identify what they need to do differently.

Tools and techniques: Get the team to create their Team Charter. Ask them to develop ways that they can review how well they are doing. Get them engaged in designing ways and means of practising. Then just do it!

6. Reflection – It helps us to learn faster if we can step onto the balcony outside ourselves and look in at what we are learning from a higher perspective. This reflection combined with practice and habit building makes the learning impact bigger. The habit of reflection from a helicopter viewpoint is an important practice to leave the team able to do this effectively.

Tools and techniques: A check-in at the end of a team interaction (be it the whole or part of the team). Take a few minutes to review how the interaction went. What worked? One thing that could be improved? How reflective of the Team Charter was it?

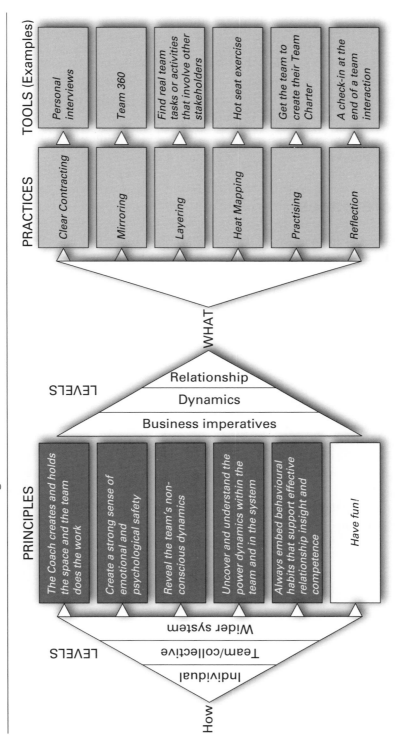

FIGURE 18.1 Linx 6 Team Coaching Model™

PRINCIPLES

The Coach creates and holds the space and the team does the work

Create a strong sense of emotional and psychological safety

Reveal the team's non-conscious dynamics

Uncover and understand the power dynamics within the team and in the system

Always embed behavioural habits that support effective relationship insight and competence

Have fun!

LEVELS
Individual
Team/collective
Wider system

How

LEVELS
Relationship
Dynamics
Business imperatives

WHAT

PRACTICES
Clear Contracting
Mirroring
Layering
Heat Mapping
Practising
Reflection

TOOLS (Examples)
Personal interviews
Team 360
Find real team tasks or activities that involve other stakeholders
Hot seat exercise
Get the team to create their Team Charter
A check-in at the end of a team interaction

Summary

Businesses will only truly solve the challenges facing them by using distributed leadership and effective teamwork. Teams are a huge source of power and a resource that effective leaders must harness. They must truly empower their teams. As leadership and executive coaches we have an important role to play and team coaching offers a useful additional tool to help and support this change.

References

Bresman, H and Ancona, D (2007) *X Teams*, Harvard Business School Publishing, Boston

Canney Davison, S and Ward, K (1999) *Leading International Teams*, McGraw-Hill, London

Caracciolo, A (1999) *Smart Things to Know About Teams*, Capstone Publishing Limited, Chichester

De Rond, M (2012) *There is an I in Team*, Harvard Business School Publishing Corporation, Boston

Fredrickson, B L (2001) *The Role of Positive Emotions in Positive Psychology American Psychologist*, **56** (3), pp 218–226

Harvard Business Review (2004) *Teams That Succeed*, Harvard Business School Publishing Corporation, Boston

Hawkins, P (2011) *Leadership Team Coaching*, Kogan Page, London

Holpp, L (1999) *Managing Teams*, McGraw-Hill, London

Huszczo, G E (1996) *Tools for Team Excellence*, Davies-Black, New York

Janis, I (1982) *Groupthink*, 2nd edn, Houghton Mifflin, Boston

Lencioni, P (2007) *The Five Dysfunctions of a Team*, John Wiley and Sons, New York

ASSOCIATION FOR COACHING

AC membership benefits

The Association for Coaching (AC) is one of the leading independent and nonprofit-making professional coaching bodies aimed at promoting best practice and raising the standards of coaching. Founded in 2002, with representation in over 50 countries, the AC has become known for its leadership within the profession and responsiveness to both market and members' needs.

Becoming a member gives you the opportunity to be involved in an established yet dynamic membership organization dedicated to excellence and coaching best practice.

Membership includes three categories:

1 Individual (aspiring/professional coaches);
2 Organizational (training/coach service providers);
3 Corporate (organizations involved in building internal coaching capability or cultures).

Areas of coaching include: Executive, Business, Personal, Speciality and Team Coaching.

Our vision

To inspire and champion coaching excellence, by being bold, collaborative and purposeful, so that we advance the coaching profession, and make a positive and lasting difference in the world.

Our core objectives

- To actively advance education and best practice in coaching.
- To develop and implement targeted marketing initiatives to encourage growth of the profession.
- To promote and support development of accountability and credibility across the industry.
- To encourage and provide opportunities for an open exchange of views, experiences and consultations.

- To build a network of strategic alliances and relationships to maximize the AC's potential.

There are many benefits that coaches and organizations can access by joining the AC:

- *Journal*: receive *Coaching: An international journal of theory, research and practice*, twice a year by post, the AC's international coaching journal.

- *Gain new customers and referrals*:* through a dedicated webpage profile on the AC online membership directory.

- *Regular seminars and events*: monthly workshops and forums across the United Kingdom on current relevant topics. This allows an opportunity to network, compare notes and gain knowledge from industry experts and colleagues. Members are entitled to discounts on attendance fees.

- *Accreditation*:** eligibility to apply for AC individual coach accreditation after being approved as a full AC member for at least three months.

- *International AC Conference*: attend the AC's annual conference at discounted rates, with international speakers drawn from top coaching experts.

- *Press/VIP contacts*: raise the profile of coaching through PR activities, through the influential honorary board and contacts across the AC.

- *Member newsletters*: increase knowledge through sharing best practice and learning in the quarterly *AC Bulletin* and *AC Update*.

- *Co-Coaching*: practise your coaching skills and learn through experience and observation at any of our many regional co-coaching forum groups.

- *AC forums*: an opportunity to participate in AC's online forums – networking and discussion groups for members to share their views and receive advice and support from others.

- *Industry/market research*: gain first-hand knowledge into the latest industry trends via the AC's market research reports.

- *Dedicated AC website*: gain access to up-to-date AC activities, members' events, reference materials and members-only section.

- *AC logo/letters*:* add value to your service offering and build credibility through use of AC logo/letters in marketing materials.

- *Ongoing professional development*: acquire CPD certificates through attendance at development forums, workshops and events.

- *Improve coaching skills*: through special invitations to professional coaching courses and participation in workshops.

- *Networking opportunities*: enjoy networking opportunities to draw on the advice and experience of leading-edge organizations that are also passionate about ethics, best practice and standards in the coaching profession.
- *Strategic partnerships*: receive member discounts, discounted training offers, and product and service deals through strategic partnerships.

* Associate level and above only.
** Member level only.

Each approved individual member will receive a member's certificate with embossed seal.

For further information on the AC or joining, please visit the membership section of the website or e-mail **members@associationforcoaching.com**

'promoting excellence and ethics in coaching'

www.associationforcoaching.com

INDEX

Note: The Index is filed in alphabetical, word-by-word order. Acronyms are filed as presented and numbers within headings are filed as spelt out. Page locators in *italics* denote information contained within a Figure or Table.